COMPARING WESTMINSTER

Comparing Westminster

R. A. W. RHODES, JOHN WANNA,
AND PATRICK WELLER

OXFORD
UNIVERSITY PRESS

OXFORD
UNIVERSITY PRESS

Great Clarendon Street, Oxford OX2 6DP

Oxford University Press is a department of the University of Oxford.
It furthers the University's objective of excellence in research, scholarship,
and education by publishing worldwide in

Oxford New York

Auckland Cape Town Dar es Salaam Hong Kong Karachi
Kuala Lumpur Madrid Melbourne Mexico City Nairobi
New Delhi Shanghai Taipei Toronto

With offices in

Argentina Austria Brazil Chile Czech Republic France Greece
Guatemala Hungary Italy Japan Poland Portugal Singapore
South Korea Switzerland Thailand Turkey Ukraine Vietnam

Oxford is a registered trade mark of Oxford University Press
in the UK and in certain other countries

Published in the United States
by Oxford University Press Inc., New York

British Library Cataloguing in Publication Data

Data available

Library of Congress Cataloging in Publication Data

Library of Congress Control Number: 2009924644

Typeset by SPI Publisher Services, Pondicherry, India
Printed in Great Britain
on acid-free paper by the
MPG Books Group, Bodmin and King's Lynn

ISBN 978–0–19–956349–4

4

Contents

List of Tables

Preface and Acknowledgements

In this book, we explore how governmental elites understand the Westminster systems in Australia, Britain, Canada, New Zealand, and South Africa. We seek to understand how and why countries that began with some shared sets of ideas developed different practices and interpretations of similar institutions; and to understand how these transplanted constitutional and governmental ideas interacted with local–political traditions and local elites. In short, the purpose is to show how local traditions interacted with the beliefs and practices of Westminster to provide the present-day forms of government.

This book is the latest in our several collaborations. Previously, we have explored the hollowing out of the state, the changing role of top public servants, public sector reform, institutional change in Australian government, critiques of the 'public value' approach in public management, and the legacies of Westminster in the Asian and Pacific regions. In all these ventures, we ranged widely but usually relied on others for country expertise. This time, for good or ill, we are our own country experts. However, we do not present a set of country case studies. Our vaulting ambition was to compare the evolution of executive government in the former dominion states of the British Empire. So, the reader looking for a detailed account of cabinet government in Britain, Canada, or Australia must look elsewhere. We provide some guidance to the basics of the several countries in our notes and references but our main concern is to compare and contrast the fortunes of executive government in Westminster systems from the late twentieth and into the twenty-first centuries.

The research for this book was made possible by a grant from the Australian Research Council (DP0208119 – Westminster and Explanations of Political Change). We acknowledge their financial support.

Along the way we have accumulated many debts. Collectively we would like to acknowledge the advice and criticism from an invited panel of country experts who attended a workshop 'Comparing Westminster' held at the Australian National University in 2006. In particular, we wish to thank Haig Patapan (who collaborated with us on our first Westminster project published in 2005), together with John Halligan, Geoff Hawker, Ian Holliday, Bob Jackson, Evert Lindquist, Elizabeth McLeay, David Marsh, John Nethercote, Paul 't Hart, Elaine Thompson, and John Uhr.

In addition, Rod Rhodes would like to thank Mark Bevir for ten years of criticism, encouragement, and good ideas, and Jenny Fleming for boundless support. He is also grateful to Sarah Binder, Robert Elgie, Andrew Gamble, Bob Goodin, Tony Lowe, Anthony Mughan, and David Richards for advice and help. John Wanna would like to thank Bob Jackson and John Uhr for detailed comments on drafts, and John Butcher, Alex Gash, and Shellaine Godbold for research assistance. He is also grateful to Jeremy Cronin, Tertius Delport, Philip Green, Kasper Hahndiek, Patrick FitzGerald, Douglas Gibson, Daryl Glasser, Motlatjie Anne Letsebe, Mandla Nkomfe, Nomvula Nzimande, and William Smith for assistance on South Africa. Pat Weller would like to thank Tanya Liebrecht and Arthur Whyte for occasional research assistance. All three authors would like to thank Mary Hapel who assisted with the arrangements for the 2006 workshop and John Nethercote for his help with copy-editing and proofreading.

While we draw on the material contained in previously published works, written either jointly or singly since 1998, the book is not a collection of our earlier pieces. Rather, these earlier publications trace the evolution of our own thinking on traditions and the core executive. They include (in chronological order):

- Bevir, M., Rhodes, R.A.W. and Weller, P. (Eds.) 2003. Traditions of Governance: History and Diversity. Special issue of: *Public Administration* 81 (1): 1–210.

- Weller, P. 2003. 'Cabinet Government: An Elusive Ideal?' *Public Administration*, 81 (4): 701–22.

- Rhodes, R.A.W. and Weller, P. 2005. 'Westminster Transplanted and Westminster Implanted: Explanations for Political Change', in H. Patapan, J. Wanna, and P. Weller (Eds.), *Westminster Legacies: Democracy and Responsible Government in Asia, Australasia and the Pacific*. Sydney: University of New South Wales Press.

- Rhodes, R.A.W. 2005. 'The Westminster Model as Tradition: The Case of Australia', in H. Patapan, J. Wanna, and P. Weller (Eds.), *Westminster Legacies: Democracy and Responsible Government in Asia, Australasia and the Pacific*. Sydney: University of New South Wales Press.

- Wanna, J. 2005. 'New Zealand's Westminster Trajectory: Archetypal Transplant to Maverick Outlier', in H. Patapan, J. Wanna, and P. Weller (Eds.), *Westminster Legacies: Democracy and Responsible Government in Asia, Australasia and the Pacific*. Sydney: University of New South Wales Press.

- Rhodes, R.A.W. 2006. 'Old Institutionalisms', in R.A.W. Rhodes, S. Binder, and B. Rockman (Eds.), *The Oxford Handbook of Political Institutions*. Oxford: Oxford University Press.

- Rhodes, R.A.W. 2006. 'Executive Government in Parliamentary Systems', in R.A.W. Rhodes, S. Binder, and B. Rockman (Eds.), *The Oxford Handbook of Political Institutions*. Oxford: Oxford University Press.

- Bevir, M. and Rhodes, R.A.W. 2006. 'Prime Ministers, Presidentialism and Westminster Smokescreens'. *Political Studies* 54 (4): 671–90.

- Weller, P. 2007. *Cabinet Government in Australia, 1901–2006*. Sydney: University of New South Wales Press.

- Rhodes, R.A.W., Wanna, J., and Weller, P. 2008. 'Reinventing Westminster – How Public Executives Reframe Their World', *Policy & Politics*, 2009: 36 (4): 461–79.

Hobart, Canberra, and Brisbane
July 2008

List of Abbreviations

ANC (South Africa)	African National Congress
APS (Australia)	Australian Public Service
CIU (Australia)	Cabinet Implementation Unit (PM&C)
CPU (Australia)	Cabinet Policy Unit
EU	European Union
IMF	International Monetary Fund
MMP (New Zealand)	Mixed member proportional (voting system)
NGO	Non-government organization
NPM	New public management
PCO (Canada)	Privy Council Office
PM&C (Australia)	Prime Minister and Cabinet (Department of the)
PMO (various)	Prime Minister's Office
RCAGA	Royal Commission on Australian Government Administration
SCU (UK)	Strategic Communications Unit (Prime Minister's Office)
SSC (NZ)	State Services Commission

1

Looking for Westminster

Of the Queen's title 'Head of the Commonwealth', a French-speaking newspaper in Quebec in 1953 declared, 'The solution of the problem is in the good British tradition; it is both efficient and devoid of logic' (Bogdanor 1991: 37, citing Longford 1983: 127).

Question – If you hear the expression 'the Westminster model', what does that mean to you?
Answer – Absolutely nothing (David Blunkett, former British Home Secretary, interview, 19 January 2007).

The Westminster system is a familiar point of reference in the political worlds of Australia and New Zealand. The Westminster heritage is also recognizable in the structure of government in both Canada and South Africa. Each of these four polities adopted Westminster as an important model on which to base their systems of government even if some local variations on the theme were incorporated from the outset. These polities still regard themselves, in part, as variants of British parliamentary democracy, originating in Westminster, despite each having subsequently undergone substantial transformation. For the British, however, to use the words of John Bright (18th January 1865), 'England is the mother of Parliaments' (Bright 1910), and the term Westminster, if used at all, is but a shorthand term for 'their' system of government. The 'British government' and Westminster are treated as synonymous. If used 'inside' the UK, its meaning is not clear to actors, as the epigraph by the former Home Secretary David Blunkett makes apparent.

Yet the term 'Westminster' remains important as a signifier in the study of comparative government. It is part of the political argot of politics and political science, and often used to distinguish a British-inspired version of parliamentarianism from other legislative and presidential systems. But what does the term mean in these several contexts and what influence does it have on those systems that acknowledge their heritage from British political practice?

'Westminster' often denotes a distinct and stable set of political institutions that are recognizable and around which there is some agreement. But, as we unpack the phrase, it begins to blur and lack precision.[1] This 'blurred' quality may be simultaneously one of its enduring strengths and inherent weaknesses. For instance, the term can be used for different purposes: as a historical description of institutional form; as a normative guide to constitutional design; and as a rhetorical device used by partisan adversaries when justifying or criticizing actions, as in 'this is in line with Westminster practice' (or 'this is not'). Some writers go in search of the 'essence of the Westminster idea', while others (as we will see) list putative attributes as a way of attempting to classify the system. It is claimed to exist in many settings, in both unitary and federal states, in constitutional monarchies and republics, in two-party and in multi-party systems, in developed and developing countries, in linguistically homogeneous and diverse cultures, and in small compact nations as well as across large continental land masses. These different settings and structures challenge the notion that there is one definitive or distinctive meaning to the term, but they also challenge us to ask why the concept is so widely used and employed by practitioners not only as a convenient label but to shape the way they approach and understand political practice.

So, importantly, we do not assume that all Westminster systems are essentially similar, or even started out as similar cases before departing. Indeed, it would be surprising if they had been identical and had remained the same. However, in exploring 'the meanings of Westminster' our book has two core objectives:

- to understand how and why countries that began with some shared sets of ideas developed different beliefs and practices; and
- to understand how these transplanted constitutional and governmental ideas interacted with local political traditions and local elites.

Westminster systems share a British heritage if not a common lineage.[2] The transplanted colonial varieties often copied their institutional design from Britain. Yet, from the start, they developed and have continued to develop separately in different ways.[3] But there remain similarities. As Butler (1973: 7) observed in relation to the British and Australian political systems some time ago:

> I could talk to clerks in Parliament House, or to civil servants in the Commonwealth Club [Canberra], or to party officials in Melbourne or Brisbane, and find myself speaking in very much the same terms as I might have been using with their opposite numbers in Westminster or Whitehall or Birmingham or Glasgow. It was not that Australia was Britain or that Australian answers to governmental problems were British answers. It was only that the questions that came naturally to someone schooled in the British system were, almost invariably, wholly appropriate questions to ask in Australia. The answers might be different but the

situations were usually similar enough for it to be possible to disentangle the reasons for the difference; in the process one could learn a great deal both about Australian politics and about British politics.

There is inevitably debate and contestability over what constitutes 'Westminster' and whether there exists a core of essential practices. Some constitutionalists and practitioners see Westminster as a set of relationships between the executive government and parliament: where the principal members of executive government should be drawn from the members of the parliament. The key feature here is that the parliament determines *who* is the government and for *how long* they are in government, and parliament limits a great deal of what the executive can do. Others will often use the term 'Westminster model' normatively and nostalgically to define the way they think government *ought* to work. They may eulogize or appeal to some long-lost 'golden age', usually Britain from the First and Second *Reform Acts* (1832 and 1867) or after the terms of Prime Minister Robert Peel (1834–5 and 1841–6). Such appeals, often used to depict how far recent polities have 'slipped' from the 'norm', are little more than rhetoric. While idealized notions of Westminster exist, such idealized models are of limited analytical value.

Yet resonances of the common heritage persist; many of the institutions that shape the nature of executive government bear the same names and work in approximately similar ways. Each set of institutions is an adaptation of the original, influenced enormously by the timing of the country's achievement of self-government (the 'take-off' point or point of departure). Adaptation has continued, and even Britain, the original variant, has evolved and changed sometimes more than its former colonies. Westminster at Westminster is itself a movable feast, clearly apparent, say, if British government under the Attlee administration (1945–51) were to be compared with the Blair regime (1997–2007), or the structures before and after the creation of the Welsh and Scottish assemblies.

Westminster *describes* how government might be conceived and organized. It provides a set of beliefs and a shared inheritance that creates expectations, and hands down practices that guide and justify behaviour. The practices of Westminster systems have shown remarkable resilience, surviving under different regimes and in different circumstances across the world.

These broader assumptions about how Westminster government should be organized have interacted with local and historical governmental traditions that necessarily shaped the way they were practised. These inherited *beliefs* and *practices* about the institutions of government include: accepted conventions and rules; attitudes to authority and legitimacy; the accountable exercise of power; the representation of citizens; and various ways to govern and integrate regionalism. These beliefs vary from country to country. We will explore their effects on the imported political beliefs and practices, focusing in particular on the organization of executive government. One of the aims of this study is to elucidate the competing doctrines and tensions found within Westminster systems: especially ideas about the role of executive government versus the parliament, and the powers of parliament versus executive government.

A focus on Westminster systems is instructive for three reasons. First, the book confronts questions that lie at the heart of the debate about the validity of comparative politics. What can be learnt by contrasting development of similar institutions under different conditions. We concentrate on nations with common institutions; that is, we adopt a 'most similar' research design (see Przeworski and Teune 1970: 47–73; Dogan and Pelassy 1982; Mill 1996 [1843] book 3, chapter 8). We avoid some of the definitional problems of multi-country comparisons of executives (Blondel 1980, 1985, and the critique in Rhodes 1993).

Second, comparison of countries with similar political systems and sets of political institutions, but different starting points and different cultures, allows us to develop an approach to comparative politics rooted in the analysis of 'traditions'. If inherited rules and practices create expectations and shape action, how and why have such imported traditions as cabinet government and collective responsibility, perhaps originally emanating from shared ideas and a common language, become markedly different? What impact have local ideas had on the way executive government is organized and run? By analysing the historical development of the various Westminster systems, we will develop explanations about the way governments are shaped and structured.

Third, normative assertions about the strengths of Westminster systems compared to both presidential and other parliamentary systems recur both in the academic literature and in the reports of would-be reformers. Many argue that (majoritarian) Westminster systems are institutionally more cohesive and coherent and, therefore, more decisive and effective than both presidential and European-consensual systems (Lijphart 1984, 1999). The book explores both the limits to such arguments and the several critiques of Westminster.

So, our departure point is the historical event of the (formal or nominal) acceptance of Westminster structures and conventions as the basis of self-government. We then seek to explain the resulting changes in political practices, nationally and comparatively. We focus on the core executive institutions of Westminster systems in those nations that were once regarded as the 'old or great dominions' (Keith 1928; Miller 1966).

BELIEFS ABOUT THE WESTMINSTER MODEL

Beliefs about government sustain conventions, sometimes becoming codified and written down by practitioners or scholars. To begin our analysis, it is useful to turn to the written record and extract core beliefs about Westminster. Our reading of the literature suggests that those writers interested in this field tend to identify *three* main clusters of beliefs about core institutions, around which there is much agreement and acceptance. These three clusters are: beliefs about the constitutional framework; beliefs about the structure and conventions of the core executive; and the nature of the party system and electoral process (for a comprehensive review see Rhodes and Weller 2005).

The classic interpretations refer to Britain alone. So Bagehot, writing in 1867, seeks to provide a realistic description of the way English cabinet government worked, in contrast to conceptions based on Montesquieu. For Bagehot the 'efficient secret' of the English constitution was the 'close union, the nearly complete fusion, of the executive and legislative powers' (1963 [1867]: 64). A form of constitutionality exists; it is simply not formalized, but is well understood by those who participate in governing. Yet, as the introduction to the second edition in 1872 showed, he, like Aristotle, appreciated the aristocratic, rather than the democratic, version of governing. Deference was a significant component of good government, as was breeding and training (1963: 272). It was important that the governing class understood the system of government and knew 'how to govern', a theme that is often echoed in subsequent constitutional texts in Britain.[4]

Dicey (1914 [1885]) deliberately sought to provide coherence (to laws and conventions) and to reduce 'the unwritten constitution to a partially written code, so fixing if not founding a new British Constitution' (Dicey 1914). He saw the evolving constitution as the foundation of English liberty and a bulwark against collectivism (Patapan 1997: 256). He emphasized the role of parliament in forming and maintaining the executive, sustained by the notion of parliamentary sovereignty. Hence,

> The principle of Parliamentary sovereignty means neither more nor less than this, namely, that parliament thus defined has, under the English constitution, the right to make or unmake any law whatever (quoted in Patapan 1997: 261).

This expressed the supremacy of parliament and politics over all other civic spheres. So the English parliament was supreme. It can make and unmake every law; it is omnipotent. Indeed, it can be irresponsible because its power is unfettered (Bryce 1921: volume 2, chapter 68). Such understandings were not unique to British government, but were modified as they were accepted in other transplanted Westminster polities.

If the cornerstone of Westminster is that parliament is considered sovereign (that is, in theory able to do whatever it likes), then British constitutionalism has accordingly placed great emphasis on parliamentary conventions and practice, with such manuals and interpretive guides as *Erskine May* (1844 and subsequent editions) enjoying quasi-constitutional status. These guides document precedent and parliamentary pronouncements, often at great length, to a practitioner readership. As a consequence they were widely read and acted upon by those participating in the system. Regarded as the 'bible' of parliamentary practice in the UK; this and other guides were influential parliamentary reference points in the former colonies even if they chose to depart from precedent at Westminster or prepare their own manuals.

Jennings, in the mid-twentieth century, derived his description of the development of key institutions, such as *Cabinet Government* (1959 [1936]), *Parliament* (1957 [1939]), and *The British Constitution* (1962 [1941]), from his reading of British history. The account is simultaneously descriptive and normative, distilling principles of proper behaviour from past practices. Even in revised editions there is no attempt to provide a general definition of Westminster and none of his principles is concerned with the wider Commonwealth practice, although Jennings, by the late 1950s, was a vice-chancellor in Ceylon and involved in constitution writing in British-influenced Nepal. Similarly, to take a more recent example, Birch (1964 and 1967), in an influential account of British government, was not concerned with particular discussion of what constituted 'Westminster', but instead emphasized the twin pillars of 'representative government' and 'responsible government'.

The various emphases of British constitutionalists are understandable. Westminster was the location of 'their' government: it was a working model with its constant change and introspective focus. Westminster was documented primarily as a self-referential explanation of practice for the benefit of practitioners and interested scholars, including for university courses in government. It was often contrasted with other systems of government (presidential, republican, formal constitutional, and continental parliamentary systems), essentially to appreciate its distinctiveness or extol its inherent virtues. Thus, one Clerk of the House of Commons regarded the British Parliament as singularly 'supreme', 'venerable', and the 'parent stock' from which all other legislative models were derived even if they subsequently departed from Westminster or were 'metamorphosed in their adaptation to their new and strange surroundings' (Ilbert 1912: 239).

As scholarly representations of Westminster have become more extensive, we are now able to provide a systematic list of the beliefs and core institutions said to constitute the Westminster model at various times. Table 1.1 attempts

Table 1.1. The Westminster model: a summary statement of academic sources articulating the key beliefs and core institutions

Beliefs	Sources
Cluster 1. Beliefs about the constitutional framework	
A centralized unitary state	Gamble (1990: 407); Lijphart (1999: 3)
No separation of powers and, therefore, no judicial review of constitution	Lucy (1985); Jaensch (1997: 98)
A bicameral parliament	Carey (1980: 227); Lucy (1985: 3)
Doctrines of parliamentary sovereignty and 'responsible government'	Weller (1989a: 6); Gamble (1990: 407); Verney (1991: 637); Campbell and Wilson (1995); Richards and Smith (2002: 48)
Unwritten constitution with flexible constitutional conventions	Weller (1989a: 5); Gamble (1990: 407); Verney (1991: 637); Mulgan (2004: 50–1)
Cluster 2. Beliefs about the structure and conventions of the core executive	
Head of state and head of government are separate roles	de Smith (1961: 3); Thompson (1980: 33); Jaensch (1997: 102); Boyce (2008)
Majority party control of the executive also described as the fusion of the legislature and the executive – with ministers drawn only from the parliament	de Smith (1961: 3); Thompson (1980: 34); Lucy (1985: 133); Gamble (1990: 407); Wilson (1994: 190–3); Lijphart (1999: 3); Richards and Smith (2002: 48)
Concentration of executive power in the prime minister and cabinet	de Smith (1961: 3); Weller (1989a: 5); Gamble (1990: 407); Verney (1991: 637); Lijphart (1999: 3); Richards and Smith (2002: 48)
Individual ministerial and collective cabinet accountability to parliament	de Smith (1961: 3); Butler (1973); Parker (1978: 351); Thompson (1980: 34); Lucy (1985: 3 and 6); Weller (1989a: 5); Campbell and Wilson (1995: 11); Richards and Smith (2002: 48)
Partnership between ministers and non-partisan officials in which ministers have the last word	Parker (1978: 352); Weller (1989a: 19); Davis et al. (1993: 73)
Cluster 3. Beliefs about the party system and the electoral process	
A two-party system based on single member constituencies	Verney (1991: 637); Campbell and Wilson (1995); Lijphart (1999: 3)
Majority party–government control of parliament, also described as 'responsible party government'	Thompson (1980: 37); Verney (1991: 637); Campbell and Wilson (1995); Uhr (1998: 66–81)
Institutionalized opposition	Weller (1989a: 6); Gamble (1990: 407); Verney (1991: 637)
Accountability and legitimacy through regular and transparent elections	Parker (1978: 353); Thompson (1980: 37); Lucy (1985: 4); Weller (1989a: 7); Gamble (1990: 407); Richards and Smith (2002: 48)

such a summary of the main present-day academic accounts (and it would be redundant to add more references). We seek instead to identify the main clusters of beliefs that prevail today.

In recent years, Verney (1991: 637), from a British perspective, includes among the characteristics of the Westminster model:

> strong cabinet government based on majority rule; the importance attached to constitutional conventions; a two-party system based on single member constituencies; the assumption that minorities can find expression in one of the major parties; the concept of Her Majesty's loyal opposition; and the doctrine of parliamentary supremacy, which takes precedence over popular sovereignty except during elections.

For Verney, this definition is both a description of the UK government and the principles of Westminster. Gamble (1990: 407) similarly essays a comprehensive definition and adumbrates a unitary state characterized by: parliamentary sovereignty; strong cabinet government; accountability through elections; majority party control of the executive (that is, prime minister, cabinet, and the civil service); elaborate conventions for the conduct of parliamentary business; institutionalized opposition; and the rules of debate. The antecedents are both ancient, dating back to Norman notions of the strength of Crown prerogatives, and recent, with universal electoral suffrage. Wilson (1994: 193) is even more focused, arguing that the defining characteristic is 'the unity of the legislature and executive secured through a disciplined political party'.

Finally, two other views from one of the former dominions have distinctive twists. A former Australian parliamentary official, Gordon Reid (1973: 513–15), regarded as a 'dead duck' discussion of how far Antipodean jurisdictions were more or less like Westminster. Instead he sought to develop a 'realistic perspective' that captured the dynamics of responsible government as a 'trinitarian struggle' or fight between three rival centres of power: the executive, the lower house, and the upper house. By contrast, Parker (1978: 349–53) focused on 'responsibility', insisting that individual and collective ministerial accountability were the 'essential elements' that lie at the heart of his 'Westminster syndrome'. There are four elements to the syndrome. The first 'essential' part is the doctrines of individual and collective ministerial responsibility. The second part is the need for officialdom. The third part concerns 'the "proper" relations between ministers and officials'. Parker is not resurrecting the age-old distinction between policy and administration. He simply wants to insist that 'in all decisions . . . the elected minister should *have the last word*' (emphasis in the original). Finally, 'the lines of accountability of the whole administration run from the lowliest official up through the minister to the cabinet, the parliament and ultimately, and only by that circuitous route, to the elector' (Parker 1978: 349–53).

These illustrations and Table 1.1 show the diversity of contending definitions. Indeed, given this variety, it would be amazing if these characteristics
could be reduced to a single system or model. But even if we avoid that
analytical dead end, how do we find some coherence in this mix? As Jackson
(1995: 5) has indicated, the debate about whether a state 'conforms' to the
Westminster model is likely to be sterile simply because there is no agreed
definition of that model. As Table 1.1 shows all too clearly, there is no single,
essentialist definition on which in the present context we can all agree. It is
probably futile to try.

COMPARING WESTMINSTER

So, how is 'Westminster' defined in this book? We needed to have some basis
on which to found our comparisons. We eschew a rigid or precise definition
imposed from the list above (because it is *the actors'* understandings of how
the system works that is important to us). Instead, following Wittgenstein
(1972), we argue that concepts such as Westminster often cover diverse
contents connected by family resemblance rather than a single, essential
idea. Notions associated with Westminster refer to a set of ideas with strong
family resemblances. These ideas will typically gravitate around many of
common features in the table, especially the constitutional fusion of the
executive and legislature (from where the principal executive officers must
be chosen) and the requirement that governments must have the 'confidence'
of the legislature, sovereign or otherwise. These ideas about Westminster have
survived the longest historically. They pre-date many of the subsequently
grafted-on ideas about regular, free and fair democratic elections, the primacy
of the lower house, written constitutions, equal representation of electors or
the dominance of two-party adversarial politics.

To enable a manageable comparison, we have chosen in this study to focus
on a select group of inter-related ideas about Westminster. We realize that
there are other ideas we could have chosen as our starting point or other ways
to 'cut' the analysis (for example, majoritarian, two-party politics). These
ideas are also important and legitimate avenues of investigation that could
add to our study, and we welcome such contributions. The prism we have
chosen to look through focuses on the *core executive* parts of the model. We
justify this focus on the grounds that we are interested in the understandings
of the *central political actors* (cabinets, ministers, and senior bureaucrats),
and so focus on the prism through which they are likely to interpret their
world. Our focus leads us to investigate *four* inter-related components of the

Westminster model as understood by its constitutive actors. These four sets of ideas are then used to structure the substantive chapters of this study.

1. We explore centralization in collective, responsible cabinet government, where prime ministers are often seen as dominant, even 'presidential', although there are few formal powers attaching to their office.

2. We examine beliefs around the core convention of 'ministerial responsibility'; the concept that the principal officers of executive government (ministers) come from and must have the confidence of the legislature and, in turn, are individually and collectively accountable to parliament.

3. We probe the notion that the professional, non-partisan public service provides continuity and accountability. And we ask to what extent it is a 'permanent element' of the Crown and acts as a 'constitutional bureaucracy' to counterbalance the 'winner takes all' characteristics of the political executive.

4. We investigate parliament's relationship to the executive: the doctrine of parliamentary sovereignty, executive–legislative relations, legislative scrutiny, the provision of a legitimate opposition as an alternative government, and the representative character of parliament and hence the executive.

This definition of the core executive of the Westminster model is minimalist but operational. These characteristics exist to various degrees in all systems that claim to be Westminster-derived. They are the starting point from which we can explore the intentions of political and administrative elites and their adaptive changes (see Chapter 2 for a more detailed discussion). Our approach allows for variations such as multiparty systems, different voting systems (plurality, preferential, or proportional representation), federal structures, and written constitutions, including judicial review of legislation, that have emerged with these executive arrangements during the last 150 years.

These core features are a source of contention and debate for both academics and practitioners. We use them here to structure the systematic comparative analysis of several countries. We want to explore how political and administrative elites (that is, the proximate decision-makers who determine how political power is organized and exercised) understand the notions of 'Westminster'. What impact did these understandings have on decisions about their application and how did they evolve? Their beliefs and practices make up our basic data. We use that lens to focus on how and why countries developed differently and how Westminster practices have mutated often with no changes in terminology or constitutional significance.

Westminster systems come in all shapes and sizes, ranging from the sub-continent of India to tiny island nations of the Pacific or Caribbean; and from unitary states to federations. Whether the system was *transplanted* and adopted by settler societies from the British heritage, or *implanted* and imposed on other colonies at independence is crucial (Hartz 1964; Patapan et al. 2005). Thus, we expect governing elites from the old pre-democratic British Empire to have different ideas from those from the post-1945 generations. In earlier times, there was a readiness to rely on mutually accepted understandings of what was proper and appropriate, in the transplanted contexts of Canada, the Australian colonies, New Zealand, and the South African Cape Colony. Later circumstances required understandings to be spelt out, often in a formal constitution that laid down the rules at a particular point in time, although often a wide range of issues were left for later settlement or open to subsequent parliaments to determine. New Zealand, with its minimalist constitution and subsequent statutory provisions, was a classic case in point. By contrast, as the other self-governing settler colonies emerged and developed politically and economically, they became 'federations', 'confederations', or 'unions', and, following Canada, were recognized as 'dominions', reflecting their particular standing with the UK. To bind these hybrid polities together, written constitutions were preferred. They were 'single constitutional documents with the force of fundamental law' (Mulgan 2004: 51) preferred by the local political elite, partly to guarantee local control and reduce the likelihood of governors vetoing legislation (see Ilbert 1912; Bryce 1921; Keith 1928). Although these new systems became major variants of any existing version of the Westminster model, their political elites still understood their governmental system as a species of Westminster based on 'responsible government'. As a former clerk of the House of Commons argued:

> In the British empire the great self-governing dominions beyond the seas have not only copied British forms of parliamentary government but have inherited British traditions, usages, and modes of thought (Ilbert 1912: 239).

The later the transition, the greater the detail in many of the constitutions, as its modernist authors sought to prescribe how national government *should* work. We have already explored the dynamics of Westminster beliefs in many of the implanted societies in Asia and the Pacific that gained independence from Britain after 1945 (see Patapan et al. 2005). In this book, adopting the most similar principle of comparison, we focus on the old self-governing dominions.

THE FIVE 'GREAT SELF-GOVERNING DOMINIONS'

> What does Dominion status mean? It would be difficult and dangerous to
> give a definition...That is not the way of the British Constitution. We
> realise the dangers of rigidity and the danger of limiting our constitution
> by too many finalities (Lloyd George 149 House of Commons Debates,
> 5s. 27–8, cited in Wheare 1953: 21).

Defining the term 'dominion' remains difficult and dangerous because the idea is
devoid of logic, but we must essay the task because we have chosen it as the
starting point of our study. It had at least three meanings. Its earliest British usage
dates from the mid-seventeenth century when it was applied to selective American colonies recognizing their loyalty to the Crown (for example, New England
and Virginia often still nicknamed the 'old dominion'). Second, it gradually
occurred in the King's title where it referred to all British territories and possessions overseas (the King's dominions overseas). From the mid-nineteenth to the
early twentieth centuries, it was then used to refer specifically to the colonies such
as Australia, Canada, New Zealand, and South Africa, which had achieved a
measure of self-government (Wheare 1960: 6).[5] Except in Canada, the term did
not become part of the formal name of the country; the preferred use was
elsewhere the Commonwealth of Australia and the Union of South Africa.

Canada emerged as the only country to have the title dominion bestowed
upon it courtesy of the *British North America Act* of 1867, where the term
'dominion' was chosen in preference to 'kingdom' or 'empire'. But the choice
was not straightforward. As Ged Martin (1995: 282) recounts:

> As late as 2 February [1867], the draft bill spoke of 'the Kingdom of
> Canada', but the foreign secretary, Stanley, objected that a monarchical
> style 'would wound the sensibilities of the Yankees'. The delegates then
> pressed for 'Viceroyalty', which Carnarvon thought 'open to grave objec-
> tion', before retreating to 'Dominion' which was 'somewhat in opposition
> to the institutions on the other side of the border', but not offensively so.
> Derby thought the term 'rather absurd', perhaps thinking of Psalm 72,
> which spoke of 'dominion also from sea to sea and from river to river unto
> the ends of the earth'. Not even British Columbia was that far away.

The title was thought necessary to refer to a separate and distinct area of
jurisdiction in North America in which the local administration was rested
with a substantial measure of self-government.

Canada's trajectory towards dominion status followed directly from Lord
Durham's report (1839) on the conflicts between the English and the French
and between the Governor General and the legislatures of both Upper and

Lower Canada that led to two armed uprisings in the 1830s. 'Radical Jack' Durham recommended setting up 'responsible government', that is, a local executive drawn from and responsible to a single parliament. Eventually, his scheme was implemented in 1847 by his son-in-law, Lord Elgin.

According to Lowell (1927: 573), the history of the term 'dominion', then, 'is best traced in the case of Canada, because there the process began earliest, has been most continuous, and whatever was achieved in her case has been adopted later elsewhere'. So, the term had a specific usage in relation to Canada but Whitehall began to use it generically and titularly when the Dominions Office was created. Canada then became regarded as 'the senior dominion within the Commonwealth' (Holland 2003: 642). It grew accustomed and warmed to the title, to such an extent that its federal government in Ottawa continued to be known as the 'Dominion Government' until well into the 1950s, when the term 'federal government' came to be preferred.

The term 'self-governing dominions' was subsequently adopted at the 1907 Colonial Conference and applied to the self-governing colonies of the Empire.[6] According to Hall (1920: 114–16), 'the most outstanding achievement' of the 1907 Session of the Imperial Conference was 'the passing of the constitutional resolution'. It set out the scope and structure of the Imperial Conference and for the first time used the phrase 'dominions' instead of 'colonies'. The official report of the proceedings of the conference note that 'Both Sir Wilfrid Laurier and Mr Deakin, the Prime Ministers of Canada and Australia respectively, insisted that the conference was "between governments and governments"'; it was not between the British Colonial Office and dependent colonies (1907: 7). From now on, the Imperial Conference comprised 'His majesty's Government and his governments of the self-governing Dominions beyond the seas' (see also Wheare 1960: 6–12). While Australia and New Zealand were classified as dominions in 1907, South Africa was not recognized as a dominion until 1910 when it formalized its union.

Dominion status was further asserted (paradoxically as it was about to be abandoned) at the Paris Peace Conference of 1919. After the sacrifices of the First World War, the dominions were not prepared to be treated as minor powers and fall in with the British delegation but wanted separate representation, eventually gaining this with a 'secretariat of Britain Dominions' – a contentious development at the time. As MacMillan recounts (2001: 52):

> The dominion leaders were most annoyed when they discovered that the British had assumed that they would tag along to the Peace Conference as part of the British delegation. Lloyd George attempted to mollify them by suggesting that a dominion prime minister could be one of the five British plenipotentiaries. But which one? As Hankey said, 'the dominions

are as jealous of each other as cats'. The real problem over representation, as Borden wrote to his wife, was that the dominions' position had never been properly sorted out. Canada was 'a nation that is not a nation. It is about time to alter it'...Lloyd George gave way: not only would one of the five main British delegates be chosen from the empire, but he would tell his allies that the dominions and India required separate representation at the Peace Conference...A reluctant Lloyd George persuaded Clemenceau and Wilson to allow Canada, Australia, South Africa and India to have two plenipotentiaries each and New Zealand one.[7]

The dispute over representation at the Conference was not one of pure formality. Both Australia (Billy Hughes) and South Africa (General Jan Smuts) indicated they might not go to war again if Britain so chose. They were expressing a nationalistic independence which would see them, (with Canada and New Zealand) incorporated from the outset into the new League of Nations as separate entities (with the blessing of the French and Americans who saw this as a way of hastening the dismantling of the old British Empire).

Present-day interpretations are less sanguine and airbrushed. Holland (2003: 633) argued that 'the 1907 imperial conference decided that the term "dominion" (hardly a new one in the realm of British overseas relationships) should have special application to the self-governing colonies of Empire', when most of the Empire was still governed from London. This innovation was 'to exorcise the old bogey of "Downing Street control"' by recognizing the special position of the self-governing colonies. It was also driven 'by a racial instinct...to erect a compartment between the white man's empire, and that of lesser breeds'. Darwin (1999: 66) encapsulated this point by referring to the 'White Dominions' and such race sentiments continued to exert an influence on dominion governments for decades to come (Todd 1880; Lake and Reynolds 2007).

So, the eventual meaning of the term 'dominion' denoted British-settled, white-ruled, self-governing colonies that were autonomous but, notwithstanding, recognized the sovereignty of the British monarch. The effect of the First World War was to give these self-governing colonies 'a heightened self-consciousness' (Hancock 1930: 1). The Australian Prime Minister of the time, Billy Hughes, saw no need 'to set down in black and white the relation between Britain and the Dominions'. He argued 'we have all the rights of self government enjoyed by independent nations'. General Smuts, Prime Minister of South Africa, observed that 'although in practice there is great freedom...the status of the Dominions is of a subject character' (both cited in Wheare 1960: 11).

It was not until 1926 with the Earl of Balfour's *Report of the Inter-Imperial Relations Committee of the Imperial Conference* of 1926, that the parties attempted to clarify the relationship. The Report declared the dominions to be:

autonomous communities within the British Empire, equal in status, in
no way subordinate one to another in any aspect of their domestic or
external affairs, though united by a common allegiance to the Crown, and
freely associated as members of the British Commonwealth of Nations.

Hall (1927: 589) declared, apparently with no discernible trace of irony, that
the Durham Report (1839) and the Balfour Report (1926) were 'likely to be
known as the two greatest state papers in the history of the British Commonwealth'. Well, great state papers they may be to some, but they were also the
source of much ambiguity. A dominion was ostensibly self-governing, loyal to
the Crown, equal in status, and a member of the commonwealth; and each great
dominion understood these criteria differently or applied them selectively.

The *Statute of Westminster 1931* formalized the position, but also included the
UK itself as one of the coequal dominions. 'It was the bible of the new imperialism, the imperialism which discovered that colonies could govern themselves
and yet remain colonies' (Jennings 1948: 55) without being subordinate to the
home country. The *Statute of Westminster* (1931, section 1) defined the dominions as the UK, Canada, Australia, New Zealand, South Africa, as well as the
Irish Free State and Newfoundland (for the authoritative commentary see
Wheare 1953).[8] These diverse polities were declared 'equivalent to the home
country' largely to assuage the sensitivities of the settler societies.

The provisions of the 1931 statute were not welcomed by all. As Darwin
(1989: 69) observed, it 'was eagerly endorsed in Dublin and Pretoria, carefully
emasculated in Canada, and comprehensively ignored in Australia and New
Zealand', neither of whom ratified the statute for more than a decade (see
Wheare 1953). Years after the event, the initial doubts continued to be
expressed about rendering into law that which should be left to custom and
practice. Robert Menzies, Prime Minister of Australia (1939–41 and 1949–66),
was a continuing critic, claiming the *Statute of Westminster* was 'open to grave
criticism'. It did a 'grave disservice' and was a 'misguided attempt' to reduce to
written form what was 'a matter of spirit and not of the letter' (Cowen 1965:
18). For the Anglophile and monarchist Menzies (1960: 6), the Crown
dominions were Great Britain, Canada, Australia, and New Zealand 'united
by a common allegiance to the Crown' because the rest of the Commonwealth
had become either republic or had its own monarch.

By the end of the Second World War, the 'vast Empire' had fallen into three
classes, according to Marriott (1948: 308). First, there were 'the Colonies with
"responsible" government, these were the great self-governing dominions or
"Sister-States"'. Second, there were the Crown Colonies which 'are all administered more or less autocratically by a Governor who is directly responsible to
the Colonial Office in Whitehall'. Finally, there were 'the Colonies endowed

with representative Legislatures but without a responsible Executive'. But by this time there was also a fourth class emerging from the Empire, the newly emerging independent nations. India (and then Pakistan) became the first 'non-white' possessions to gain independence in 1947, adopting implanted notions of parliamentary government from Westminster. India managed to sustain Westminster while a more Cromwellian legacy has persisted in Pakistan. Interestingly, India was belatedly offered dominion status in 1942 by Sir Stafford Cripps in exchange for support in the war effort, but the offer lapsed through lack of agreement.

However, the term 'dominion' had started to fall into disuse after the Second World War (Wheare 1960: 13–17). As a label it was soon overtaken by phrases such as 'independent status' or 'full member of the Commonwealth' (de Smith 1954: 19). And, as many former Crown colonies became independent, the need for a special 'dominion' status within the Commonwealth diminished.[9]

Our study of the dominions takes as its empirical starting point and its focus the 'five great self-governing Dominions' (Hall 1927: 589), the UK, Canada, Australia, New Zealand, and South Africa. We take the shared temporal status of dominion as the baseline from which to explore the subsequent and continuing divergence in their patterns of executive government. They were all white, British autonomous polities, including the 'motherland' and four relatively rich settler societies, all of which ruled over the original indigenous inhabitants or other 'coloured' races who were largely disenfranchised, in South Africa's case until 1994. Each of these settler societies consciously (and in many respects unquestioningly) adopted the Westminster system of government between 1848 and 1910, understood at the time as British governmental traditions. All four settler societies became independent between 1852 and 1910 with no great normative debates about opting for 'responsible government' or how it should work. The major exception was Australia, which accepted 'responsible government' but debated its relationship with federalism in designing its proposed structures. They internalized shared assumptions of how government worked that were largely taken for granted.

OUR APPROACH

In this study we are interested in revealing how governmental elites understand the Westminster model today. We explore how traditions shape the exercise of power in Westminster systems. What stories are told about the changes and their causes? We will seek to explain the different outcomes by examining the competing governmental traditions. There are several key questions:

- What are the dominant national traditions in the five former dominions?
- How did the several traditions respond differently to challenges?
- How did the executives change in response to the challenges and attendant crises or dilemmas? How do traditions change?
- Did these changes have unintended consequences?
- Do traditions explain these consequences?

In short, the purpose is to show how local traditions interacted with the often blurred beliefs and practices associated with Westminster to provide the present-day forms of government. We are not seeking to provide commentary on contemporary events, so we have taken our examples mainly from the period 1910 to 2007.

In Chapter 2, we locate this argument in the broader context of the academic study of comparative politics, especially of the political executive. We review that literature, arguing that the study of Westminster systems has been an intellectual backwater, divorced from the study of comparative politics. The reasons for this, we believe, are that research on Westminster systems has tended to be one of its kind. It has focused on how far various polities have departed from idealized notions of Westminster, on evolving constitutional and conventional practices, and on internal power shifts that have occurred. Moreover, there has been little engagement between the comparative politics scholars and those studying national executives. We argue for an approach grounded in formal–legal and historical analysis focused on traditions, dilemmas, and court politics.

In Chapter 3, we survey the dominant political traditions and the key debates about governance in our five dominions. We identify four discernible traditions: the royal prerogative; responsible government; constitutional bureaucracy; and representative government. They set the scene, determine the shape of politics, and create much of the rhetoric and expectations. We explore how constitutional traditions have struggled with the dilemmas of centralization versus decentralization; party government versus ministerial responsibility; professionalization versus politicization; and elitism versus participation. We stress the competing interpretations of the constitution and the fluctuating fortunes of the several traditions.

Then we turn to the workings of the institutions. Each chapter begins with a different country. We seek to show how Westminster concepts have mutated in different countries, while still legitimately described as Westminster. We do not begin by asking how far they may have moved from British practice.

Chapter 4 addresses variations in executive arrangements. We look at the formal roles of the prime minister and cabinet organized around the argument there has been a trend towards ever-greater prime ministerial power. This argument is often referred to as the 'presidentialisation thesis'. We think that is a mistake. Prime ministers are frequently more powerful than presidents. In practice, the thesis expresses concern that power has become centralized in the persons and offices of prime ministers; that power is now individual, hence presidential, rather than collective. We argue there is no such uniform centralizing trend in the Westminster systems of the dominion countries. Rather, there is evidence of an ever-changing balance of power within core executives characterized by dependence and contingency between centralization and decentralization.

In Chapter 5, we start with the classic constitutional doctrines of ministerial and collective responsibility to parliament. In some versions of constitutional theory, ministers should resign for policy failure and the administrative mistakes of their departments. In practice, ministers go if and only if prime ministers judge that the political costs of a minister staying outweigh the costs of going. There is a trade-off between the exigencies of party government, with the need to manage the media and the electorate, and ministerial responsibility to parliament. Thompson and Tillotsen (1999) have attempted to demarcate when conventions of ministerial responsibility apply by using the simile of ministers left holding 'smoking guns' – one for personal improprieties and one for policy or maladministration. We not only explore how the actors interpret and reinterpret this doctrine, but also argue that ministers are embedded in webs of accountability.

The changing role of the public service both formally and in practice is the subject of Chapter 6. For a long time, public servants had a near-monopoly of advice and were safeguarded by their expertise, and by the conventions of neutrality and permanence.[10] For many they became 'statesmen in disguise', with a reputation for giving frank and fearless advice. Ostensibly, their advice was impartial, expert, and experienced. As with parliamentary government, commentators sometimes look back with nostalgia to a golden age for the public servants, regarded as the mid-twentieth century when distinguished figures were known by insiders, but not by the general public, as significant influences. They wish those circumstances could continue. But that was not to be. Due to demands variously described as responsiveness, politicization, and personalization, the public service was to be curbed. Professionalization met politicization and the demand that the public servants be 'on tap' but not 'on top'. Yet, the extent of the changes varied among the dominions. This chapter explores the aftermath of the managerial revolution; commencing in Canada, but strongest in the Antipodean countries, and applying selectively in the UK. In the developing South African context, there remains an ambivalent attitude towards a non-partisan bureaucracy in the post-apartheid or 'post-liberation' era.

In Chapter 7, we explore the constitutional primacy of parliament. We ask what implications do enduring notions of parliamentary sovereignty have for political practice, and what erosions to sovereignty have taken place? Is sovereignty now, at best, 'qualified' or, at worst, reduced to an 'elective dictatorship' (Hailsham 1978). Do political elites see this as 'qualified sovereignty' or competing sovereignties within their polity? We also question how far notions of an institutionalized and legitimate opposition prevail in the five former dominions. Furthermore, representativeness has long been a feature of Westminster, but in recent decades identity politics, ethnic politics, regional politics, and subnational forms of independence have had an impact on both the composition of the executive and its scope for action. We ask how parliaments are composed, what understandings of representation they display, and how these affect executive power.

Finally, in Chapter 8, we explore the uses to which the concept of Westminster is put and ask why it continues to have such resonance. We conclude the family of ideas we customarily refer to as 'Westminster' is variously constructed in the light of the divergent and competing governmental traditions within and between the dominions. Even if there is no such unambiguous thing as 'Westminster', with each country having markedly different trajectories and traditions, thus confronting common problems with divergent responses, we still need to understand some of the implications of the concepts. Lijphart (1999) and Strøm et al. (2003), among others, have challenged the traditional view that Westminster governments bring benefits: majoritarian governments, political stability, policy cohesion, and constructive parliamentary–executive relationships. We ask whether there is indeed evidence for the benefits of Westminster systems and to what extent they are the result of different traditions and variable understandings of the role of institutions. We ask whether there is a reliable and easy way to determine the effectiveness of the regimes or are all such measures both contingent and country specific and ill-suited to comparative generalizations. Traditions shape not only what is done and why, but also the outcomes of executive government.

NOTES

1 We use the phrase 'Westminster model' to refer to the beliefs and practices of the Westminster tradition and the phrase 'Westminster systems' to refer to the countries studied in this book.

2 There are no countries in the world that regard themselves as a Westminster system that do not share a British heritage. In most cases they were under British rule for some period. However, in the 1990s the President of Kazakhstan, Nursultan Nazarbaev, in the post-Soviet era, thought the Westminster system was an attractive model of stable democracy. After announcing he would implement it, and holding elections for a legislature in 1994, he promptly sacked the representatives, dissolved the parliament and resumed unilateral control of the republic, which he enshrined through a second post-Soviet constitution.

3 Historically, political movements from various parts of the UK determined not to follow Westminster practice, such as the Irish, the Chartists, and Guild Socialists.

4 Jennings's discussion of the personal qualities of Sir Robert Peel, William Gladstone, and Benjamin Disraeli are good examples of this viewpoint.

5 For a comprehensive bibliography see Larby and Hannam (1993). The authoritative study of dominion status is Wheare (1953). The indispensable study of the British Empire in the twentieth century is Brown and Lewis (1999).

6 See for further details: COI (1957: 4–5); Holland (2003: 633); Kendle (1967: 45–57); Wheare (1953: 2–4 and chapters 2 and 3); Wheare (1960: 6–12).

7 Arguably, by the period 1907–19 there were five categories of dominion in the British Empire – each with its own status and forms of political rule. These were:

1. The self-governing 'great' dominions – the 'white' settler colonies of Canada, Australia, New Zealand, and South Africa.
2. The Indian Empire – a separate empire with the monarch as emperor, not enjoying self-rule.
3. The 'home rule' regions – Ireland, Southern Rhodesia, Malta and perhaps Newfoundland (although this was later counted as a dominion briefly).
4. Colonies – British possessions in Africa, the Caribbean, and South Pacific.
5. Crown Colonies – such as Gibraltar and Hong Kong.

8 The last two countries did not remain dominions for long. Newfoundland's dominion status was temporarily suspended in 1933 because of economic difficulties. In 1949, Newfoundland became the tenth province of Canada. The Irish Free State lasted for but a few more years. In 1936, it removed all references in its constitution to the monarchy and in 1937 a new constitution was enacted establishing Eire as 'a sovereign, independent, democratic state'. It did not join the Allied cause in the 1939–45 war, and in 1949 Eire left the Commonwealth.

9 Although the term 'dominion' fell into disuse, it still resonated in the former colonies. For instance, in South Africa the pro-British white party in the Second World War named itself the Dominion Party (1939–48). In New Zealand, one of the country's major daily newspapers is called *The Dominion Post*, while, in Canberra, Dominion Circuit partly surrounds Parliament House on Capital Hill.

10 There were a few examples of outsiders being 'brought in' for policy advice, such as the role of various economics professors (including Keynes) in the Great Depression and its aftermath.

2

Comparing Westminster

A myth does not take hold without expressing many truths – misleading
truths, usually, but important ones: truth for one thing, to the needs of
those who elaborate and accept the myth; truth to the demand for some
control over complex realities; truth to the recognition of shared values
(however shakily grounded those values may be in themselves). Even the
myths that simplify are not, in themselves, simple (Wood 1997).

...and what should they know of England who only England know?
(Rudyard Kipling, 'The English Flag' (1990 [1891]).

Much of the literature on executive government in parliamentary systems has
been produced by writers other than political scientists. Often it is more racy
and fun to read precisely because it is *not* written by scholars. The authors are
practitioners, journalists, or popular historians. There are the biographies of
individual prime ministers with varying degrees of lurid detail about their
private lives. There are psycho-biographies probing childhood and other
formative experiences. There are the journalists recording the comings and
goings of our leaders, with an eye for a story that is rarely discomfited by an
inconvenient fact or the need to articulate frameworks and methods. There
are the glossy magazine accounts of 'court politics' and tabloid exposés, with
the stress on human interest and experiences, and on the husband's or the
wife's viewpoint. There are novels and dramas based around real characters or
events but with concocted storylines of intrigue and plot.

But, against this panoply of reportage, where are the theories, the models,
and the typologies of executive government in parliamentary systems that
distinguish political scientists from their more racy rivals. The academic
political science literature is limited – much more so than readers might
expect or the importance of the subject warrants. The reasons for this lie in
the problems of access to executive government, which is often shrouded in
secrecy, and in fickle academic fashions. Executive government in parliamentary systems was often regarded as an academic backwater, whereas presidential or semi-presidential government became the 'sexy' area. There is also a
continuing need to break free of worn-out debates, especially in the analysis of
Westminster systems. The study of executives in parliamentary government

would be far more vibrant *if* it engaged with core debates in the comparative politics literature.

We try to build such bridges in this chapter. Conceptual ambiguity and contestable assumptions lie at the heart of most current classifications and definitions of regimes (Elgie 1998). However, we start with Shugart's (2006: 348) definition that 'pure' parliamentary democracy is defined by two basic features: 'executive authority, consisting of a prime minister and cabinet, arises out of the legislative assembly'; and 'the executive is at all times subject to potential dismissal via a vote of "no confidence" by a majority of the legislative assembly'. But parliamentary government is a broad church (see Shugart 2006: table 18: 1). Westminster is one manifestation of parliamentary government with its own variants. Here, we are concerned not with the generic notion of parliamentary government but with that specific variant known as Westminster.

The first section of this chapter considers the limits of existing approaches to the study of executive government. We identify four main schools:

1. The idealized Westminster genre based on particular formal–legal notions of executive government.
2. A comparative–empiricist strand that contrasts executive institutions and behaviours across nations.
3. The functionalist depiction of the core executive based on activities and roles.
4. Principal–agent models of executive relations informed by rational choice institutionalism.

These four approaches and their variants dominate the political science literature. In contrast to them, we argue for an interpretive approach based on a revamped formal–legal, historical analysis of traditions and beliefs. We stress the need to be genuinely comparative and to use the authoritative voices of political elites rather than secondary analytical observations from 'object-ive' analysts. We argue for the production of narratives based on the language and meanings of the proximate political actors derived from contemporary primary sources. Finally, we identify a series of predominant debates and challenges emerging from practice but prevalent in the contemporary study of parliamentary executives. These debates often concern disquiet over pre-sumed trends and tendencies within the parliamentary executive. We will later explore these debates in the context of our five former dominion Westminster systems. We identify: the presidentialization of prime ministers; deficits in accountability; the politicization of the public service with impli-cations for its policy advice and policy capacities; and executive dominance of the legislature.

COMPETING APPROACHES

By the latter half of the twentieth century, *Westminster studies* was a distinctive genre in the broader study of parliamentary government. The genre embodied both descriptive and normative aspects. Many of its claimed attributes went back to archaic times and episodic clashes between monarchs and parliamentarians, framed by Burkean or Whig notions of evolution. We summarized this family of ideas in Table 1.1. If an unwritten constitution framed the system, practitioners were still constrained by the 'understood constitution'. Prior to 1914, the unwritten elements were taken for granted and accepted across almost the entire political spectrum of parties and opinion. Participants and observers were socialized into formal–legal rules and powerful bipartisan conventions. However, majority control over the legislature was fundamental and to some extent could reshape the conventional rules over time. It was also accepted that small 'c' constitutions did not reflect reality; and much of the subsequent codification of Westminster was promulgated by academics, constitutional lawyers, or government intellectuals. It was of necessity *idealized.*

Over time, lists of defining characteristics were created which invariably included the 'efficient secret' of 'the closer union, the nearly complete fusion, of the executive and legislative powers' (Bagehot 1963: 65). The party or parties with a majority in the lower house of parliament formed the executive, and assumed the key positions of prime minister, cabinet and, later, the penumbra of junior appointments. Cabinet is collectively responsible for its decisions, and its members (or ministers) are individually responsible to parliament for the work of their departments. The Westminster approach often assumes that power lies with specific elected positions and the people who occupy those positions – they are believed to initiate policy and have the last word in decisions. The literature is dominated by such topics as the relative power of prime minister and cabinet, and the relationship between the executive and parliament.

The *modernist–empiricist approach* drew heavily on social science behaviouralism, and treated political executives as discrete objects that could be compared, measured, and classified (Bevir 2001). Its core assumptions were that institutions in various national settings could be regarded as objects to be counted to produce 'law-like generalisations' (Bevir and Rhodes 2006). Early cross-national studies focused on political elites, especially the notion of political leadership (Mughan and Patterson 1992; Elgie 1995).

There has also been a plethora of country-specific case studies collected into comparative volumes. The popular topics of comparison include: the recruitment, tenure, and careers of prime ministers and ministers; ministerial and prime ministerial relationships with bureaucracy and other sources of policy advice; their links with political parties, the media, and the public; and the resources and personal qualities of ministers and prime ministers (Blondel and Thiébault 1991; Jones 1991). While valuable as compendia of information, such studies are not genuinely comparative and tend to rely on experts in one jurisdiction. Others of a more comparative bent drill down to examine the impact of certain key variables. Blondel and Müller-Rommel's (1993*a*: 15) work on Western Europe studies 'the interplay of one major independent variable – the single-party or coalition character of the cabinet – with a number of structural and customary arrangements in governments, and of the combined effect of these factors on decision making processes' in 12 West European cabinets. It is 'a fully comparative analysis' with data drawn from a survey of 410 ministers in nine countries; and an analysis of newspaper reports on cabinet conflicts in 11 countries.

The *functionalist approach to the core executive* was developed in the analysis of British government (Dunleavy and Rhodes 1990), but it has travelled well (Elgie 1997). It defined the executive in functional terms. So, instead of asserting which position is more or less important by some external measure, it asked which functions define the innermost part or heart of government. For example, if the core functions of the British central executive are to pull together and integrate central government policies and to act as final arbiters of conflicts between different elements of the government machine, those functions can be carried out by institutions other than the prime minister or the ministers in cabinet; for example, by departments such as the Treasury or by officials in the Cabinet Office. By defining the core executive in functional terms, the key question becomes 'who does what?'

But power is contingent and relational; it depends on the relative power of other actors and events. Most ministers depend on the prime minister for support in getting funds from the Treasury. In turn, the prime minister depends on ministers to deliver the party's electoral promises. Both ministers and prime minister depend on the health of the world economy (and especially the US dollar) for a stable currency and a growing economy to ensure the needed financial resources are available. This power-dependence approach focuses on the distribution of such resources as money and authority in the core executive and explores the shifting patterns of dependence between the several actors (Rhodes 1995*a*; Elgie 1997; Smith 1999).

The term '*core executive*' thus directs our attention to two key questions: 'who does what?' and 'who has what resources?' This approach also tends to assume the answers to these questions will vary from arena to arena. If the answer for several policy areas and several conflicts turns out to be the prime minister who presides over the coordination of policy, resolves conflicts, and controls the main resources, we will indeed have prime ministerial government. But, otherwise, we may wish to qualify notions of presidentialization.

Principal–agent explanations of executive relations have come in many guises but were increasingly focused on the analysis of prime ministers and cabinets. Contract theory, bargained relations, rational choice theory, and methodological individualism are at the heart of this approach. Here, one example will suffice. Strøm and his colleagues have developed a principal–agent theory of delegation and accountability in parliamentary democracies (see also Cox 1987; Laver and Shepsle 1996; Tsebelis 2002). Strøm et al. (2003) conceive of parliamentary democracy as a chain of delegation from principals to agents; from voters to their elected representatives; from legislators to the chief executive; from the chief executive to ministerial heads of departments; and from ministers to public servants. Principals and agents are in hierarchic relationships and both act rationally to gain exogenously given preferences. No agent is perfect. So, agency loss occurs because the actual consequences of delegation diverge from the principal's initial intentions. There are two main causes of agency loss. First, there may be a conflict of interest between the principal and the agent who may have different policy objectives. Second, there may be limited information and resources and, for example, the principal may not know what the agent is doing. When principals know less than agents, two problems occur: moral hazard and adverse selection. Moral hazard arises when an agent takes actions of which a principal disapproves. Adverse selection occurs when an agent is unwilling or unable to pursue the principal's interests. A principal can use *ex ante* mechanisms, such as screening of applicants, to control adverse selection problems, and *ex post* mechanisms, such as contracts, to deal with moral hazard. For Strøm, such a framework can be used to analyse the strengths of Westminster parliamentary systems, which they found to be heightened coordination and efficiency.

Each of these approaches has limits. Westminster's idealized formal–legal approach ignores larger debates both in the study of comparative politics and in political science. It can revel in archaism, taking its stance from Burke, Bagehot, and Dicey (Bogdanor 1999: 175). The sheer scale of Blondel's modernist–empiricism is impressive but it is the scale that poses problems. Dogan and Pelassy (1990: 116) comment that such comparative studies disappoint because 'comparability is very low'. Citing Blondel's (1980) analysis of all 'heads of government in the post-war period', they ask: 'what sense is there in comparing the "regular ministerial career" in the Middle East and in the Atlantic and communist worlds? Aren't we here misled simply by verbal similarities?' The 'core executive' approach can also be reductionist, covering too few functions of the core executive; for example, ignoring the representative function of cabinets. As we argue below, it needs to be extended to include the varieties of 'court politics'. It would then be able to pick up the ironies and unpredictabilities of politics, including luck, accident, unintended consequences or misunderstanding. Ignoring the general criticisms of the rational choice approach (Green and Shapiro 1994; Hay 2004), there are the specific limitations of principal–agent theory when applied to the study of executives. For example, the reified assumption of top-down hierarchy does not hold. Ministers are embedded in webs of vertical and horizontal dependences and only the former can be conceived as principal–agent chains. Webs or networks are absent despite their centrality to both delegation and accountability.

AN ALTERNATIVE INTERPRETIVE APPROACH

In contrast to the four dominant approaches outlined above, our point of departure is an *interpretive approach* to political science. All political scientists wish to offer us 'their' interpretations, which are authorial, objective, and law-like. But interpretive approaches differ in offering interpretations of interpretations. They concentrate on meanings and beliefs, not laws and rules, correlations between social categories, or deductive models. So, an interpretive approach asks about the meaning of something, and in this book the 'something' refers to the beliefs and practices of elite actors about the Westminster model. We prefer to think of meanings as 'beliefs' that inform practices. To explore and explain webs of beliefs we employ the concepts of tradition and narrative, hoping to uncover how political elites make sense of their world and to discover what internalized navigation points they use to guide their practice (Bevir and Rhodes 2003, 2006).

Traditions, Agency, and Myth

In this book, we do not seek to write another series of national studies of government. Rather, across all five countries, we explore how political elites adapted and used, rhetorically and practically, the concepts at the heart of the Westminster system. We are interested in the history of the political ideas that drive political action and the uses to which they are put. Our historical analysis will be built around the notions of received traditions and their relationship to the governmental practices.

A governmental *tradition* is a set of inherited beliefs about the institutions and history of government (Perez-Diaz 1993: 7). For Western Europe it is conventional to distinguish between the Anglo-Saxon (small 'l' liberal state) tradition; the Germanic *Rechtsstaat* tradition; the étatist French (Napoleonic) tradition; and the Scandinavian tradition which mixes the Anglo-Saxon and Germanic. There is already a growing body of work on the impact of such traditions. Bevir, Rhodes, and Weller (2003*b*: 202) commented that Westminster systems embody traditions that support strong executive government thus enabling governments to force through reform in response to economic pressures whereas in the Netherlands, with traditions of consensual corporatism, there is no reform without formal coalition agreement. France provides another contrast. The combination of departmental fragmentation at the centre, coupled with the 'grand corps' tradition and its beliefs about a strong state, meant that any proposed reform rested on the consent of those about to be reformed and this was often not forthcoming. So, we agree with Helms (2005: 261) that a historical and comparative perspective is the best way to explore the analysis of core executives and the variety of political practice within and between regime types. This is the analysis of traditions by another name (as is the analysis of path dependences in Pierson 2004).

A tradition is a set of understandings or orthodoxies that someone learns or receives during socialization. Although tradition is unavoidable, it is a starting point, a first influence on people. But traditions are *living* constructions that are constantly interpolated orally and renegotiated inside actors' heads. As living traditions they constantly percolate and change. They are not long-dead 'traditional customs' or ceremonial pomp handed down to functionaries as if they were mere automata or cyber-beings. Traditions usually only influence, as distinct from govern, the nature of individuals and are thus products of individual agency. Consequently, although individuals will start out from an inherited tradition, this does not mean they cannot break free or seek to adjust it. When we confront the unfamiliar, we have to extend or change our heritage to encompass it and, as we do so, we develop our heritage. Every time we try to apply a tradition, we have cause to reflect on it perhaps to try to understand it afresh in today's context or circumstances. By reflecting on it, we give dynamism to traditions and open them to innovation. Thus, human agency can produce change even when people think they are sticking fast to a tradition they regard as enduring or sacrosanct.

A particular relationship must exist between beliefs and practices if they are to make up a tradition. For a start, the relevant beliefs and practices must have passed from actor to actor, generation to generation, and have practical application (an abstract set of beliefs that were not passed on would form a contemporaneous record, not a living tradition). Such socialization may be intentional or unintentional. The continuity lies in the themes developed and passed on over time. But as beliefs are passed on, they are adapted and extended, and many may take on a relatively recent characterization.[1] In many cases we will be able to trace a historical line from the start of a tradition to its current finish. However, the developments introduced by successive generations might result in the beginning and ending having little in common apart from the links over time.

As well as suitable links through time, traditions must embody suitable conceptual links. The beliefs and practices a teacher passes on to a pupil must display a minimal consistency. A tradition could not have provided someone with an initial starting point unless its parts formed a minimally coherent set, but it does not have to be as coherent as a recognized political ideology. Indeed, while the recognized ideologies (e.g. liberalism, conservatism, and socialism) form traditions, not all traditions form ideologies (e.g. traditions of nationhood and territorial expression). Similarly, traditions cannot be made up of purely random beliefs and actions that successive individuals happen to have held in common.

Although the beliefs in a tradition must be related to one another, both temporally and conceptually, their substantive content is less important. Because tradition is unavoidable, all beliefs and practices must have their roots in perceived tradition. They must do so whether they are aesthetic or practical, sacred or secular, legendary or factual, premodern or scientific, valued because of lineage or reasonableness. This idea of tradition differs, therefore, from that of political scientists who associate the term with customary, unquestioned ways of behaving (Oakeshott 1962: 123 and 128–9) or with the entrenched folklore of premodern societies. At the heart of our notion of tradition are individuals using local reasoning consciously and subconsciously to reflect on and modify their contingent heritage (Bevir, Rhodes, and Weller 2003*a*).

A suitable emphasis on agency and local reasoning also makes us wary of essentialists who equate traditions with fixed essences to which they credit variations. Dicey and Greenleaf illustrate clearly the difference between an essentialist notion of tradition and our own. For Britain, Dicey (1914: 62–9) divided the Victorian period into three parts. The first, 1800–30, was an era of legislative quiescence or an era of old Toryism. The Benthamite spirit of inquiry and governmental reform typified 1825–70. Then 1865–1900 was the era of collectivism, irresistible yet unwelcome to the author. There have been many challenges to Dicey's account of nineteenth-century administrative history but his defence of individualism against collectivism continues to influence interpretations of British government. Likewise, Greenleaf (1983: 15–20) describes the British political tradition as the dialectic between libertarianism and collectivism. But Greenleaf's categories of individualism and collectivism are too ahistorical. Although they come into being in the nineteenth century, after that they remain static. They act as fixed ideal types into which individual thinkers and texts are then forced. In contrast, an emphasis on situated agency encourages a view of tradition as a starting point for a historical story. It suggests that later instances cannot be constructed by comparison with the allegedly essential features of a putative tradition.

So, in our Westminster systems, traditions provide a set of maps, a language, and historical narratives about government that over time captures those essential features we would now group under the heading 'the Westminster model'. These systems have been relatively stable and enduring, and so evolution, longevity, myth, and nostalgia form a major part of the mainstream story. We disagree that Westminster is a fantasy, as Hughes (1998: 328) maintains. It is better seen as a set of evolving traditions couched in myth. And as the epigraph to this chapter explains, myths express many truths about shared beliefs and practices; they are constructed and disseminated to explain praxis. In our interpretive approach, myths are handed down from generation to generation as a way of understanding beliefs and practices. Traditions associated with Westminster express such beliefs in both their mundane routine form and in their 'heroic' qualities.

How Traditions Change

The interpretive approach encourages us to examine ways in which individuals create, sustain, and modify social life, institutions, and policies. It encourages us to recognize that institutional norms or some behavioural logic do not fix the actions of individuals. Rather, actions and strategies arise from the beliefs individuals adopt against the background of traditions and in response to the challenges they come to face.

It is through challenges or, in Bevir's (1999: 221–64) terms, 'dilemmas', that agents are able to bring about changes in beliefs, traditions, and practices. Here we use challenges and dilemmas interchangeably. Any existing pattern of government will have some failings although different people will have different views about these failings because they are not given by experience, but constructed from interpretations of experience infused with traditions. When people's perceptions of failings conflict with their existing beliefs, they pose 'dilemmas' that push them to reconsider their beliefs and the intellectual tradition that informs those beliefs. Because people confront these challenges in diverse traditions, there arises a political contest over what constitutes the nature of the failings and what should be done about them. Exponents of rival political positions or traditions seek to promote their particular sets of theories and policies, and this political contest leads to a reform of government. So, any reform must be understood as the contingent product of a contest of meanings in action.

As the practices of government are reformed by this complex process, they will begin to display new failings, pose new challenges or dilemmas, and subsequently be the subject of competing proposals for reform. There will be a further contest over meanings, a contest in which not only will the perceived challenges often be significantly different, but also the traditions will have been modified because of previous accommodations. At particular points in time, laws and norms prescribe how all such contests should be constructed and conducted. Sometimes the relevant laws and norms have changed because of simultaneous political contests over their content and relevance. Yet, while we can distinguish analytically between a pattern of government and a political contest over its reform, we rarely can do so temporally. Typically, governing continues during most political contests, and most contests occur partly within local practices of governing. What we have, therefore, is a complex and continuous process of interpretation, conflict, and practice that produces ever-changing patterns of governance. Sometimes these changes are incremental and evolutionary, but occasionally they transform the polity – such as the shift to a mixed member proportional voting system in New Zealand in 1994 or the fundamental rewriting of South Africa's constitution in 1995–6.[2]

Thus, the political challenges posed by the increasing role, size, and scale of government fuelled changes to the 'unwritten' British and New Zealand constitutions. As a result the meaning was fragmented. They had no special procedures for amendment, and no written constitutions, as in Australia and Canada, to slow down change. In the unitary states, it no longer seemed credible to conceive of the constitution as rooted in a minimalist, caretaker role for the state. The dominant liberal interpretation of that constitution was Dicey's formalist, normativist style of public law, which stressed a rule-oriented conception of public law about government. The key functions of constitutional law were adjudication and control of the executive, which nevertheless enjoyed certain privileges and immunities. This stress on the separation of powers and the subordination of government to law confronted the functionalist style in public law that emphasized law as part of the apparatus of government, playing a regulatory and facilitative role and sustaining an instrumentalist social policy (Loughlin 1992: 60). The liberal view of the constitution and its key doctrines of parliamentary sovereignty and ministerial accountability was decisively transformed by the functionalist or Whitehall view of the constitution with its emphasis on executive power and the role of the executive as the guardian of the national interest and a defence of 'strong government'. Indeed, Britain can be said to have invested in 'strong government' rather than constructing a 'strong state'.

Similar expansions in the role of government placed strains on written constitutions over the coverage or inclusion of issues, who had responsibility for new policy areas, and whether one government's desire to intervene could be overturned by another. 'Old' constitutions were often notoriously hard to change and update, and often even mild amendments proposed by governments were seen as self-serving and opposed by the citizenry. However, written constitutions are contested and subject to evolving interpretations, so meanings can change over time especially in relation to both powers and the principles or conventions on which government rests (Birch 1964; Rees 1977; Smiley 1980; Loughlin 1992). Expanding roles and heightened expectations that governments would 'solve problems' caused Australian and Canadian governments to explore ways to get around their constitutions – by funding deals, reinterpretations of constitutional provisions, resort to external or emergency powers, or by fiat or negotiated agreement. The consequence is that governments may now be operating in areas where they have limited or no constitutional authority. By contrast, South Africa, with a history of punctuated constitutional change, has adopted a constitution that is amenable to change although the 13 amendments up to 2007 have been technical and institutional rather than policy related.

Traditions in Comparative Perspective

Not only are traditions living and evolving, but analysis of them is brought more into relief by genuinely comparative research. The distinctive nature of traditions in various national settings becomes more apparent as we compare across polities. So, for instance, traditions of liberalism may be evident in, say, Britain and New Zealand but they differ markedly in how particular beliefs are marshalled and how those operating in the tradition may confront challenges. Moreover, common institutional terms such as cabinet, the prime ministership, or ministerial accountability, while ostensibly similar, will be infused with local traditions, meanings, and possibilities. It is precisely this complexity that gives the interpretive approach to traditions a sharper analytical edge.

The focus on traditions and the belief systems of practitioners allows us to be genuinely comparative. Our criticism of much of the existing literature is that it is not genuinely comparative analysis. For instance, much of the published work on Westminster systems is not strictly speaking comparative, but compilations of country studies reporting separate cases (but cf. Weller et al. 1997; Weller 1985). Even though the modernist–empiricist school collects extensive cross-national data sets, by accepting institutional labels such as 'cabinet' at face value it is often reduced to comparing apples and oranges, and changing the level of analysis (say from cabinet to ministers) does not solve the problem (see Blondel and Thiébault 1991). Most comparative research has preferred to contrast regime types, not (as in this volume) focus on variations within one regime type and explore how different understandings shape behaviour. Perhaps one of the most sterile and misleading comparisons has been between American presidents and UK prime ministers. It is not revealing to be told, as Rose (2001: 237–44) says, that there are similarities (for example, the media's impact on leaders and campaigning) and differences (such as recruitment, careers, terms of office) between these positions. To conclude that there are big differences in the powers of prime ministers over time, big differences in the powers of presidents, and big differences between prime ministers and presidents is hardly informative. The comparative analysis of prime ministers and cabinets must compare like with like and explore meanings.

To explore traditions in cross-national terms we also need to explore specific traditions in specific countries. We do so by focusing on the core executive – the apex of formal government. Otherwise our task would not only be daunting but well nigh impossible. It is also helpful to open some key themes and questions with which we interrogate the traditions. Our main themes are centralization, accountability, bureaucracy, representation, effectiveness, and how each changed and continues to change. And when we explore change, we find Elgie's typology of possible power relations in the core executive suggestive. He identifies six varieties of court politics:

- *Monocratic government* – personal leadership by prime minister or president.
- *Collective government* – small, face-to-face groups decide with no single member controlling.
- *Ministerial government* – the political heads of major departments decide policy.
- *Bureaucratic government* – non-elected officials in government departments and agencies decide policy.
- *Shared government* – two or three individuals have joint and equal responsibility for policy-making.
- *Segmented government* – a sectoral division of labour among executive actors with little or no cross-sectoral coordination.

The key advantage of this formulation is that it gets away from bald assertions about the fixed nature of executive politics. While one pattern of 'court politics' may operate in one arena at one time (in relation, say, to foreign policy), there can still be fluidity over time as one pattern succeeds another or in another arena of politics (such as domestic politics). We are not interested in 'finding' the precise patterns in practice, or in explaining which one might prevail. Rather, we seek to widen the scope of analysis and allow for several patterns of 'court politics' in the core executive. Those studies that presuppose and then demonstrate that there has been an unprecedented growth in prime ministerial power are analytically limiting. By contrast, Elgie's six patterns (1997: 231) remind us of the richer possibilities in explaining similarities and differences in executive politics. Our key point here is that the comparative analysis of executives must not, as in the case of much of the writing on Westminster systems, become inward looking and oblivious to developments elsewhere in comparative politics.

HOW WE STUDY EXECUTIVE GOVERNMENT

The formal–legal study of political institutions is central to the identity of the discipline of political science. Eckstein (1963: 10–11) points out:

> If there is any subject matter at all which political scientists can claim exclusively for their own, a subject matter that does not require acquisition of the analytical tools of sister-fields and that sustains their claim to autonomous existence, it is, of course, formal–legal political structure.

Similarly, Greenleaf (1983: 7–9) argues that constitutional law, constitutional history, and the study of institutions form the 'traditional' approach to political science, and he is commenting, not criticizing. With the behavioural revolution in American political science and then the arrival of the so-called new institutionalism, formal–legal analysis was reduced to the role of Aunt Sally. It was the butt for the criticisms of the new arrivals, often caricatured, rarely understood or even cited accurately.[3] However, formal–legal analysis has its own distinctive rationale and, understood as the analysis of *the historical evolution of formal–legal institutions and the ideas embedded in them,* it remains the defining characteristic of the political science contribution to the study of political institutions. Such texts as constitutions and their allied customs constitute the governmental traditions that shape the practices of citizen, politician, administrator, and political scientists alike. So, we read constitutions as text for the beliefs they embed in institutions. We also explore the related conventions by observing politicians and public servants at work because observation is the prime way of recovering ideas and their meanings.

If institutions are to be understood through the beliefs and actions of individuals located in traditions, then historical analysis is the way to uncover the traditions that shape these stories. We seek to reconstruct the meanings of social actors by recovering other people's stories (Taylor 1971; Geertz 1973). The aim is 'to see the world as they see it, to adopt their vantage point on politics' (Fenno 1990: 2). Shore's (2000: 7–11) cultural analysis of how European Union elites sought to build Europe uses participant observation, historical archives, textual analysis of official documents, biographies, oral histories, recorded interviews, and informal conversations as well as statistical and survey techniques. The techniques are many and varied but the aim is always to recover other people's meanings. In effect, we draw on three sources of information:

> the pattern of practice, talk, and considered writing – the first is the most reliable, the second is the most copious and revealing and the third is the most difficult to interpret (Oakeshott 1996: x).

Although we rely on a similar battery of methods, we cannot employ participant observation in a historical study. Rather we start with our revamped formal–legal analysis that explicitly relies on the views and actions of key actors, reflected in what they said, wrote, and did. In examining the beliefs and preferences of political and administrative elites, we will explore elite beliefs about how government works, their explanations for the causes and extent of change, differences between the first and present-day systems, and the effects of the differences.

Governmental elites can enact their beliefs and preferences in many arenas; the political party, elections, in the media, or on the international stage. Our arena is the core executive itself, the political and administrative rela-tionships at the heart of government. We believe that by exploring the contingencies of political life, the shifts in the core executive, and the ways in which individuals modify their inherited beliefs and practices when they confront the dilemmas of governance, we will better understand the shifting patterns of executive leadership. Hence, we commence our analysis by exam-ining five key debates.

KEY DEBATES

We identified five recurring debates among government elites and scholars in the analysis of Westminster systems. These debates represent the shifting tectonic plates of Westminster systems, the most pronounced dilemmas for accepted traditions and beliefs. They also structure the book, each the subject of a subsequent substantive chapter. They are:

1. the growth of prime ministerial power, also referred to as the 'presidentialization thesis';
2. the decline in individual and collective ministerial accountability;
3. the politicization of the public service with perhaps an attendant loss of policy capacity;
4. executive dominance of the legislature; and
5. the broader debate about the overall effectiveness of Westminster as a system of government.

We address this final debate in the conclusion to this book. These debates parallel our core themes of power, accountability, bureaucracy, representation, and effectiveness.

Presidentialization

The institutions of prime minister and cabinet are as much creations of practice and convention as of constitutional law. That said, conventions are widely recognized and accepted beliefs and practices. Thus, 'first among equals' and 'cabinet government' are well-known clichés, and clichés that once said something significant. In the second half of the twentieth century it became commonplace to challenge these sedimented beliefs. So, the prime minister is no longer 'first among equals' in the government but the new overlord or, in Crossman's famous phrase evoking classical rule, the elected 'first magistrate' (Crossman 1963: 22–3; Mackintosh 1968: 627). There is also said to be a corresponding decline in 'cabinet government'. The debate is no mere historical anachronism. It is alive and well today. For their 13 country study, Poguntke and Webb (2005*a*: 1) claim 'it is hard to avoid the impression that perceptions of personalization, and in particular, the "presidentialisation" of politics have become more widespread in recent years', citing Tony Blair, Gerhard Schröder, and Silvio Berlusconi as recent examples. It is difficult to overstate the scale of this debate in the academic literature. It is the defining debate of the Westminster approach and refers to three main claims: there has been a centralization of coordination, a pluralization of advice, and the personalization of party leadership and elections. The presidential argument is common to Westminster systems such as Australia, Britain, Canada, New Zealand, and South Africa and it is also found in many West European parliamentary systems.

Central coordination is seen not only as an internal process of consistency and collaboration, but also a strategic platform about the government's stance on wider agendas and policy issues. In place of cabinet coordination, the prime minister is believed to have concentrated coordinating powers around his or her office through systems of control, greater initiation and monitoring of policy by the centre, additional advisers and support staff attached to the prime minister's office, and shared agreement on priorities among central agencies. The pluralization of policy advice is thought to have eroded the capacities of departments while placing presidential prime ministers in positions to initiate, select, and arbitrate. Against arguments that the demands on the core executive exceed its capacities, the concern for prime ministers has been to get more and better advice. Prime ministers have augmented their own sources of advice through advisers and think-tanks to enhance their agenda-setting influence at the expense of their ministers or line departments. Control over these levers of power has enhanced the capacity of prime ministers to make decisions and determine the directions of their governments.

In addition, prime ministers have also centred attention on themselves as a presidentializing device. Citing Thatcher and Blair, Foley (2000), writing from within the modernist–empirical genre, has described prime ministers as using 'spatial leadership' techniques to bolster their power. They have become 'flagships' detached from their own government, dominating media coverage, and developing a personal rapport with the public to enhance their authority. Their party remains under tight control and has far less real authority than the leader. Similar arguments have been made about prime ministers Jean Chrétien, Bob Hawke, John Howard, and Helen Clark, and President Thabo Mbeki. We explore these contentions through the beliefs of the proximate players in Chapter 4.

Accountability – Individual and Collective Ministerial Accountability

Two debates stand out in this area: the degree to which ministerial accountability exists in practice (as opposed to fanciful, idealized notions); and the degree to which ministerial accountability is becoming extra-parliamentary in nature.

In theory, ministerial responsibility is 'one of the fundamentals' of the Westminster system. It means that 'some Minister of the Crown is responsible to Parliament and through Parliament to the public, for every act of the Executive' (Morrison 1964 [1959]: 332). In practice, the doctrine of ministerial responsibility resembles 'the procreation of eels' (Marshall 1986: 54). It is often said to be honoured only in the breach. Ministers often seek to evade responsibilities and not 'answer' for actions taken in their name. They rarely resign or stand aside unless the prime minister feels it more expedient for them to depart than remain. Politics, not ethics, governs the convention. There may be a 'smoking gun', it may be in the minister's hand, but that does not mean he or she will resign. As Thompson and Tillotsen (1999: 56) argue, 'if individual ministerial responsibility ever meant that ministers were expected to resign for major policy blunders or for serious errors of maladministration by a government department, it is dead'. Similarly, in terms of collective responsibility, a rule of political prudence, it was once thought essential that cabinets abide by the principles of cabinet solidarity. Yet today, 'Cabinet may have a policy, if it wishes, of permitting public disagreements between Ministers even on matters of major policy without endangering constitutional principles' (Marshall 1986: 225). In short, despite much formal subservience to the rhetoric, ministers do not resign and cabinets can openly disagree in public. So, the extent to which these notions of ministerial responsibility and collective responsibility are applied depends on the political standing of the minister and the judgement of the prime minister (Woodhouse 2003). So, in the UK, ministerial responsibility now means only that ministers account to and are answerable before parliament for their department's policies and actions. They resign only if they mislead parliament (Hansard 1997 cols 1046–7). This 'restatement' means ministers do not resign for departmental mistakes or maladministration. There is an important proviso. Woodhouse (2004: 17–18) reviews some recent cases of resignations in British government, arguing the key factors were 'the media and the minister'. She concludes that the 'constitutional principle has not been totally overcome by political pragmatism'.

Today, moreover, the focus on the accountability of individual ministers to *parliament* may obfuscate other developments affecting how ministers approach their roles. It is claimed that ministers are not singularly responsible to parliament but instead are locked in a myriad of competing responsibilities and accountabilities, as are both the departments they administer and the range of other public and non-public bodies involved in policy-making. Arguably they are all embedded in webs of accountabilities; in the institutional complexity of networks; in sets of organizational relationships; and cascading sets of legal and administrative law imperatives. Ministers may be but one player in this matrix in which many levels of accountability operate: legal, professional, and managerial as well as political. Ministers may be becoming more accountable to their constituencies or to clients through the courts rather than through the legislature. So, how far do these developments shape the beliefs of ministers in office? We return to these debates in Chapter 5.

Bureaucracy: Politicization of the Public Service

Formally, since the turn of the nineteenth century, Britain had a constitutional bureaucracy or

> an unpolitical civil service whose primary connection is with the Crown,
> and which, while subordinated to party governments, is unaffected by
> their changes: the two permanent elements, the Crown and the civil
> service, which not by chance together left the political arena, supply the
> framework for the free play of parliamentary politics and governments
> (Parris 1969: 49).

It was duly exported. However, during the Thatcher premiership, fears were expressed that the civil service was becoming politicized. They have not subsided since. The Royal Institute of Public Administration (1987: 43) cautiously concluded 'the appointment process has become more personalised' but 'we do not believe that these appointments and promotions are based on the candidate's support for or commitment to particular ideologies or objectives'. Other critics found it more difficult to hold the sanguine view that it was 'personalisation not politicisation' (Plowden 1994: 100–9).

In Australia, since Labor's 1972–5 term of office, claims have been made about a 'creeping politicization' (Weller 1989c: 369). By the late 1990s, the crescendo had escalated to the point where many critics believed ministers were no longer receiving 'frank and fearless' advice from their officials. Political control of the public service became the order of the day. The language of reform called for 'responsiveness' by public servants to the needs and wishes of ministers and three-to-five-year contracts for top public servants were instituted to reinforce the message. Suddenly, public servants were accused of becoming 'ultra-responsive' to their political masters, prepared of their own volition to act in the minister's name, anticipating their likely political interests, and telling them only what they wanted to hear. In reforming the public sector, the system has become far more open to ministerial involvement in the recruitment and appointment of senior executives than before.

Pollitt and Bouckaert (2000: 155) identify similar structural trends in Canada. In New Zealand, Norman (2003: 143) has described how, with the new public management (NPM) reforms (see Chapter 6), the quest of cabinet ministers for greater control over the bureaucracy produced a system that was marked by compliance and a 'climate of fear'. Local politicians told executives: 'we don't trust you but we want to build public service capability' and 'we want you to be innovative but don't make mistakes and don't take risks' (2003: 161). South Africa has devised its own twist on politicization; since the

African National Congress (ANC) assumed power it has sought a high degree of professionalism from its officials but not expected neutrality; the government has insisted on a quasi-partisan 'loyalty' to the new regime and greater representation to 'redress the imbalances of the past'.

If creeping politicization has come to characterize ministerial attitudes to the public service (although there is as yet less evidence of any overt party-politicization in any country) it has come at some cost. Notions of 'loyal competency' and mutual interests have flourished and long-standing traditions of 'institutional scepticism' may well have become attenuated (Plowden 1994: 104). Rhodes and Weller (2001: 238) put it another way in their six-country survey. Top civil servants, they argue, 'are selected and kept in part because of their style and approach, in part because of their policy preferences, and in part because ministers are comfortable with them'. All these characteristics attest to the malleability of the top echelon.

Politicization was not only seen to rock the fabric of the institution of the public service, it also led to claims that policy advice to ministers was also becoming more politicized and selective. Moreover, public sector reforms tended to magnify rather than impede such political biasing. In Australia and New Zealand, there has been much criticism of officials 'protecting the minister', creating firewalls that protect them not only from outside criticism but also from his or her department, from unpleasant and unwelcome information, and from parliament (Marr and Wilkinson 2003).

Then there is the question of the quality of advice from the civil service. Sir Richard Wilson (1999), former head of the British home civil service, questioned how good top civil servants were at policy advice and how often their advice had been evaluated. It was a rhetorical question. There were no formal mechanisms for holding the civil service to account for its policy advice, and this was increasingly seen as a problem. Prime Ministers Paul Martin in Canada, John Howard in Australia, and Helen Clark in New Zealand all made comments about how they were underwhelmed by the quality and reliability of public service advice.

Hence, the public service's monopoly of advice came under challenge, with governments often finding official advice wanting. Gradually, they chose to supplement public service advice with a plurality of sources and advisers. Campbell and Wilson (1995: 59–61 and 294–6) regarded this trend as the death of the Westminster system. However, rather than death we have seen the role of the public service change to suit the new conditions. We now have competing streams of advice and coordination, with the public service putting together packages of advice from many sources, insisting not on their monopoly but on staying 'in the loop' and proffering dispassionate commentary on alternative sources of advice.

Clearly, we now have plural sources of advice, ministerial advisers who are here to stay, and this creates its own problems that will not go away. Codes of conduct and some codification of these roles may have occurred. However, is there effective management of their roles? Are they accountable for their actions?

The accountability of public servants for their management work is scarcely any better. In theory, responsibility (for management) can be delegated to agency chief executives, while accountability (for policy) remains with the minister. But this distinction hinges on clear definitions of both policy and management and of the respective roles and responsibilities of ministers, chief executives, and senior public servants. As the British Cabinet Office (1994: 24) observes: 'it is not always possible to separate clearly policy and management issues'. It also comments that 'some Chief Executives, especially the ones from the private sector, are very conscious of being in what they consider to be a fairly precarious position'. Again, similar problems have occurred in Australia, New Zealand, and Canada (Aucoin 1995; Weller 2001). Pollitt and Bouckaert (2000: 157) dryly observe that 'politicians have not been spectacularly willing to relinquish their former habits of detailed intervention'. Allied to ministerial intervention, public management reforms have created an 'anarchy of aggressive competitive accountability' that undercuts performance (Behn 2001: 216). We return to these topics in Chapter 6.

Representation–Executive Dominance of the Legislature

Mulgan's survey (2003: 113) of accountability documents how government accountability is 'seriously impeded' by an executive branch that 'remains over-dominant and too easily able to escape proper scrutiny'. This dominance is thought to undermine the formal–legal sovereignty of parliament, relegating it especially in Question Time to a theatrical PR arm of the executive for the purposes of point-scoring. There are criticisms both ways: that the executive treats parliament with disdain, if not contempt, and that too often parliament is not interested in exercising its powers, or in strengthening its capacities. The 'fusion' argument, implying the 'closer union' of executive and legislative powers, has turned full circle. Whereas 'fusion' was once considered the constitutional heart of the system and its essential political strength, it is now considered an 'elected dictatorship' especially when single-party, majoritarian governments elected by first-past-the-post voting take little heed of contrary views or consultations. Indeed, the main opposition can come from the majority party's own back-benchers either voting against government legislation or using the threat of a back-bench revolt to wring concessions from the government (Cowley 2005).

Moreover, notions of unitary nationhood expressed through a national sovereign parliament have also been eroded by a loss of national powers to supra-state entities such as the European Union (EU) or the World Trade Organization (WTO). National governments also have to contend with territorial demands for autonomy and decentralization. Some of these trends are not new. In South Africa, Australia, and Canada (and originally New Zealand), territorial interdependence was formally built in from the beginning. Devolution in Britain, giving semi-sovereign status to Scotland, Wales (and eventually Northern Ireland), is a more recent example of such forces. Increasingly, it is argued, national executives dominate more and more over less and less.

Finally, the ways in which parliaments, and thus executives, are constituted affects their practices and priorities. Representation of different social groups has been a constantly evolving phenomenon. The entry of women into the legislature and then the ministry reputedly changed the way politics was played. Indigenous representation either through designated seats or via party pre-selection increased the visibility of their status and interests. Territorial representation and the need to balance ministries from across the nation also had major effects on governments. Racial and ethnic representation and multilingualism changed the way politics were played and how problems were understood. Each time the politics of representation altered, the pool of available talent aspiring to the ministry also changed. These new recruits may also shape the traditions and beliefs of the system as they progress through its ranks. We return to these topics in Chapter 7.

Westminster Myths of Effectiveness

One of the prevailing myths found in comparative executive studies is that Westminster systems have strong leadership and, as a consequence, they deliver more effective government. Lijphart (1999 [1984]) has made a career out of plumbing this distinction. He has produced the most systematic comparative attempt to measure, rather than merely assert, the differences between majoritarian and consensual parliamentary governments. He asks whether consensual political cultures make a difference. He challenges the conventional wisdom on the trade-off between quality and effectiveness in which proportional representation and consensus government provide better representation whereas plurality elections and majority government provide more effective policy-making. He concludes that consensus democracies outperform majoritarian democracies. However, because the statistical results are 'relatively weak and mixed', he couches his conclusion negatively: 'major-itarian democracies are clearly *not* superior to consensus democracies in managing the economy and in maintaining civil peace' (Lijphart 1999: 274, emphasis in the original). However, consensus democracies deliver better women's representation, great political equality, higher participation in elections, and 'gentler qualities', such as persuasion, consultation, and 'more generous policies' (see Strøm et al. 2003).

So, the good news is there is no trade-off between effectiveness and democracy. The bad news is that 'institutional and cultural traditions may present strong resistance to consensus democracy' (Lijphart 1999: 305). Also, as Peters (1999: 81–2) argues, the advantage of majoritarian government is that the executive can act as it wants; prime ministers can shape policy more effectively. The fact that they are less effective could well be a function of poor policy choices, not of institutional differences; in a phrase, 'leaders do not know best'. However, in reply, it is possible that policy choices would be better if the product of persuasion and consultation rather than adversary politics. (On leaders knowing best and the ensuing policy disaster, see Butler et al. 1994.) In other words comparisons based on aggregate data result in sweeping generalizations that are too remote and do not allow for more fine-grained analysis of individuals, roles, and systems over time. We will seek to provide that fine-grained analysis in Chapter 8.

CONCLUSIONS: CORE THEMES REVISITED

Why does the study of executive government and politics matter? We care because the decisions of the great and the good affect all our lives for good or ill. So, we want to know what prime ministers and ministers do, why, how, and with what consequences. In other words, we are interested in their reasons, their actions, and the effects of both.

We can now return to our core themes. We can rephrase them using our analysis of tradition, dilemma, and court politics.

The centralization of a collective and responsible cabinet

What are the formal roles of prime minister and cabinet? What is the meaning of presidentialization? What is cabinet government? How are these notions constructed within the several traditions within and across the dominions? Who makes the claim? What roles and functions does cabinet serve in the polity? How have core executive politics changed and why?

The accountability of ministers

What roles do ministers play and what functions do they perform? Are these roles and functions variously constructed within the several traditions? By whom? What are the meanings of ministerial and collective responsibility? How are these interpretations enacted in court politics?

A constitutional bureaucracy of non-partisan and expert public servants

What is the formal role and function of the public service? How is it constructed within the several traditions? Is it understood to be a 'constitutional bureaucracy'? How has this notion changed and why? Has there been a politicization of the public service? Who makes this claim?

Relations between the executive, the legislature, territory, and identity

What is the meaning of parliamentary sovereignty? How do the several traditions interpret the constitutional position of parliament? How do their conceptions of executive control of parliament differ? Who holds to these interpretations? Do the executive and the opposition hold to different accounts of the role and functions of parliament? What are the shared understandings of parliament? How have they changed and why?

Do the differences make a difference?

What are the consequences of these differences in the organization, beliefs, and practices of the core executive for policies and their effects on citizens? Do variations in their court politics affect how government works and what government does? Are there any shared understandings about the meaning of 'making a difference'?

However, before exploring these themes in detail, we need to identify the relevant living traditions for constructing the meaning of executive government in our Westminster systems.

NOTES

1 For instance, while traditions insisting ministers should be answerable to parliament are long-standing, the doctrine that ministers should resign for errors made on their behalf by departments is of relatively more recent origin.

2 For a detailed discussion of the mixed member proportional (MMP) system in New Zealand, see Chapter 7.

3 We cannot provide a history of the study of political institutions here. For a comprehensive survey of the study of political institutions, see Rhodes et al. (2006). For a defence of formal–legal analysis, see Rhodes (1995*b*, 2006).

3

Living Traditions

> The British on the whole prefer to see a strong government of which they disapprove, rather than a weak government whose political structure is more complex and whose power to govern is limited (Hogg 1947: 303–4).

> The accumulation of all powers, legislative, executive and judiciary, in the same hands . . . may justly be pronounced the very definition of tyranny (James Madison, *The Federalist*, 1887).

This chapter describes the living traditions in our five dominions and their recurring dilemmas. We are interested only in *live* traditions; that is, those key traditions that underlie the beliefs and shape the practices of elite actors of the core executives in the respective polities. It is not important for our purposes to show there is much agreement within these traditions or that elites work from common definitions and shared assumptions. These living traditions are broad churches or families of ideas that may be expressed with differences in emphasis or nuance both within and between similar Westminster systems. It is important for our analysis that these traditions inform the mental political map that political actors carry with them.

We are far less interested in former or 'dead' political traditions that may have flourished and died some time ago. Such dead traditions as Chartism, syndicalism, communism, Christian socialism, or pre-war fascism are important historically and are intrinsically interesting. But they are not today expressed regularly in the language and beliefs of key elite actors that shape political practice.

We are, however, interested in the recent trajectories of these living traditions: how they have developed over time, adjusted to changes, confronted political challenges, or rebuffed other contending fashions. They are resilient if nothing else. So we focus on how these traditions construct and shape current political beliefs about the formal–legal nature of politics, about how the system works or should work, and about what latitude for political action exists in any given circumstance.

The aim of the chapter is to identify the main traditions and the recurring dilemmas that shape political beliefs in the dominion countries. Specifically, we ask what impacts these traditions have had and continue to have on the beliefs and practices of executive government in Westminster systems. We are not interested in comparing and contrasting the many traditions in each of the dominions, highlighting differences of form or content.

It is important to be precise. We are keenly aware that we omit many traditions. There is much written on, for example, the politics of identity and the political marginalization of indigenous people, or of women, in parliamentary democracies. But the traditions that inform our understanding of indigenous and identity beliefs and practices have less impact on executive government than on (say) the composition of political parties and of parliament.[1] In other words, we define traditions pragmatically. Political scientists can locate an individual in various traditions depending on what questions they seek to answer; we can appeal to all kinds of traditions at many levels. In this book, we seek to explain broad shared beliefs and actions across five dominions, so we appeal to such general traditions as representative and responsible government. However, if we wanted to explain conflicts and differences in Australian or Canadian politics, then our purpose would be better served by appealing to several more specific and competing traditions (see Bevir and Rhodes 2003: chapter 6). The choice of traditions must be justified by their capacity to shape executive government.

We identify four living traditions as central to the present-day evolution of executive government: the legacy of royal prerogative or hierarchy; responsible government; constitutional bureaucracy; and representative government. Each tradition has a recurring dilemma. In the monarchical tradition, it is the see-sawing balance between the centralized executive prerogative and various checks and balances, including federalism. For the responsible government tradition, it is the conflicting demands of party government and ministerial responsibility. For constitutional bureaucracy, it is the tension between professionalism in policy-making and implementation and the demands for responsiveness to political leaders. For the representative government tradition, it is conflict between elite and participatory notions of representative democracy.

THE ROYAL PREROGATIVE

The executive is heir to two living traditions that are constantly competing for weight. Both are deeply embedded in the governing institutions and in the customs and modes of behaviour that drive political practice.

The first is the royal tradition of executive authority. The royal prerogative tradition is not just an artefact of history and it cannot be overstated as the basis for the exercise of political power. Traditions of royal prerogative in England and elsewhere in Europe followed the triumph of Christianity. Such traditions gradually became institutionalized from the early medieval period but the political antecedents have roots further back to the 'kingdoms' of Northumbria, Kent, Mercia, and finally Wessex. The royal prerogative was premised on notions of divine right and allegiance to the crowned leader. Monarchs claimed to be God's temporal rulers on earth, but if divine authority was the source of their authority, the mace was the means of their power. Barons, knights, and magistrates (and then the other social orders) owed allegiance, imposed order, paid taxes, provided armed forces for campaigns, and administered their lands. Bloodlines and primogeniture became the inherited principles of the Crown ruptured only by invasion and usurpation. It was a tradition created through a bloody legacy.

Our inheritance from the royal prerogative can be discovered in the way power is organized, in the assumptions that underwrite government authority. The reality of a monarchy is that power flows *down*; it is a *hierarchic* order. When governments act in the name of the Crown, they evoke a royal authority that long pre-dates electoral legitimization. In the place where the monarchs once held sway, the prime ministers now stand supreme and often unchallenged, the single power at the top. The prime ministers and the executives continue to hold and exercise many royal prerogative powers.

- The sittings of parliament are normally determined by prime ministers, derived from the right of the Crown to 'call' parliament, a procedural power and matter of great administrative convenience.

- Prime ministers decide when an election will be held, a great political asset.

- The executive acting in the name of the Crown determines the proposed appropriations, borrowings, and taxes, the essence of its resourcing powers.

- The executive determines appointments for everything, from the High Court to departmental heads to numerous statutory positions without any external check or analysis.

- The executive runs the departments of state that report exclusively to ministers.

- War can be declared without the permission of parliament or the people; treaties and international commitments are part of the executive prerogative.

- The royal prerogative assumes the proceedings of the Crown are secret and so reinforces a culture of secrecy within government. Neither parliament nor the public need to know what is happening in the core executive. Executive deliberations are still withheld from public view for 30 years or more. The more recent provision of freedom of information is a privilege granted (not a right).

Every one of those powers was used by Stuart monarchs to bypass parliament; to assert the royal prerogative without restraint. They were the powers against which the parliament fought and won. And although the Stuart doctrine was circumscribed by the constitutional settlement of 1688–9, it is those powers that are now exercised by the executive itself. The Glorious Revolution not only overthrew the reigning Stuart monarch, but it also ended the doctrine of divine right of kings and absolute rule, and began the slow process of forging a constitutional monarchy, with a bill of rights granted the citizenry.

The monarch's continuing influence can be seen in the constitutional role of the governors-general who retain some nominal reserve powers, usually undefined (see Finn 1987; Low 1988; Butler 1991). Thus, the Australian Constitution states: 'The executive power of the Commonwealth is vested in the governor-general'. No one takes it literally, but the legacy remains even though the prime ministers speak on behalf of 'Her Majesty's government'. Even today, the governor-general as head of state has three functions. First, in Low's (1988: 22) memorable phrase, constitutional heads of state are the 'chief ribbon bestowers and chief ribbon cutters'. The importance of such ceremonial should not be underestimated; it burnishes the myth. Second, there is also the formal public role; for example, opening parliament or receiving foreign dignitaries. Finally, there is their contribution to the everyday working of the polity, which is frequently routine, such as giving assent to bills.

Boyce (2008) argues that the governor-general in Australia (and to some extent also in Canada and New Zealand) had 'reserve powers' that were exercised without ministerial advice. In theory, the Crown's representative could dissolve the lower house, decide whether conditions for a 'double dissolution' had been met (in Australia), and dismiss a prime minister for illegality or breach of the constitution. However, these powers have been progressively narrowed, although Boyce sees a penumbra of doubt over what the head of state can still do. Routinely, the governor-general enjoys the three tacit prerogatives first identified by Bagehot in 1867 with respect to the British executive: to encourage; to warn; and to be consulted. When they *do* exert their reserve muscle, as the Australian governor-general did in 1975, their actions will always be contested and controversial. The occurrences are fortunately rare (see Low 1988; and Winterton 1983). The key point here is the *continuing* role of the head of state and, as Butler (1991: 8) concludes in his survey of governors-general, the simple fact is that 'every country is a special case. Each governor-general operates under special rules or customs, developed in response to some special local situation or by mere chance.'

When the Australian, Canadian, New Zealand, and Cape Colonies gained self-government, they expected that parliament and the executive would broadly act in the same way as Westminster. Federation or unification brought no change either. Three of these governments may be restrained by written constitutions, but the workings of government are implied, not explicit. Within those bounds lie sets of assumptions and practices that duly reflect the practices of the British parliament and government and their conventions. Indeed, at times, Canadian or Australian practices have become even more frozen than those of the 'mother'. These nations essentially operate behind a façade of language which assumes a royal prerogative even if real power is exercised elsewhere. It is never constitutionally prescribed, never precise but somehow known and understood.

Royal tradition helps to explain other characteristics of executive government. It is hierarchical; participants look to the leadership for guidance and assume a degree of authority: not quite the Stuart version of divine right, but sometimes a level of obeisance that comes close. Prime ministers can appoint; prime ministers can fire. Power is centralized; it may have moved from the monarch to the prime minister or cabinet, but power-sharing comes hard even within the traditions of collective government.

Hierarchy also assumes a unitary government, following the British model. It may be true that power in Britain is now shared with assemblies in Wales, Scotland, and Ireland, that the British polity is 'differentiated' in practice, characterized by networks and a segmented core executive (Rhodes 1988 and 1997). It is true that Canada, Australia, and South Africa have federal systems that share power territorially, with many government responsibilities maintained by the states or provinces. In their cases, a central state did not capture outlying territories, rather the composite self-governing polities voluntarily agreed to enter into a differentiated polity. So power is sometimes distributed and sometimes shared. But within each of those polities, federal or provincial, can be found the traces of monarchical centralized power. South Africa choosing in 1961 to become a republic and not recognizing the British monarch as the head of state merely transferred these prerogative powers to the president.

There was nothing democratic about this process. Power was ceded from the monarch long before any extended suffrage applied, let alone universal suffrage appeared. Parliamentary rules and practices were settled when governing was the pastime of the nobility and less than 2 per cent of the male population had the vote (and prior to 1896 no women). But some of the formal obsequies remain. Certain executive decisions still go through the charade of requiring authorization from the nominal, but not real, power: the privy council or executive council.

Ministers, thus, exercise the modern version of royal power. Power remains hierarchical, centralized, and sometimes delegated by statute. The responsibility of the cabinet is to administer the country, with the prime minister (or president) proxy for the monarch. The dominions adopted similar myths in their rhetoric, and similar practices in their cabinets.

But, secondly, there was an alternative tradition driving the polities: the demand that the executive be supported and legitimized by parliamentary means. This was a long and slow process of adaptation, involving rival claims to legitimacy stressing notions of parliamentary sovereignty (rather than popular sovereignty) and representative government increasingly based on the consent of the ruled.

Cabinet is now the forum where majoritarian (or quasi-majoritarian) support intersects with the prerogative power. As parliament had long exercised authority over funding (initially revenues and then expenditures), governments had to maintain political support. Prime ministers chose ministers from among their supporters to provide cohesion and a continuing majority. The necessity for ministers to be elected or appointed from upper chambers (and, in South Africa at least initially, elected to the Assembly) ensured the link between the executive and the parliament. The need to maintain 'confidence' requires prime ministers to select their leading politicians, the 'big beasts of the jungle', in their cabinets, even though they may be rivals for power. They were initially needed to maintain parliamentary support as a prerequisite to maintaining their position in government. Later, such leading politicians were usually drawn from a subset of the cohesive majority political party. Parliament became the gatekeeper to office; the career route for the ambitious; the theatre of political performance. In the main, political actors had to be in parliament to become a minister, although there could be exceptions.

Of course, there is the reality that a party must retain a majority in parliament and in that sense the power of the executive can be held in check. But disciplined parties have made that at best a nominal power, to be used in the last resort and not as a routine check on particular actions. Indeed, we need only note the energy with which governments of all persuasions rail against even a minimal exercise of power by the upper houses to appreciate that the government's belief in executive prerogative remains untrammelled.

It is an interesting combination of form and socialization. Parliament gives rights to members, and provides the rites of passage. Parliamentarians are wont to believe that elections select the wise and provide those representatives with wisdom. Even upper house parliamentarians, who may never have had to face the people, sometimes believe that just being there gives them the knowledge and experience of all that is required to govern effectively. The royal hubris of divine right can infuse the neophyte governors in the assembly.

So, historically power shifted once: from monarch to the executive supported by a majority in parliament. But what parliament won in the process, it was not about to give up. The prerogatives ceded by the monarch were to be exercised by the executive answerable to a sovereign parliament. The franchise may have been extended, but the exercise of power still retains its monarchical character. Power was transferred not to the people but to the executive. As parliament increasingly came under the control of political parties, its capacity to continue the fight against the prerogative power declined. Representative government needs democratic support; but it is *representative* not plebiscitary. The executive decides, the parliament supports, and the people vote every three to five years. There have been attempts to expand and increase accountability, but the inherited structure of institutions and traditions from Westminster has proved persistent and durable.

In summary, the royal prerogative and democratic powers intersect in the executive cabinet: the core and the powerhouse of Westminster government. Bagehot's 'efficient secret' was the intersection of legislative and executive power. The cabinet is the buckle or hyphen that fuses the party to the government. It thus creates the continuing dilemma for governments faced by the two competing imperatives of government. On the one hand, governments need to develop and implement policies to administer the country (derived from the royal prerogative). On the other hand, they need to maintain political support for the government (derived from the demand for parliamentary support – and much later for democratic legitimacy).

The fusion of these two traditions in cabinet does not provide a blueprint for how the executive should be run. It does not prescribe the powers of prime ministers or the procedures and influence of cabinet. It does not determine what will be decided by the prime ministers in conjunction with the core executive, rather than with ministers in 'full cabinet'. It does not determine what should be approved by parliament or authorized by executive authority. These are settled case by case, country by country.

The traditions themselves are inevitably imprecise about administrative detail or procedure. They create expectations about decisive and coherent governments (their capacities and record), maintaining a common view (collective responsibility), and answerable to whomsoever can make them answer (parliament, external bodies, or the media). They allow prime ministers to shape their power and seize what authority they can. When one prime minister was asked what his priorities were when he first won office, he responded, 'I did what I had to do'. There were expectations, procedures, imperatives created by tradition and history that shaped his paths, but did not predetermine all his actions.

So, our challenge is to identify the following:

1. How prime ministers and cabinets interpret and utilize these traditions in the way that they govern their countries.
2. The way that these traditions shape expectations and practices.
3. How they differed from country to country and how those distinctions are determined by the development of local conditions and traditions.
4. How dilemmas and local traditions shape and constrain practices.

Our interest is how prime ministers and cabinets responded to these expectations and whether they maximized the opportunities thus provided.

The key dilemma of the royal prerogative is the oscillating balance between centralization and decentralization.

Centralization and Decentralization

The Westminster model presupposes a hierarchy, whose exemplar is the unitary state. This phrase refers to the politically sovereign, centralized governments of unified nation states. It is an institutional and constitutional notion. Politically, sovereignty refers to international recognition that a government rules a specified territory. It is centralized because the decision to decentralize can be revoked by the central authority. The roots of the tradition in Westminster systems lie with the British monarchy and the origins are there for all to see today.

England forged a centralized unitary state within the British Isles over centuries and at great military cost. It had suppressed and subsumed Wales by military force in 1282, then, after centuries of warfare, absorbed Scotland through the *Treaty of Union 1707*, and finally incorporated Ireland with the *Act of Union 1800*. All these Acts of Union had occurred before traditions of responsible government took hold in Westminster. In other words, Britain claimed territorial integrity over the British Isles before either responsible or representative government became the prevailing norm. In the nineteenth-century, Britain became an archetypal imperial nation state, controlling the land mass of the British Isles and building an empire of some 60 colonial possessions. Later, British governments gradually ceded back degrees of sovereignty to its distinct domains. Ireland, after more than half a century of anti-English rebellion finally broke free in 1948, becoming a sovereign nation but keeping many of the features of a Westminster-style political system. In more recent times under parliamentary and electoral pressures, Westminster ceded a gradual devolution of powers to its peripheral nations. The Scottish Office headed by a cabinet minister was created in 1885. Wales did not get its cabinet minister and the Welsh Office until 1964. The Scottish Office had significant control over the distribution of its budget from the 1970s. By contrast, the Welsh Office is best seen as an example of administrative deconcentration. Finally, after two referenda, the Blair government legislated for devolution to Scotland and Wales in 1998, with Scotland getting its own powers of direct taxation (see Rhodes et al. 2003).

However, following Rokkan and Urwin (1982: 11), it is important to distinguish between the unitary state and the union state. The unitary state is 'built up around one unambiguous political centre which enjoys economic dominance and pursues a more or less undeviating policy of administrative standardisation. All areas of the state are treated alike, and all institutions are directly under the control of the centre'. In the union state 'integration is less than perfect ... (and) ... while administrative standardisation prevails over most of the territory... in some areas pre-Union rights and institutional infrastructure ... preserve some degree of regional autonomy and serve as agencies of elite recruitment'. In a similar vein, Bulpitt (1983: 235–6) argues that the central operating code of the national political elite focused on the high politics of the national economy or foreign affairs. So, 'national and local polities were largely divorced from one another'; the contacts which did exist were 'bureaucratic and depoliticized' and the centre's aim in centre–periphery relations was 'relative autonomy from peripheral forces to pursue its "High Politics" preoccupations'.

Further, Rhodes (1988, 1997, and 2007) argues that Britain is a 'differen-tiated polity' characterized by policy networks, governance, a segmented core executive, and hollowing out. He argues there has been a shift from govern-ment by a unitary state to governance through and by networks. Differentia-tion became more extensive in the 1980s and 1990s, which saw significant changes in the functional and territorial specialization of British government. Networks have multiplied as an unintended consequence of marketization. Devolution to Scotland, Wales, and Northern Ireland strengthened political decentralization. The degree of international interdependence is greater. National sovereignty was constrained by membership of the European supra-state union. As a result, the core executive's capacity to steer is reduced or hollowed out. In short, centralization and control are incomplete and Britain is best viewed as a differentiated polity – a disunited kingdom.

All of these versions of British government and its challenges revolve around the limits to centralization. The centralized unitary state has both political and administrative problems. On the political front, the centre has to confront political movements on the periphery. On the administrative front, the centre lacks local knowledge and the capacity to respond to local circumstances; red tape frustrates flexibility. Decentralization increases the efficiency of the centre by freeing top management from routine tasks and reducing the diseconomies of scale caused by congestion at the centre. So, there is a continuing oscillation between the search for more effective central control and decentralizing decision-making to local and regional authorities. That tension was resolved by creating the union state that offset political centralization with administrative decentralization. Latterly, with devolution to Scotland, Wales, and Northern Ireland, Britain has entered a phase of political decentralization. Such oscillations are not peculiar to the UK. They are a feature of all dominions. The key point is that even in this most centralized polity, political elites confront the recurring dilemma posed by the conflicting beliefs and practices of centralization and decentralization. In the former dominion federations, managing this dilemma is a way of life.

Decentralization is one of the more emotive terms in politics, almost rivalling democracy and equality in the heat it can produce. Not only is decentralization 'good' but centralization is definitely 'bad' (Fesler 1965). It is a romantic term, offering the prospect of the 'good society' (Smith 1985, chapters 2 and 5). However, the 'big federations' of the British Commonwealth are as much products of a pragmatic 'socio-economic federalism' (Hueglin and Fenna 2006) as of romantic political principles. The federations of Canada and Australia began as decentralized colonial polities that were pushed or chose to federate and form a central government, which later claimed the title 'national government'. This socio-economic process of federation was not about principles of government or which conventions of Westminster to adopt or retain. It was a series of brokered arrangements among the constituents, political deals, trade-offs, shares in the new institutions, and commercial arrangements to sustain support for the merger, with notions of some limited union (confederal as in Canada or federal as in Australia). The most crucial aspect of this process of territorial integration was the division or allocation of codified policy powers with appeal mechanisms to a 'higher authority' that could arbitrate and reach a definitive verdict if disputes occurred. In federating, all were conscious that they were dividing sovereignty and surrendering some unspecified proportion of the national parliament's claim to sovereignty.

In these 'great federations' territorial and regional politics shape their national political cultures. They are woven throughout their constitutions and subsequent constitutional debates. Territorial representation is not an 'add-on'; it is fundamental to their political fabric. It is interwoven with debates on national identity, especially in Canada.[2] Such debates encompass the national polity (how national unity can be maintained) and diversity (who makes up the polity). Governments have to ensure representation from across the regions, select ministers with regional connections, and negotiate relations with subnational jurisdictions and their political complexions. Canada is perhaps the most heterogeneous polity with linguistic differences overlaying provincial cultures of great economic variability. Regional politics tend to magnify the 'social qualities that differentiate people rather than the human qualities that make them the same' (Porter 1963 cited in Ullman 1979: 3). Some have argued that this underlies the 'national unity obsession' (where certain topics are off-limits; for example, republicanism or a redistribution of Senate seats). Alternatively, extreme regionalism is blamed for breaking the party system and fuelling a 'spoils system' of representation and regional benefit (see Young and Archer 2002). Others have argued that it adds to political capriciousness and parliamentary instability when there is a high level of electoral competitiveness based on first-past-the-post voting and few safe seats (Lovink 1973). The Canadian Senate is composed of provincial representation appointed by the governor-general at the bidding of the government so it has rarely been a conduit for provincial attitudes (Smiley 1976).

Both Australia and Canada are political hybrids. They melded the royal prerogative with American beliefs about federalism. They fused the incompatible: the all-powerful executive able to impose strong authority with traditions of regionalism, spatial checks and balances, and countervailing power structures to central power. Central political elites were often ambivalent about federalism. Sir Robert Menzies, Australia's longest serving prime minister and ostensibly a defender of states' rights by instinct, bemoaned the limits imposed on the Commonwealth by federalism:

> how true it is that as the world grows, as the world becomes more complex... it is frequently ludicrous that the National Parliament, the National Government, should be without power to do things which are really needed for the national security and advancement (Menzies 1967: 24).

In effect, federalism is a historical curio and potential encumbrance. This view of federalism is all too prominent in the Australian Labor Party. It sees it as an impeding conservative block to government. Peter Wilenski (1983: 82–7), a high-level adviser to Labor governments and later secretary of the Department of Foreign Affairs and Trade, argued: 'Federal constitutions make difficult those changes desired by a majority of electors but resisted by minorities in the smaller constituent states. That is the price paid by the majority to the smaller constituents for their entry into federation' (Wilenski 1983: 84). It was a 'frustration with the obstacles in the path of their programs to improve social conditions... that led Labor leaders to support a philosophy of centralism' (Wilenski 1983: 85). Even the Liberal Prime Minister Malcolm Fraser (1975: 25) conceded that: 'A federal system of government offers Liberals many protections against those elements of socialism that Liberals abhor.'

Yet the founders of the Australian state sought to balance federalism and responsible government from the start. Brown (2003*a*, 2003*b*) argues that federalist ideas were current in Australia from 1822, long before the proposals for union in the 1840s and the federation debates of the 1880s and 1890s. He argues there are two federalisms. The first federalism dates from the 1820s and called for an active programme of territorial decentralization. The second federalism dates from the 1840s and is a non-theoretic pragmatic, or utilitarian, federalism associated with partial centralization. It may well be true the authors of federation were not theorists but practical men defending their interests. Nonetheless, 'Australians seem always to have been in search of *both* a high level of national unity *and* serious political decentralisation' (Brown 2003: 31, emphasis in the original).[3]

The recurring dilemma of centralization and decentralization is played out at every level of the federations, fuelled by the tyranny of distance. In other words, great distances from the centre to the periphery sustain decentralization, local discretion, rival power centres, and even insularity. Such fragmentation disaggregated these polities. They resembled a loose network of subnational idiosyncratic regimes, often centralized, susceptible to boss-politics and with questionable commitments to open democratic government (as in the cases of Alberta, British Columbia, Newfoundland, New South Wales, Queensland, and Western Australia). There was the inevitable reaction to such fragmentation with the national political elite inventing schemes for central control. They sought to preserve the 'nation' to equalize conditions and opportunities, to equalize access to markets, to equalize costs or charging schemes; for example, the Canadian rail-freight schemes such as the Crows Nest Pass Agreement, or the Australian Grants Commission's horizontal equity formula for funding. These schemes sought horizontal equity and were the centre's response to the decentralization of the hybrid of Westminster federalism.

Fundamental institutional reform of these great federations is notoriously difficult. It is nigh impossible to change the composition of states and provinces or to redraw the boundaries to make 'more sense' today. While theoretically possible, the admission of new states or provinces, or divisions of existing states and provinces, is politically impractical. Changes in political decentralization are changes in the distribution of power and there are always enough losers to frustrate change. It is more feasible to create territories. Administrative decentralization is less threatening. Both Australia and Canada created and accepted new territories – two and three, respectively. It is difficult to see either Australia or Canada dispensing with its historical voting system for the lower houses (as New Zealand did in 1994–6) and opting for a radical proportional system. In Australia, there have been two equal increases in Senate representation (from the original 6 seats, up to 10, and then to 12 for each state). It is not possible to change the relative representation of the six states despite enormous population differences. Tasmania elects the same original number of senators as New South Wales but its population is only 490,000 compared with seven million in the latter. Similarly in Canada, while the Conservatives (now in government) have campaigned on Senate reform – the three 'E's of elected, equal, and effective – it will be difficult to reapportion representation because of the winners and losers problem. Although most attention usually focuses on proposals for an elected upper chamber, the disproportionate shares of Senate seats are a constant sore for the western provinces, which are under-represented compared with Ontario and Quebec.

So, in many political and administrative guises, in all the dominions, the dilemma of balancing the competing beliefs and practices of centralization and decentralization recurs.

TRADITIONS OF RESPONSIBLE GOVERNMENT

It is at best a half-truth to claim that Britain developed the conventions of responsible government and then the dominions replicated the system when granted self-government. When colonial administrations began to rule themselves they selectively adopted components of Westminster that suited them. They adapted these as they considered appropriate, and added other elements as they saw fit. So, all systems were hybrids and all systems, including the UK, had evolving conventions.

British traditions of responsible government emerged through accretion. Separate and different conventions were amassed slowly into a recognizable but ever-changing form. Gradually, the constitution that dare not speak its name took shape (although Jennings (1959: 1) remarked: 'it is a trite observation that there is no such constitution'). Characteristically, the main constitutional conventions were not articulated by the participants but rather by 'onlookers' – journalists, parliamentary officials, academics, and constitutional lawyers who produced systematizing commentaries.[4] Constitutional law and responsible authority were founded on and allied to opinion, consent, and acquiescence. However, commentators would often discuss specific elements of convention, without providing a succinct definition of responsible government. For instance, in over 1,200 pages of his *Responsible Government in the Dominions*, Keith (1928) never once succeeds in providing a concise definition of the concept, and indeed he frequently conflates responsible government with representative government.

Principles, understandings, and conventions were inherently political and, in Dicey's famous phrase (1914: 20–1), 'not inquiries which will ever be debated in the law courts'. Such understandings were combinations of history and custom. They were fundamentally political in nature, not rules of law or subject to legal interpretation or legal enforcement. They were above and outside judicial review. Yet, inherited understandings of political practices were conventionally respected and obeyed as if law. Actors internalized and became indoctrinated with these understandings and rules, changing them as circumstances warranted. The bipartisan commitment to and consolidation of such political practices formed the heart of the Westminster constitutions, surviving the comings and goings of parties and governments. By the 1860s, the foundational principles of British responsible government were in place.

The conventions of responsible government are an 'essential feature' of British government and 'signify the accountability of ministers, or of the government as a whole, to an elected assembly' (Birch 1964: 20). Collective responsibility, essentially a convention based on practicality, has 'acquired that status of a sacred principle of British government' (Birch 1964: 136). So, the terms collective and individual ministerial responsibility refer to a family of ideas.

For the UK, we cannot better Marshall's (1986: chapter IV) summary.

1. The prerogatives of the Crown are exercised on the advice of ministers (except in such cases as they are not).
2. The government resigns when it loses the confidence of the House of Commons (except when it remains in office).
3. Ministers speak and vote together (except when they cannot agree to do so).
4. Ministers explain their policy and provide information to the House (except when they keep it to themselves).
5. Ministers offer their individual resignations if serious errors are made in their departments (except when they retain their posts or are given a peerage).
6. Every act of a civil servant is, legally speaking, the act of a minister (except those that are, legally speaking, his own).

Why so many exceptions? The answer is simple. Responsible government predates the two-party system of a mass democracy. So, its tenets conflict with the exigencies of party government. Or, to put it more brutally, when the demands of responsible government conflict with the party political needs of the government, the latter usually wins. We explore the consequences of this recurring dilemma between the beliefs and practices of party government and those of responsible government in Chapter 5.

If our summary of responsible government in Britain seems a tad ambiguous, if party government seems to reduce constitutional conventions to fictions, then the variations in the dominions make the UK a model of clarity and predictability.

New Zealand, more than any other of the dominions, accepted the fundamental premises of the tradition of responsible government. After an initial flirtation with provincialism, it adopted a unitary state model with a high degree of centralization. It became an 'extreme' form of Westminster (McLeay 1995; Wanna 2005), with unchecked power, and arguably the 'fastest law in the west' (Palmer 1979). Its 'winner takes all' character reached perhaps its apogee under prime ministers Muldoon (1975–84) and Lange (1984–9), but while its political elite often bullied their way through political confrontations, they remained loyal to notions of constitutional law.

While the basic principles of responsible government have not often been disputed in New Zealand, campaigns to make the system more accountable and responsive have periodically posed challenges to the dominant regime. The nature and limits of the Westminster system are a feature of local political debates (Mulgan 2004: 54–8, 63–71). The three-yearly electoral contest was seen as the sole effective check on power. Hence, proposals for electoral reform, especially for proportional representation, simmered away for decades, only to be rebuffed by the political establishment. Campaigns to 'improve New Zealand's democracy' were concerned not with franchise issues or with urging higher turnouts at polls, but with fundamental ways of making the political institutions more responsive to people's wishes. Two of the proposed reforms are of particular relevance here: reducing the power of the two dominant political parties over both pre-selection and over their back-benchers; and replacing plurality voting with proportional representation (especially given the unicameral system). In other words, the reforms sought to redress the balance between party and responsible government by weakening the former and strengthening the latter. The introduction of the mixed member proportional electoral system (MMP) induced some important changes in the practices of collective responsibility (see Chapter 5).

The Australian constitutional debates before Federation record much discussion of the conventions of responsible government, especially on whether to include them in the written Constitution. But various proposals to include formally some aspects of responsible government were rejected. The notion that ministers had to have a seat in parliament at the time of their appointment was rejected, as was the phrase holding 'office subject to their possessing the confidence of the House of Representatives' suggested by Sir Henry Parkes. Also rejected was the description of ministers as *responsible ministers* of the Crown for the 'Queen's ministers of state'. However, section 64 of the Constitution requires them to be in parliament within three months of appointment as minister, so the effect was the same. No minister has been appointed from outside. Nominally, the Australian parliament consists of the governor-general, the Senate, and the House of Representatives. The governor-general is taken for granted. The one signifier of responsible government in the Constitution was the term 'federal executive council'. It is a counterpart to the Privy Council, also referred to as the governor-general-in-council. It consisted of a council of ministers (at least two) advising the governor-general. But its activities have always been formal. The main reason for the reluctance to enshrine such principles was that powerful arguments were put not to specify responsible government, and not to be too prescriptive. Robert Garran (1897: 149) pleaded at the time of Federation that it was wrong to

> attempt to fix the present pattern of responsible government as a thing to
> be clung to for all time; we must allow scope for its development... To
> try to crystallize this fluid system into a hard and fast code of written law
> would spoil its chief merit; we must be careful to lay down only the
> essential principles of popular government, leaving the details of form as
> elastic as possible.

There was also awareness that, with the Constitution open to judicial interpretation, codifying political conventions (that were constantly evolving) would potentially give the High Court the power to interpret, not parliament.

Australian politicians have returned to this theme in subsequent constitutional reviews. In discussing the nuances of the Australian system of government, an advisory committee of politicians and lawyers in 1987 argued that Westminster did not adequately describe the local system and their preferred term was a 'parliamentary executive' system of government. This term, they believed, captured 'the differences between the Westminster system and the system which operates in Australia' in that the role and powers of the Senate were unique but that still the 'executive government retains office only so long as it can maintain the "confidence" of the lower house' (Constitutional Commission 1987: 12). These practitioners rejected specifying the notions of responsible government in the Constitution. They did recommend that the Constitution should state that 'the governor-general shall appoint an officer to head the government, to be known as the prime minister'. However, the recommendation was never put to referendum. The prime minister is still not mentioned in the Constitution; the position is based on convention.

Finn (1987: 45) argues the 'two political principles of ministerial responsibility, the collective and the individual, coexist uneasily'.[5] 'Local circumstances were to accentuate the importance of collective responsibility.' The effect was that 'Coalition ministries called upon collective responsibility as cement to their union' and faction leaders used it to control their administrations. In short, 'in its devaluation of individual ministerial responsibility in favour of the collective, it suggests an adherence to principles of political responsibility which to this day accord with Australian parliamentary practice' (Finn 1987: 53). 'Cabinet and ministerial government was the prize of the colonial constitutions' (Finn 1987: 164). So, Australian constitutional conventions stress cabinets sticking together (except when they disagree), and not leaking (except when they do).

Twentieth-century debates about responsible government in Australia focus on its contradiction with both federalism and party government. Reid (1981: 312–16) talks of the 'three distorting influences' that federalism exerts on responsible government: namely, legalism, an elected Senate, and a formal division of powers. Lucy (1993: 292) prefers the term 'responsible party government', meaning the cabinet is in practice more responsible to the governing party than it is to the lower house of parliament or, indeed, any other institution such as the media. His conception is incompatible with Australian federalism. For Lucy, the defining characteristic of Australian government is the struggle between responsible party government and the separation of powers, the 'twin eaglets model' of Australia's government (Lucy 1993: 325). So, debates about responsible government still echo down the years, taking on local colouring. The key points are, first, there is a continuing debate; the tradition is alive and well. Second, the demands of party government stalk that debate; for example, the call for individual ministerial responsibility is resurrected whenever the opposition and the media scent ministerial blood (see Thompson and Tillotsen 1999 and Chapter 5 below).

Canada, too, assumed traditions of responsible government but without the notion that they were copying exactly Westminster. Indeed, Canadians believed they were blending Anglo-French parliamentary and legal systems that were separately organized but combined in a confederation. It was never just Westminster. Even if certain assumptions were derived from Westminster practices, it was impolitic to admit as much. After Durham's report, the *Union Act 1840* provided for coequal political representation within a single polity, which soon recognized English and French as coequal languages. Within twenty years, federalism was grafted on to these traditions of responsible government. The 1867 *British North America Act* (BNA Act, which was rarely referred to as the constitution) stipulated at great length the relative representation of the various provinces and territories. It provided for a council to advise the governor-general, 'styled the Queen's Privy Council for Canada'

(1867, s. 11), although the language of the document gave the governor-general power to appoint at pleasure. There was no statement that ministers must be in parliament, although governments had to have their annual budgets authorized by both houses of parliament. The closest the 1867 *BNA Act* came to an expression of responsible government were the two statements: 'a Constitution similar in principle to that of the United Kingdom'; and 'It shall be lawful for the Queen, by and with the Advice and Consent of the Senate and House of Commons, to make laws for the Peace, Order and good Government of Canada'.

If the written constitution is silent, the notion of responsible government is numbered among Canada's constitutional conventions with the allied practices of ministerial and collective responsibility. So, ministers are expected to support government policy in public and to take the blame for what goes wrong in their departments. Constitutional proprieties are followed except when it is not in the governing party's interest to do so. But, as in Australia, beliefs about responsible government are shaped by the impact of federalism and party government. For instance, Canadian governments believe that all provinces should be represented in cabinet and that all ministers ought to be of cabinet rank. This has led to a practice of nominating large, almost unwieldy cabinets that were too cumbersome for regular decision-making, thus creating conditions for enhanced prime ministerial authority.

In South Africa, four colonies (two British and two Dutch-Afrikaner) had been granted self-rule prior to Union in 1910 (Cape Colony in 1872, Natal 1893, and after the Second Boer War, Transvaal 1906 and Orange River Colony 1907). The *South Africa Act 1910* established the national parliament elected by a restricted white (British and Afrikaners) electorate. Given the legacy of the immediate civil war, South African parties assumed a militaristic character until well after the Second World War. The new central state coexisted uneasily with strong notions of provincial autonomy. It adopted the forms of responsible government based on strong executive, parliamentary majorities, and oppositional parties (to the Second World War), but with restrictive suffrage (all adult whites gaining the vote first in 1931 but with all other races excluded). While the institutional structures were recognizably British in form, in practice the new South African state was governed and administered by the majority Dutch-Afrikaners and their kaleidoscopic nationalistic parties. As a consequence, the South African government was, along with Ireland, always the most stridently independent dominion seeking complete separation from imperial rule (a goal of all the major parties). As a nation, it did not formally adopt multilingualism, although it tolerated separate regional languages. Much later, it forced the Afrikaans language on to the local indigenous population, a move that magnified dissent.

In short, all the dominions had their version of responsible government from the outset and those notions have evolved under the twin forces of federalism and party government. Because of the rise of the 'electronic glut' and the growing importance of the media in 'selling politics' (Seymour-Ure 2003: 9), the exigencies of party government and of electoral success triumphed over constitutional convention. Ministerial responsibility encounters the dilemma posed by party government.

THE TRADITION OF CONSTITUTIONAL BUREAUCRACY

The eighteenth-century civil service 'was not permanent, it was not civil, and it was not a service' (Parris 1969: 22). Civil servants did not keep their jobs 'during a change of government'; there was no civil service 'as distinct from the political, or parliamentary, service of the Crown'; and it was not 'a body of full-time salaried officers, systematically recruited with clear lines of authority and uniform rules' about terms and conditions of employment (Parris 1969: 22–7). The permanent, non-partisan civil service that evolved in the latter part of the nineteenth century was a key support of Britain's constitutional monarchy:

> As monarchy rose above party, so the civil service settled below party. Constitutional bureaucracy was the counterpart of constitutional monarchy (Parris 1969: 49).

Constitutional bureaucracy has several entwined strands, the generalist and the specialist, which underpinned the growth of professional administrative bureaucracies with strong norms, precepts, and values. Such administrative traditions have roots in the bureaucracy but must coexist with the political traditions. So, evolving conventions of responsible government are complemented by evolving ideas about professionalism, degrees of independence, expertise and technical proficiency, management, and preferred patterns of recruitment and workforce composition.

For more than a century all dominions have entertained beliefs about the desirability of a professional non-partisan public service. However, the conception of professionalism changed. When Lord Bridges (1950), Head of the British Home Civil Service (1945–56), drew his 'portrait of a profession', he was describing the generalist civil servant or the belief

> that men who have been engaged, up to one or two and twenty, in studies which have no immediate connexion with the business of any profession, and of which the effect is merely to open, to invigorate, and to enrich the

mind, will generally be found, in the business of every profession,
superior to men who have, at eighteen or nineteen, devoted themselves
to the special studies of their calling (Parris 1969: 287).

So, the preference for the all-rounder prevailed over a preference for relevance
from the first competitive examinations. But the speed of change must not be
overstated. The apogee of the generalist civil servant was not the nineteenth
century but occurred between the two world wars when first Sir Warren Fisher
and then Sir Edward Bridges were Heads of the Home Civil Service. During the
interwar years, the 'blend of intimacy and informality which has characterised
the higher echelons of Whitehall' was created (Chapman and Greenaway 1980:
113; see also Beloff 1975; Chapman 1988; and O'Halpin 1989).

Bridges captures the essence of the generalist. He identifies four 'skills or
qualities' needed by civil servants. First, they must have 'long experience of a
particular field'. Second, they must have the specialized skills of the administrator who can 'assess the expertise of others at its true worth, can spot the strong
and weak points in any situation at short notice, and can advise on how to
handle a complex situation'. Third, the civil servant should possess the qualities
associated with the academic world: 'the capacity and determination to study
difficult subjects intensively and objectively, with the same disinterested desire to
find the truth at all costs'. And, finally, the civil servant must 'combine the
capacity for taking a somewhat coldly judicial attitude with the warmer qualities
essential to managing large numbers of staff' (Bridges 1950: 50–2 and 55–7).

Hence, administration was, for Bridges, not a science but an art, and
recruits would acquire the relevant qualities by experience and learning on-
the-job. What the administrator needed was 'a general understanding of the
main principles of organisation' or 'a kind of rarefied common sense'. The
departmental secretary was a 'general manager', comparable to 'the conductor
of an orchestra'. The analogy was with rowing. You cannot become a good
oarsman by studying diagrams and angles. You learn to row 'from the mere
fact of rowing in a good crew behind a really good oarsman, for the good style
and rhythm proved as catching as measles' (Bridges 1956: 6, 14, and 23).

The Committee on the Civil Service (1968) was to rant famously about this
cult of the amateur with its subordination of the specialist to the generalist
(see also Ridley 1968; Macleod 1988). The committee was much criticized at
the time and subsequently (see Fry 1993), but it did herald the end of an era.
The last third of the twentieth century witnessed recurrent bouts of reform
designed to make civil servants, professional managers, and the civil service
responsive to its political masters.[6] We explore changes in the public service in
the dominions in more detail in Chapter 6. Whether the reforms are seen as
strategic decision-making by political and administrative leaders or a process

of muddling through in which there was a wide discrepancy between rhetoric and reality, it matters not. Our only point of concern here is the simple fact that there have been waves of reform which produced new conceptions of professionalism and demands for a more politically responsive public service. These tensions were not peculiar to Britain.

Australia prized the qualities listed by Bridges: dispassionate analysis and providing advice (Crawford 1954 and 1960). The Coombs Commission sought to build a professional public service with service-wide norms, rules, efficiency, and capacities. So, while the object was to 'build a profession', that phrase did not encompass the occupational professions. Generalists outnumbered specialists, and decades of training on-the-job prepared the brightest telegraph boys to aspire to be permanent head later.[7]

Moreover, these generalists were 'statesmen in disguise'. Assessments can rise to eulogistic heights. A report into the *Public Service Act* opened with the claim: 'The Australian Public Service is a national asset' (McLeod 1994). Prime ministers argue that 'no government "owns" the public service ... The responsibility of any government must be to pass on to its successors a public service which is better able to meet the challenges of the day than the one it inherited' (Howard 1998: 4 and 11). In Australia there was a lively debate in the late 1950s and 1960s over whether Australia had a peculiar 'talent for bureaucracy' (Davies 1958) and for turning to bureaucratic solutions in preference to other types of solutions. A group known collectively as the 'Seven Dwarfs', all of whom were men small of stature but considerable intellect, were said to have ruled for decades at the top of the Australian public service. They numbered Roland Wilson, Richard Randall, H.C. Coombs, Frederick Shedden, Allen Brown, Henry Bland, and John Crawford, or so one listing goes; like all myths, the precise membership of this fabled company is disputed. They were scarcely a united team, but they were able to monopolize the provision of advice in an environment where there was little intellectual or institutional challenge to their position. The most dominant, Sir Roland Wilson, was secretary of the Treasury for 15 years and periodically participated at cabinet as if he were a senior minister.[8]

The picture was no different in New Zealand. Its constitutional bureaucracy helped pioneer nation-building but it was increasingly criticized. Geoffrey Palmer (1988: 1), speaking at a time when he first entered office as Labour deputy prime minister, commented that the bureaucracies were 'not responsive', 'not flexible, and 'they tended to be inefficient'. He continued:

> We found as a new government that we were not actually in control of them in any real sense, and that came as a surprise, because as people who believed in the orthodox theory of the Westminster system we were confronted with the reality that it does not work.

Indeed, Palmer admirably illustrates both the continuity of the Westminster tradition of constitutional bureaucracy and the pressures for change.

So, all the dominions had permanent, non-partisan, and professional public services. Mostly, these public services eschewed direct involvement in political life. Civil servants did not run for office, give political speeches, or campaign for one side or the other. Only in Canada is there an acceptance that public servants might declare their interests for one party and stand for office: Indeed, two former deputy ministers (permanent secretaries in the British parlance) eventually became prime minister. And on occasion, senior public servants have been appointed directly to the ministry.

It is more common, however, to deploy statutory boards to preserve the independence of the bureaucracy. Public service boards or commissions administer their respective services, with ministers not usually in a position to determine senior appointments in their department. Politicians have at various times stipulated their requirements and preferences for an apolitical career service. Thus, the 1902 *Public Service Act* in Australia provided for a neutral public service. Almost a century later the third, new Act stipulated that the 'APS is apolitical, performing its functions in an impartial and professional manner' (1999: s. 10.1[a]). It is 'openly accountable for its actions, within the framework of Ministerial responsibility to the Government, the Parliament and the Australian public' (1999: s. 10.1(e)). Such statements are not just rhetoric; they have legal standing and affect the culture of the bureaucracy.

The public services of today – though still recognizable to their forebears – have had to confront two major challenges: politicization or responsiveness and managerialism. With the arrival of mass two-party politics, came the era of the professional politician determined to set the policy agenda for his or her ministry. One Australian minister summed up the demand for greater responsiveness to political directions and preferences as follows:

> There has been a transition over 25 years from the final days of an imperial public service to a public service which is focused on policy advice and service contracts, as an enterprise operating in a competitive environment where governments have alternative sources of advice and service provision ... [I]t was an institutional struggle between the democratically elected governments and the public service for control over the public service. And in that struggle the elected governments have won (cited in Weller 2001: 81).

The public services were also challenged by managerialism in two main guises: marketization or demands for privatized and outsourced services; and managerialism or businesslike and client-oriented ways of working. These challenges have not wiped out traditions of a career civil service based on neutrality and permanence, but they have wound back the breadth of the 'administrative service' and changed the way governments deliver services to the community. Nowhere was the change more dramatic than New Zealand. Canada, by contrast, has been more cautious, maintaining more traditional language, even if the effect is seen to be dramatic, with Donald Savoie claiming governments have 'broken the bargain' with their civil service (Savoie 2003).

TRADITIONS OF REPRESENTATIVE GOVERNMENT

The traditions of representative government based on parliamentary sovereignty have grown both as a counterfoil to the royal prerogative tradition and as an inheritor of its majesty. Parliamentary sovereignty usurped monarchic absolutism while preserving the constitutional authority of the Crown as the hierarchical apex of legitimate power. The gradual adaptation to representative forms of government, eventually extending to universal suffrage, completed a gradual transfer of legitimate authority to the non-permanent, or elected, elements of the central state.

Let us recall the English heritage of competing traditions. From Simon de Montfort's rebel gathering in 1265, parliaments fought for more than 400 years with the monarch over the right to be heard, the right to complain, and the right to approve taxation. The ability to present their grievances was intended to precede the voting of supply. It was far from certain whether they would succeed. The Stuart kings were able to govern for years without parliament meeting at all. Those battles were finally won after 1688, when a Dutch stadtholder ascended the English throne and was far more interested in raising taxes and troops to defend his native land than with the maintenance of any royal prerogatives. The *Mutiny Acts* gave him the authority to raise a standing army and the taxes he wanted, but only for a year, thus ensuring that parliament had to meet every year to renew the supply of money and men. Annual meetings of parliament were born.

Since 1689 the 'elected' have gradually encircled and disempowered the monarch while keeping the Crown, assisted by one new king who spoke no English and others whose health prevented any royal decision. Since the monarchs depended on the parliament for funds, they could not govern without the parliamentary representatives. Prime ministers then emerge, from Sir Robert Walpole onwards, as the link between king and parliament. Cabinet also emerges as a device to curtail royal authority, initially as 'pre-meetings' of ministers who felt it necessary to agree a common line and prevent the king from adopting a strategy of 'divide and rule', and later as a political device to maintain collective solidarity under representative government.

Parliament was where power lay and where governments were formed. Because English parliamentarianism became robust from the mid-sixteenth and seventeenth centuries through to the modern era, traditions grew around notions of parliamentary sovereignty, at least in the liberal view of constitutionality (Birch 1964). Parliament, not 'the people', was considered sovereign; it was a representative institution composed of popularly elected representatives renewed periodically. The classic constitutional doctrines of Westminster in the nineteenth century stressed that government was founded on the sovereignty of parliament as it historically emerged and through evolving conventions – not on constitutions and law. So, each parliament was meant to be autonomous and unable to 'bind' its successors; parliamentary decisions were not subject to challenge outside the chambers; and parliament acted as the highest political and legal authority in the land. Each house of parliament controlled its own affairs and could not automatically regulate the other.

The British constitution developed as a series of understandings of how the 'chain of command' worked in practice from the electorate, to the parliament, to ministers, and to public servants (Birch 1967: 30). If the constitution is no more than a mixture of convention and some important statutory law, then parliament itself can eventually decide what the constitution means and any additions, amendments, or reinterpretations were not formally justiciable. Significantly, Britain's uncodified constitution was largely consolidated and articulated by constitutional thinkers outside parliament, such as Bagehot, Dicey, Laski, Jennings, and, later, Wade and Hood-Philips, Hennessy, Birch, and Armstrong. They interpreted and rationalized the practices they observed, articulating them as evolving political conventions (the parliamentary composition of the executive, governing by consent and representation). They were often trying to construct seminal references for practitioners and students, or to distil the essence of Westminster compared with other systems, or later prepare manuals to assist British colonial administrations in running government. Erskine May and other parliamentary officers codified parliamentary practice within a legacy of shared notions of responsible government, such that today's practitioners and scholars frequently quote such texts as if they are constitutionally authoritative sources.

In this sense, Britain *invented* its own constitution piecemeal and even now continues reinventing it. Accordingly, when a contemporary Whig scholar, such as Peter Hennessy, searched for 'the constitution' or explored the making of the constitution, he finds himself asking questions such as: What would happen if a hung parliament eventuated? Should prime ministers necessarily resign if they cannot command a majority after an election? Within the confines of traditions, the key actors themselves (and sometimes 'commentators') often make it up as they go along.[9] Under such circumstances a briefing note from a permanent head on some topic can be said to be the British constitution 'in the making' (Hennessy 1986 and 1989). But *if* these principles and conventions form a constitution, it is a weakish one that exists so long as shared understandings and accepted practice persist. Cynics will argue that Westminster conventions are a convenience to be maintained until it is in the interests of one side to change them or break them, thus creating new conventions.

Other Westminster systems, perhaps because they were deliberately 'born' rather than evolved, have codified their constitutions, either minimally or extensively. Colonial and later independent constitutions were principally a means towards, and an expression of, nation-building, based on formalized 'deals' negotiated extensively in the period leading up to self-government. New Zealand has had two constitutions, in 1852 and 1986, providing for the 'peace, order and good government of New Zealand'. The constitution was repatriated in 1986, but the repatriated Act was passed adopted by parliament, with the required level of support, not by referendum, which is itself a statement of intended parliamentary sovereignty. Together, these constitutions have provided a minimalist description of the legislative arrangements, though arguably the *Treaty of Waitangi* (1840) and the *Electoral Act 1993* have more bearing on government today (see Chapter 7).

Australia, Canada, and South Africa have more extensive constitutional provisions that both limit the sovereignty of the national parliament and cede power to the judiciary to rule on the validity of legislation.

Australia's Constitution was enacted by the UK parliament in 1900 and came into effect in 1901 after 20 years of debate about what it would, and would not, include. The politicians of the day believed parliament should be quasi-sovereign and subordinated in three important respects. The Australian parliament was unable to overturn or breach the provisions of the constitution. Parliament itself could not ignore or overturn High Court judgments on matters of constitutionality except by means of a popular referendum. And, the Australian parliament was given many concurrent powers with state governments, meaning it shared the national stage with autonomous state governments. The Constitution also contains statements such as 'until parliament otherwise decides', preserving traditions of sovereignty within certain confines.

The constitution of modern Canada unfolded in three principal stages. The *British North America Act 1867* brought the Dominion of Canada into existence based on four colonies. It was followed by the *Statute of Westminster 1931*, which provided for local autonomy, and then the repatriated constitution expressed in the *Canada Act 1982* that effectively confirmed Canada's independence. Even so, the 1867 Constitution enshrines royal prerogative and talks more about the relative numerical representation of the various provinces rather than principles of government.[10] The Constitution lodges executive power in the Queen, without mentioning parliamentary sovereignty. There have been subsequent constant attempts (such as the *Meech Lake Accord* (1987) or the *Charlottetown Accord* (1992)) to alter the Constitution to accommodate Quebec, but without success. In the process, Canada's constitutional architecture has locked in place the undertakings assumed from colonial times while legalizing much of the way the system works.

South Africa's new 1996 constitution was passed by the Constitutional Assembly (parliament) in the post-apartheid period after extensive review by the constitutional court. As a liberationist regime, modern South Africans became enormously proud of their Constitution and hold it in high esteem; popular celebrations were held in 2006 to commemorate its first decade in operation. It is a frequent topic of discussion among the political elite, who, unlike the other Westminster systems, know its many clauses and sentiments in detail (such as those 'recognising injustices of our past', 'united in our diversity'). Unlike the historical constitutions of the other dominions, South Africa's most recent constitution enshrines a number of important principles of government, such as 'democracy', 'respect for human dignity', multiparty recognition, and 'cooperative government'.[11] Significantly, the constitution declares the 'supremacy of the constitution' and that 'this constitution is the supreme law of the republic' (Chapter 1, sections 1 and 2). The National Assembly is 'elected to represent the people and to ensure government by the people under the Constitution' (Chapter 4, section 42.3). Yet the assembly is able to amend the Constitution without referenda, and has frequently done so since its establishment (some 13 times in just over a decade).

Linking the traditions of representative and responsible government, Birch's book of the same title (1964: 243–5) provides an astute analysis that remains relevant to this day. Birch argues that an 'important tradition' is the belief that 'the government of the day should be given all the powers it needs to carry out its policy' (1964: 243). It is also accepted that 'a government should not be deterred from pursuing policies which it thinks right by the fact that they are unpopular' (1964: 244). As one might expect, 'this tradition that the government should have both the powers and ability to provide strong leadership plays a major part in determining the nature of political responsibility in Britain' (Birch 1964: 245). Thus, if the various forms of political responsibility were to be ranked,

The British political tradition would clearly determine the order as, first, consistency, prudence and leadership, second, accountability to Parliament and third, responsiveness to public opinion and demands (1964: 245).

This responsible leadership tradition 'explains and supports the system of disciplined party government' (1964: 245). A disciplined party government requires only a limited notion of representative democracy. The function of the representative system is to legitimate the party that forms the government of the day, to give the electorate a choice between the retiring government and the opposition, and to provide an occasional channel of communication between government and electorate. This interpretation can be accurately labelled an elite or top-down view of representative democracy that will have no truck with participatory ideas about democracy (Marsh 1980). Our next section explores this conception in more detail, looking at political parties and parliament and their relationship to the executive.

Political Parties

The political culture of the former dominions was distinctly majoritarian with preferences for the concentration of power in key institutions. Their systems could be described as being 'excessively majoritarian' because they have few checks and balances on executive power. Governments inherited virtual autocracies. Yet they tempered this rule with a liberal understanding of the constitution and state–citizen rights and freedoms. On losing power, governments ceded political office to their opponents, and no mass electoral boycotts or coups took place during this period. South Africa from 1910 to the 1990s and New Zealand from 1908 to 1996 had the most extreme forms of majoritarian rule with terms such as 'military state', 'elective dictatorships' (a phrase coined by Lord Hailsham, Lord High Chancellor of Great Britain, in 1976), and 'state authoritarianism' bandied around (Mulgan 1992; McLeay 1995; Boston et al. 1996; Wanna 2005). Both, in different contexts, were a product of low electoral competitiveness and a high degree of hegemonic party rule. In South Africa, with the exception of a decade in the 1920s to 1930s, the nationalists never surrendered power until 1994. In New Zealand after 1908, the non-Labour side held power for 72 years. Canada has a similar pattern with the Liberals in power for 77 years from 1900 to 2006. In Britain, Labour was in power for only 32 years after 1900 and in Australia for just 22 years.

Yet majoritarianism is not the principal defining characteristic of these regimes. Rather, it is class-based party organizations that changed the nature of political practice. Class schisms are the key to the two-party stability that underpins many Westminster practices.[12]

As the franchise was gradually widened, class-based, disciplined mass political parties came to dominate the parliament in the UK, Australia, and New Zealand. Not only was class the main basis of political identification, but the socialist parties established by the trade union movement also became established players with a stake in the system (see Castles 1985). By entering parliament these parties accepted parliamentary government and came to share many of its core traditions and practice. They helped legitimize the system of government through their participation, even if they interpreted some of the conventions differently.

With disciplined socialist parties entering parliamentary politics they brought with them beliefs about 'parliamentary socialism'; that is, collective resolve, caucus unity, and representatives as delegates rather than Burkean 'independents'. They also brought with them notions of how politics should be conducted: by disciplined interest groups, leaders serving the party and removable at the collective will, consociational politics inside the party, regular party meetings, and internal political and policy debates. It was still a top-down view of representative government. Some Tories claimed the salaries paid to MPs allowed Labor parties to flourish, recruiting the 'hack politician whose chief aim is to keep his seat', and 'who earn a comfortable living from their services and are completely subservient to the caucus' (Keith 1928: 412–13). Labor had already argued that without salaries no working person could enter parliament and it would be left to the wealthy. Usually its members saw nothing anomalous with their acceptance of the decisions of caucus (Hughes 1909). Most significantly, these left-of-centre parties caused a predictable reaction from the non-labour political parties and factions (conservative, liberal, protectionist, free trade, reform, and nationalist). Once class-based politics occupied the two-party 'space' it became difficult for third parties (especially non-class parties such as social credit, democrats, and religious parties) to prosper or for non-party candidates (independents) to win seats. No third party has formed government in any of the five former dominions since 1910 until New Zealand changed its electoral system to proportional representation in the mid-1990s.[13]

Interestingly, while the socialists reconfigured the party system and shaped its disciplined two-party characteristics, they were not the natural party of government. In the UK, Labour had to wait until 1945 to form a government with a majority. Although Australia's Labor governments pre-date those of other countries, often by decades, these early governments were restricted by the limited notion of government incorporated in the Constitution and tended to split over the seismic issues of war and economic depression.[14]

New Zealand Labour has been even less successful, capturing office only five times since 1908 (twice for only one term), although it did hold office continuously between 1935 and 1949. Altogether it has governed for only 26 years.

The other significant influence of the socialist parties was to turn policy debates towards social disadvantage and state provision and regulation. As parties with a distinct ideology, they were strong adherents of majoritarianism, awaiting their chance to implement their preferred platforms. Legislation on progressive taxation, unemployment, and family benefits were largely a function of the influence of these parties, although occasionally, as in the UK, Liberals introduced such measures earlier. Labour parties favoured expanding public ownership either to solve market failure or to provide state competition against private oligopolies (e.g. public banks). These bodies also provided employment, regional development, and stabilized economies. In short, Labour parties spurred the expansion of government responsibilities.

South Africa and Canada are major exceptions to this pattern. South Africa had a short-lived traditional Labour Party in the early decades of the Union, forming government once in coalition after which it gradually lost influence and was disestablished in the Second World War, largely because its potential working-class base was excluded from participation in the political process. It never managed to rival the nationalist racial-purity parties in holding electoral appeal. Moreover, the nationalist parties tended to represent the white yeomanry in regional areas and mining and service industry administrators in the major cities. The other exception with respect to South Africa is that after the Second World War it did not develop a tradition of a loyal opposition in parliament. Although there was some white liberal opposition in the parliament and in the media, its main opponents were the outlawed African National Congress (ANC) formed in 1912.

Canada is the other exception where class has never been the basis of electoral contests. Canada never developed a socialist party capable of challenging for government in the national arena. Electoral politics in Canada appear as an extension of 'American exceptionalism', where individualism rather than collectivist politics characterized party politics. As a result, adversarial politics are not a struggle between left and right with competing partisan platforms, but a subterranean dialogue. Canadian parties are more fluid, more convergent, with fewer ideological differences. The cult of leadership, in the guise of formidable prime ministers like Mackenzie King, Trudeau, and Chrétien, often imposed itself on party politics and determined the policy preferences of governments. Arguably, this feature has contributed a sense of stability to the competitive nature of national electoral politics.

Canadian scholars have debated these issues in their own distinctive way. In the 1960s and 1970s, the dissident John Porter initiated a debate over the absence of class parties. He argued the absence of 'creative politics' dulled the capacity to innovate and initiate change. Politicians were accused of playing a brokerage role, tic-tacking between powerful interests and searching for compromises. Parties were seen as representing the status quo, interested in brokerage rather than social change. At the time there had been six minority governments since 1945 (and now eight), reinforcing the pattern of brokerage politics. So, distributional politics triumphed, with its 'conditional grants', joint funding schemes, equalization payments, and social assistance pro-grammes. While the spoils system is seen as the normal way of doing business, occasionally it can appear as a form of graft and semi-official corruption and offend notions of propriety.

For most of the dominions, class-based disciplined parties have added stability and reduced electoral competition. In the UK there has been no significant change in the electoral systems nationally. In Canada, without a class-based electoral cleavage, the fragmented nature of the federation has paralysed notions of change for fear of breaking former compromises or creating noisy losers. Australia started with several electoral innovations: compulsory voting, preferential ballots, and later public funding, all without seriously undermining the class nature of political representation. However, in New Zealand, the class-based party system became discredited and dys-functional. Many believed that a non-representative elite had a stranglehold on representative politics. So New Zealand adopted a new and previously unconsidered mixed member proportional system and in doing so went from an 'archetypal transplant' of Westminster to a 'maverick outlier' (Wanna 2005). But this outlier illustrates one possible resolution to the recurrent dilemma posed by a top-down or elite view of representative government. It was a decisive shift to a more participatory form.

CONCLUSIONS

Taking these four governing traditions together, the logic of our argument is embedded in Table 3.1.

We argued in Chapter 1 that four key sets of embedded ideas (or institu-tions) defined the Westminster model (see Column 1). We argued in Chapter 2 that changes in the ideas (or beliefs and practices) of elite actors in the core executive occurred when traditions (or inherited beliefs and practices) con-fronted challenges from or conflicts with other traditions. It follows that we

Table 3.1. Traditions and dilemmas in executive government

Institutions	Traditions	Dilemmas	Debates
Prime minister and cabinet	Royal prerogative	Centralization vs. decentralization	Presidentialization
Ministers	Responsible government	Party government vs. ministerial responsibility	The smoking gun
Public service	Constitutional bureaucracy	Professionalization vs. politicization	Politicization and managerialism
Parliament	Representative government	Elitism vs. participation	Elective dictatorship vs. theatre of action

cannot explain how Westminster changes by a formal description and comparison of these institutions; there are innumerable country-specific textbooks to provide that basic information. Rather, we explain the changes by analysing traditions and their recurring dilemmas (see Columns 2 and 3). This chapter identifies and describes the relevant traditions and dilemmas. We have shown how the tensions between centralization and decentralization, party government and ministerial responsibility, professionalization and politicization, and elitism and participation recurred throughout the last century. The next step is to explore how these dilemmas continue to shape executive government by examining present-day debates (Column 4). These debates have their roots in at least one of the traditions and its recurring dilemma. We do not claim the debates in Table 3.1 are the only ones that illustrate the recurring dilemmas, just that they do so. We now turn to each institution and its associated debate.

NOTES

1 The politics of identity may have changed the political agenda, distilling a new set of issues for leaders to address. It has also impacted on the composition of the executive (for example, the gender balance within the political executive and in the bureaucracy) and with the inclusion of indigenous representation in the legislature. But the impact of identity politics is as nought compared with the impact of the tradition of responsible government or the two-party system on executive government. Indeed, the more important effect we observe is the way executive government shapes, even to the point of limiting or excluding, the politics of identity.

2 The Scots, the Welsh, and the Northern Irish can and do debate national identity both at length and with arms. The English can mount an occasional sortie but, like

sex and religion, it is not deemed a suitable dinner table topic. The only variant that can excite the English is the debate about a 'federal Europe'; they do not like it! The Conservative Party was divided between Euro-sceptics and those favouring integration. Interestingly, this debate is normally constructed not in terms of English national identity but of British sovereignty. For the English, the two are indivisible. Not so for the other constituent nations. The Scots are pro-Europe; it is seen as a way of furthering their nationalist ambitions. British sovereignty is but an arcane abstraction. There is almost no political debate on national identity in Australia and New Zealand. The Australian republican debate in the late 1990s caused a flurry of interest. There were marches and public debates. But the debate had little continuing pulling power.

3 However, while browsing through the six-volume review of the Constitution (1986), we were struck by the diverse views expressed and the unsystematic nature of the analysis compared to the Federalist Papers. It was not just federal theory that was absent. Equally, there was no substantial measure of agreement or clarity over the notion of ministerial responsibility. We had some difficulty resisting the thought that the Convention papers can be used to support any position.

4 See for example, Bagehot (1963); Dicey (1914); May (1844); Keith (1928); and Todd (1880).

5 Finn's view only holds if one sees collective responsibility as a principle of government, not a rule of political prudence. He does illustrate the point that when party (collective responsibility) and responsible government (individual responsibility) clash, the former usually succeeds. When individual ministers are under challenge the first hurdle in survival is to win the support of the prime minister and ministerial colleagues (see Chapter 5).

6 On the UK, see Fawcett and Rhodes (2007); Hennessy (1989); and Rhodes (2001). For an authoritative worldwide survey see Pollitt and Bouckaert (2000). For individual case studies of reform, see Rhodes and Weller (2001).

7 Of course some specialists rose to the top, most notably engineers, but the phrase 'on tap but not on top' is a fair generalization about the role of specialists in the public service.

8 See, for example, Weller (2001: 37–52 and 183–8) and Weller (2007: 100 and 113). There is no overall study of the 'Seven Dwarfs' but some individual studies include: Arklay et al. (2006); Coombs (1981); Cornish (2002); Edwards (2006); Horner (2000); and Rowse (2002).

9 A good example is Mackenzie (1961) who argued that local government was part of the British constitution. This assertion gained some acceptance at the time of writing but in more recent times (post-Thatcher) constitutional experts do not so regard local government.

10 The 1982 schedule to the Constitution lists a series of guarantees of democratic rights and freedoms, including equity and languages, but does not articulate principles of government. They are assumed to be understood.

11 Canada's new schedule to its constitution, the *Canada Act 1982*, also now contains basic rights and freedoms.

12 South Africa is the major exception here where parties were racially divided and for over 80 years the majority black working class was excluded from representation.

13 In 1941, a Country-party-led coalition ministry in Australia held office for five weeks before it fell. It was a coalition government led by the minority party.

14 Because early Australian Labor governments tended to split on such issues they reacted by imposing a 'pledge' to which all MPs had to swear allegiance. They also culturally castigated 'splitters' (or 'rats' in Labor parlance) and regarded party divisions in public as a heinous crime. As a consequence of this, notions of collective responsibility were often used to enforce unity among cabinet members, and back-bench disquiet tends to take place within the confines of the party room rather than on the floor of the legislature. New Zealand Labour shares some of these characteristics, but these notions of party unity at all costs are different from UK Labour traditions where sizable back-bench votes against the leadership (and occasionally ministers) are not uncommon and usually not regarded as a 'confidence' issue.

4

Executive and Cabinet

An extraordinary affair. I gave them their orders and they wanted to stay and discuss them (Duke of Wellington on his first cabinet meeting as prime minister in 1828, cited in Peter Hennessy 1986: 121).

The Cabinet...is a board of control chosen by the legislature, out of persons whom it trusts and knows, to rule the nation (English economist and political journalist, Walter Bagehot 1963 [1867]: 67).

If we mean by presidential government, government by an elective first magistrate then we in England have a president as truly as the Americans (Labour parliamentarian and later cabinet minister, Richard Crossman 1963: 22–3).

A strong and practical Cabinet is absolutely essential for Australia at present and will be so for years to come. A Cabinet made up of light-weight figures confused about policy priorities and equipped with little more than rhetoric and ideology would produce a disastrous outcome for the nation (Australian prime minister, Paul Keating, 1991, Higgins Memorial Lecture, 15 May 1991, quoted in *The Age*, 16 May).

Cabinet has evolved from a decision-making body under Pearson to a university-type seminar under Trudeau, to a focus group under Trudeau in his later years in office and also both Mulroney and Chrétien (Canadian senior public servant, cited in Savoie 1999: 1).

This chapter asks a deceptively simple question: 'how do we understand the relationship between the chief minister, cabinet, and the rest of the Westminster system?' That question is not just about people, but about institutions, rules, conventions, and the political traditions that shape the decisions of individuals. It is concerned with the interplay between the collegial doctrines that underlie cabinet government and the contrasting claims of prime ministerial centralization. This chapter has three aims. First, it reviews long-standing assertions that Westminster systems have witnessed expanding prime ministerial power verging on presidentialism. Second, it reviews the interpretive evidence supporting such claims and shows that the claims for, and critiques of, presidentialism are variously constructed. Third, in identifying three alternative explanations, it explores competing political traditions and shows where and how they shape and constrain the capacity of prime ministers and the form and expectations of cabinet in Westminster systems.

REVIEWING THE CLAIMS – CANADA'S DICTATORSHIP

The leading Canadian journalist Jeffrey Simpson published a book in 2001 called *The Friendly Dictatorship*. He argued that Jean Chrétien (prime minister of Canada 1993–2003) was merely the last, and most obvious, manifestation of dominant prime ministers able to govern with few constraints on getting their own way. Cabinet had become little more than a focus group in which some issues might be considered, but it did not meet for long and was not a deliberative or decision-making institution. Cabinet committees could, in theory, 'decide' on policy initiatives, but they were not funded or announced at that time. Rather, these 'decisions' were put into a basket of possible initiatives and the prime minister and the minister of finance would determine at budget time what would be taken up. Within their portfolios, ministers were left alone, but whenever the prime minister wanted to become involved, he determined the direction and content of policy. Simpson argued that 'cabinet government presupposes collective decision making and responsibility, a collection of equals, with some inevitably being more equal than others because of the importance of their portfolios' (2001: 62). But the prime minister had become far too powerful for this description to apply now.

Simpson's polemic builds on Donald Savoie's magisterial work *Governing from the Centre: The Concentration of Power in Canadian Politics* (1999). Savoie's book provided a detailed account of the growth in the power of the central agencies in Canada, and the significance of the prime minister and his office. Without resorting to presidential language, Savoie (1999: 3) summarized his argument as follows:

> The centre of the federal government has…been largely redefined in thirty years – it is now considerably larger and extends its influence over more activities than ever before. Yet power has also shifted within the centre itself…[T]he prime minister, with the support of advisers in his own office and senior public servants in central agencies, has gained a great deal of power while the cabinet has lost influence.

Cabinet still has a series of set agenda items: discussion, presentations, nominations, and then the endorsement of committee decisions that are rarely disputed (Savoie 1999: 647). But it did no more. Cabinet is bypassed as a decision-making body (Savoie 1999: 362; Bakvis and Wolinetz 2005: 217). Savoie built a case that these changes mean the prime minister is '*Primus*: there is no longer any *Inter* or *Pares*'. So, Trudeau, Mulroney, and Chrétien are all seen as dominant figures able to impose their will over multiple domains. For instance, it is claimed that the Canadian prime minister 'dominates the legislature ... to a degree that is substantially greater than is the case in the UK and other Westminster systems' (Bakvis and Wolinetz 2005: 216).

We challenge whether the sensationalized picture Simpson and Savoie present is indeed new. In Canada's past, Prime Minister Robert Borden could recall in 1917:

> The discussion was lengthy and eventually became so wearisome that I interposed, informing my colleagues that they had made me sufficiently acquainted with their views, that the duty of decision rested with me, and that I would subsequently make them acquainted with my conclusion (Bliss 1994: 80).

Similarly, with R.B. Bennett, prime minister 1930–5, and simultaneously finance and external affairs minister, 'the story went round that when Bennett was seen mumbling to himself, he was holding a cabinet meeting. "He was not above asking the opinions of others ... he was only above accepting them"' (Bliss 1994: 113). Gordon Robertson (2001: 62), later secretary to the Canadian cabinet, has written that the political colossus Mackenzie King (prime minister 1921–6, 26–30, and 35–48) lost interest in cabinet in his later years:

> More than once he left his ministers arguing over some point in a cabinet meeting while he went around the corner to his office in the East Block to have tea. Both he and his colleagues knew that they could reach no conclusion without him.

At the least the prime minister's approval and consent was needed. King was always determined to get his own way. Robertson (2001: 100) cited the view of cabinet secretary and later minister Jack Pickersgill on Prime Minister Louis St Laurent (1948–57):

> As St Laurent hated to waste time, cabinet meetings were exceedingly business-like ... No minister was restrained from presenting his views for fear St Laurent might take offence, but I believe some ministers were restrained by the fear of appearing to be ill-informed or ineffective. More than any prime minister I have known, St Laurent dominated his cabinet, not by imposing his authority, but by his sheer intellect, his wide knowledge, and his unequalled persuasiveness.

Such prime ministerial power has now been expressed formally. The latest guidelines for Canadian ministers starts with the bald statement:

> Ministers of the crown are chosen by the Prime Minister who may ask for their resignation at any time.

Nothing could be clearer or blunter. Canada has a long history of prime ministers who dominated, sometimes even ignored, the cabinet over which they presided.

TALES OF PRESIDENTIALISM GAIN
CREDENCE ELSEWHERE

Presidential tales are told of many prime ministers in many ways. It is a common story in Westminster systems with long antecedents. For the UK, many would agree with Peter Hennessy's (2000*b*: chapter 19) judgements on post-war prime ministers. He treats Clement Attlee and Margaret Thatcher as the two great 'weather makers'. Edward Heath and Tony Blair are seen as 'system-shifters'. Winston Churchill and James Callaghan are seen as 'seasoned copers'. Harold Macmillan and Harold Wilson fall into the 'promise unfulfilled' category, although post-Iraq many might move Blair to this box (Riddell 2005; and 2001: 40). Alec Douglas-Home is a 'punctuation mark', John Major was 'overwhelmed' and Anthony Eden was a 'catastrophe'. So, of the 12 post-war prime ministers prior to Gordon Brown, only three attracted the epithet 'presidential': Harold Wilson (1964–70), Margaret Thatcher (1979–90), and Tony Blair (1997–2007).

Judgements about their presidentialism among their colleagues have varied over time and with the personal standing of the minister with the prime minister. Three brief but contrary examples must suffice. Richard Crossman wrote of the growth of prime ministerial power in his famous 1963 introduction to Bagehot's *The English Constitution*.[1] He depicted prime ministers in the first half of the twentieth-century as dominant and controlling.

In more recent decades, three of Thatcher's senior colleagues (Michael Heseltine, Nigel Lawson, and Sir Geoffrey Howe) resigned ostensibly because of the way she ran her cabinet. Sir Geoffrey Howe, Chancellor of the Exchequer, then Foreign Secretary, then Leader of the House of Commons, criticized the way she ran her government, especially her 'roman intemperance' on European Monetary Union, which led her to criticize publicly her own government's policy. His cricket analogy has passed into parliamentary folklore: 'it is rather like sending in your opening batsman to the crease only for them to find, the moment the first balls are bowled, that their bats have been broken before the game by the team captain' (Howe 1994: 641, 666; see also Lawson 1992: 955–6, 960–1; Heseltine 2000: 312).

By contrast, other ministers disagree with these assessments. Nicholas Ridley (1991: 30) held several cabinet posts. While acknowledging the reasons for the Heseltine, Lawson, and Howe resignations, he professed: 'I . . . have no complaints to make about the way Margaret Thatcher ran her Cabinet' (see also Carrington 1988: 276; Walker 1991: 202–3). He also observed that 'in many respects it was Willie Whitelaw's Cabinet which she first appointed' in

1979. Only after the Falklands War and the 1983 election victory was the cabinet hers. In her later years, she lost cabinet colleagues to dramatic effect; when she needed their support in the leadership contest of November 1990, it was not forthcoming. Her pre-eminence was contingent on the support of the public, the parliamentary party, and the cabinet. So, beliefs about prime ministerial power vary between individuals, over time, and with the personal relations between the prime minister and other ministers.

Tony Blair was described as presidential from the moment he became prime minister. Jonathan Powell (No. 10 chief of staff) famously warned senior civil servants to expect 'a change from a feudal system of barons to a more Napoleonic system' (cited in Seldon 2004: 437). Blair's No. 10 aides asserted: 'Cabinet died years ago ... we want to replace the Department barons with a Bonapartist system' (quoted in Kavanagh and Seldon 2000: 291). Blair's ministerial critics did not demur (Mowlam 2002: 356, 361; Short 2004: 272, 278). 'President Blair' disagreed, arguing such claims have been made 'about virtually every administration in history that had a sense of direction ... Of course you have to have Cabinet Government' (*The Observer*, 23 November 1997; see also Hennessy 2000c: 11 and n. 70). Indeed, after the feuding with his Chancellor of the Exchequer, Gordon Brown, and the invasion of Iraq, the presidential moniker began to ring hollow. Journalist Andrew Rawnsley (2001: 292–4) initially subscribed to the 'command and control' view of Blair, but after six years in office he wrote of 'a prime minister who is not looking in the least bit presidential' at the head of 'a government displaying signs of drift' (*The Observer*, 15 June 2003). In similar vein, Riddell (2001: 40) commented: 'If Mr. Blair has been a Napoleonic figure, he has been a frustrated rather than a commanding one'. As Blair retired to his Elba, his legacy remained controversial and was 'bitterly contested' (Riddell 2005: 208; Seldon 2007).

In Australia, the presidential debate takes the form of prime ministerial dominance that can be traced back to the First World War (Weller 2007).[2] The journalist Mungo MacCallum (2004: 2) may opine that 'the office of prime minister, once regarded as no more than first among equals, turned into an unaccountable commissariat ruling by absolute fiat'. But passion overrides judgement and memory is short. Few would deny that a centralization of government occurred under John Howard, prime minister from 1996 to 2007, but it was not because the incumbent was 'a sluggish and rather stupid predator' who 'kills by treachery', as MacCallum suggested (2004: 2). Howard was a traditionalist who did not bypass cabinet or the regular 'party room' meetings – indeed, he admitted that he aimed 'to run a proper cabinet system' (*The Australian Magazine*, 11–12 December 2004).[3] His prime ministerial dominance was *based on* cabinet. Kelly (2005: 3) makes the points succinctly by arguing 'good prime ministers must be good team leaders' (citing Fraser, Hawke, and

Howard as dominant but team players) and that 'the main instrument of Howard's Prime Ministerial power is the cabinet'. His cabinet is 'tight, secret and collective' and it is 'an instrument of collective responsibility' (Kelly 2005: 3). Other commentators agree. In his first two terms 'Howard's persistence and his capacity to achieve goals were a factor in his dominance of cabinet' (Singleton 2000: 9). Weller (1992: 5, 27) similarly observed: 'executive government is collective in its form and its expectations' and 'the development of cabinet government to a higher level of activity and authority has...been a crucial factor in extending the prime minister's authority and span of control'.

A second example of cabinet government comes from the Keating era (1991–6); a domineering prime minister with little interest in the processes of government (see Watson 2002). Neal Blewett was social security minister under Paul Keating from 1991 to 1993. His diary (1999), in the genre of the Crossman Diaries, is a day-to-day record of life as a cabinet minister. He records all manner of meetings and decisions as he sought 'to capture the immediacy and intimacy of cabinet government' (1999: 1). One immediate conclusion can be drawn: despite different styles of leadership, Australia continues to produce cabinet government under its various prime ministers.

In New Zealand, journalists talk of Prime Minister Helen Clark as 'Queen Helen' who enjoys 'absolute power' or, in the words of her own website, 'unlimited sovereign power' (Wishart 2008: 6 and 314). Even a favourable biography described how her colleagues refer to her as a 'control freak' (Edwards 2002). Officials have also detected a growing emphasis on the leader. McLeay (1995: 155), writing within the idealized Westminster genre, quoted an internal briefing note to the incoming prime minister written in the measured tones of the bureaucracy.

> A number of factors have combined to build up the role of the Prime Minister in New Zealand. The television concentration on the heads of political parties and the Head of Government is one. But there are others. The scope of Government activity has widened. It has grown more complex. And many of the big issues – fostering growth, protecting the environment – are of a multi-sectoral nature. All of this calls for a central head who can inject coherence into a range of Government policies. In short, the Prime Minister is increasingly required for functional as well as political reasons to be a co-ordinator, an integrator and a mediator on policy issues as well as a leader of a political party.

Thus, officials feel the role of the prime minister has expanded as the need for policy coherence and political leadership combine to push items on to the prime ministerial agenda. But prime ministers also feel the job has changed. Helen Clark, prime minister of New Zealand (1999–2008), has argued (cited in Sykes 2008: 17):

> What's happened...is that parliamentary systems are transforming themselves almost into presidential systems...We're the head of government as prime ministers just as the American president is head of government. So there are certain functions that go with being head of government – and sitting around parliament for hours isn't one of them.

Apparently, MMP is no safeguard against presidential trends. Clark may be no less dominating than some of her predecessors, Robert Muldoon or even Richard Sedden.

In South Africa, adoption of an executive presidential model (established under the old apartheid regime in 1984 and cemented under the new Constitution of 1996) has given rise to talk of an emergent 'imperial presidency', especially under the post-apartheid presidents Nelson Mandela (1994–9) and Thabo Mbeki (1999–2008). Some of this critique is a response to the development of a new black 'political elite' and the ANC's Leninist traditions of 'democratic centralism'. It has also become an obsession with the liberal media, with occasional critiques also emanating from dissident politicians. Political and official insiders have argued that there is little evidence of substantial centralization of power. Indeed, the reverse may be more apparent as the National Assembly has decentralized powers and responsibilities to the provinces. There is also much debate among the political elite about the need to avoid the 'Zimbabwe path' where President Robert Mugabe has clung to power, turning the nation into a degenerative one-man state. Paradoxically, debate about the potential for presidential power has nurtured a post-apartheid discourse among practitioners on the need for a separation of powers and separate institutional realms of authority.[4] National and provincial politicians as well as the Constitutional Court have lent most weight to such arguments, widely canvassed in the local media.

In short, although the terminology varies from time to time and place to place, the debate about the power of the chief minister and the analogy with presidents is common to all Westminster countries. There are nuances in analysis; for example, some authors pay more attention to the constraints on prime ministerial power than others. We now explore not only the nuances but also the dilemmas posed by the presidentialization thesis.

THE PRESIDENTIALIZATION THESIS

The presidential analogy contrasts the individual position of presidents with the nominally collective role of prime ministers. Writing in the modernist empiricist tradition, Foley's (2000) analysis of the rise of the British presidency is the most comprehensive and thorough elaboration of the presidentialization thesis. He recognizes there are important constitutional and structural differences between the UK and the United States,[5] but argues that the analogy is not merely useful but essential if we are to understand general trends in the pattern of political leadership. He insists that 'prime ministerial leadership has undergone changes of such profundity that they amount to a qualitative shift in the type of leadership which is now viable in British government' (Foley 2000: 25).

The key shift is to 'spatial leadership' or 'the way in which political authority is protected and cultivated by the creation of a sense of distance, and . . . detachment from government' (Foley 2000: 31). Notions of 'presidential activism' are replaced by the 'president as outsider', exploiting public discontent with the system for his or her own electoral benefit. Thatcher is seen as the pioneer in Britain. From the start, she was an outsider in her own party with an unconventional political and policy agenda with populist appeal. She became distanced from her own government, respected by the public for her leadership while few supported her policies.

Blair then dared to be Thatcher (Foley 2000: 98). He, too, was distanced from his party and, in government, 'he raised the concept and application of spatial leadership to unprecedented levels of development and sophistication' (Foley 2000: 110). The key methods are 'going public', or building support or even coalitions by appealing to the public over the heads of government colleagues and entrenched interests, and 'getting personal', or using the media in all its forms to build personal rapport with the public independent of party and government. This drive to occupy the public arena distances leaders from their colleagues. They are no longer leaders but 'flagships' (Foley 2000) dominating media coverage, waging permanent election campaigns, and exercising a major influence over election results. The party remains under tight control and the leader often reminds the party not only of their duty to the public but of the leader's special link or 'contract' with them.

In sum, 'spatial leadership, outsider politics, competitive populism, personal projection, media management, individuated party images, the "permanent campaign", and the contractual and affective linkages between leaders and their public constituencies' (Foley 2000: 330) all confound conventional collective nostrums about leadership in British government. There is no inevitable *process* of presidentialization, no sudden shift from cabinet to presidential government. Rather, there is 'an emergent hybrid that fuses presidential characteristics with the forms of parliamentary democracy and cabinet government' (Foley 2000: 351).

Others have taken similar approaches to the public leadership of prime ministers. Pryce (1997: 1 and 197) argued that 'the rise of the British presidency in electoral terms has led to the presidentialization of the prem-iership, at least in respect of advice'. For Mughan (2000: 9–11), presidentia-lization refers to the 'personalisation of electoral politics', encompassing both the ways in which 'political parties choose to present themselves to the public'; and the 'impact' or 'the behavioural effect party leaders have on the voting patterns of citizens'. Poguntke and Webb (2005*a*: 5–7) suggested presidentialization has three distinct faces: the executive face, the party face, and the electoral face. Presidentialism occurs when there is a shift of 'political power resources and autonomy to the benefit of individual leaders' along *each* face and a corresponding loss to such collective actors as cabinet.

These authors seek to show how prime ministers, with all the institutional advantages that US presidents do not have, are able to bring decisions into their own grasp. In all these cases the better term is not 'presidential' but 'centralized'. Power is concentrated. Indeed, presidents, faced with a separ-ation of powers, limited terms, and far more open government, are far more constrained than prime ministers.

ASSESSING THE EVIDENCE

Whatever the perceptions surrounding the presidentialization thesis, there are four contested and contestable claims:

- The *lack of formal–legal constitutional rules* applying to the chief minister's position and powers has allowed power to shift in a centripetal direction.
- The *centralization of policy-making and coordination* has reinforced the capacities of leaders.
- The *pluralization of advice* has empowered the chief minister within the government over ministerial colleagues.
- The *personalization* of party leadership and electoral strategies have focused intense attention on the leader.

Each of these claims provides challenges to the dominant traditions of Westminster collective style. Also, none of those espousing the presidentiali-zation thesis explores counter-trends, especially the pressures for decentral-ization. So, our analysis focuses on these criteria for determining the degree to which prime ministers have increased their authority. In assessing the presidentialization thesis, we do not intend to describe the changes in central government in detail. Such accounts are available elsewhere. We concentrate on the *limits of the thesis*. We primarily compare and contrast the UK,

Australia, and Canada because they provide instructive insights about the basis of centralization in Westminster systems.

The Lack of Formal–Legal Constitutional Rules

Whether there is a codified or uncodified constitution almost all Westminster systems are remarkably silent on the constitutional standing of prime minister and cabinet. For the UK, Turpin (2002: 222) has provided a standard description:

> The office of Prime Minister is the creation of convention, and the role and powers of the Prime Minister still depend mainly on convention and political circumstances. Few powers are vested in the Prime Minister by statute – the office is barely acknowledged in legislation – but like other ministers, although without pre-eminent authority, the Prime Minister may make use of prerogative powers which have devolved upon ministers or are exercised by the sovereign only on ministerial advice.

He added (2002: 228):

> The modern Cabinet is a result of the slow growth of constitutional convention and has received only incidental recognition from the law (for example, in the *Ministerial and Other Salaries Act 1975*, Schedule 1).

With the partial exception of South Africa now,[6] the same interpretation could be applied to the core executive in the other countries.

Other descriptions can be even more succinct. In Canada, commentators have argued the cabinet 'remains an institution not described nor mentioned in any law of the land' (Matheson 1976: 1), although it remains a committee of the Privy Council (*Constitution Act 1867*, s. 11 cited in Heard 1991: 48). In the UK, 'the Cabinet, like the office of Prime Minister, has no identifiable legal source' (Loveland 1996: 335). The situation becomes more complex and disputatious when we unpack the notion of constitutional conventions (Marshall 1986 and 2003). Some, such as the modern-day convention that the prime minister should be a member of the lower house, need delay us no further.[7] Others, such as the conventions surrounding collective and individual ministerial responsibility, will be considered in more detail in Chapter 5.

According to Jackson and Jackson (2006: 266), in Canada 'the pre-eminence of the prime minister and the Cabinet, has evolved more from tradition than from any specific part of the Constitution or statute'. Australian and New Zealand prime ministers and cabinets appear 'nowhere in the written parts of the constitution' (McLeay 1995: 13). Executive practices are shaped by local conventions and practices, a theme that dominates Encel's (1962: Part II) account of the constitutional background to cabinet government in Australia.

Only in South Africa is formal recognition extended to the position of 'president'. While formally head of state, the president acts mostly as head of government and is a prime minister by another name. But there is one important variation. The president must be elected *from* the National Assembly but, once appointed, does not continue to sit in the parliament (and has no legislative vote), although may occasionally address the Assembly and be questioned by members. The 1996 constitution lists the formal responsibilities and powers of the president both as head of state (ceremonial and 'dignified' functions) and head of government (executive authority and 'efficient' functions). It stipulates that the president is head of cabinet, a formal body with prescribed accountabilities in the constitution. Even more significantly, the president is limited by the constitution to a maximum two terms (usually of five years).

If prescription cannot be found in constitutions, partial guidelines that shape the behaviour of prime ministers and cabinets do now exist. These are the operational procedures and conventions that prime ministers promulgate in documents such as: *Ministerial Code* (UK formerly known as *Questions of Procedure for Ministers*); *Accountable Government: A Guide for Ministers* (Canada); or *A Guide to Key Elements of Ministerial Responsibility* (Australia), the *Cabinet Manual* (New Zealand).[8] They appear to be simply a set of instructions to ministers about how to behave. But they are suffused with assumptions, value judgements, and the exercise of prime ministerial authority. These guides are, in effect, prime ministers defining *their* powers (over their colleagues, parliament, or cabinet), expressed in the dry language of bureaucratic procedure. Prime ministers determine what is included and retained, and how and when these guidelines will be enforced (for the UK history, see Baker 2000; for Australia, see Weller 2007).

Nevertheless, we should acknowledge three important points here. First, codification has increased in every jurisdiction. Second, constitutional conventions have been codified as governments have attempted to provide guidelines for politicians and officials. And, third, the codification of conventions and practices has blurred the distinction between written (codified) constitutions and unwritten constitutions.

But these evolving guides are essentially enumerations of conventions and practices. As a former secretary to cabinet in Britain noted of the *Questions of Procedure for Ministers*:

> I don't regard it as having a constitutional force at all...it would be perfectly possible for an incoming Prime Minister to scrap the whole thing and to devise entirely new rules. The fact that it has now been

published, would, of course, lead to debate about that and he would, no doubt, be questioned about the reasons for the change. But it is entirely at the discretion of the new Prime Minister to ... deal with the administration in the way that he chose (cited in Hennessy 1995: 33).

As public documents in regular use, these codes may have gained greater weight; however, prime ministers can and do amend them to suit their convenience. The key point here is that there are few formal–legal rules or constraints on the power of the head of government. The job is largely a creation of convention. Such conventions rest on accepted practices interpreted through long-standing traditions (Loveland 1996: 334) that have no authoritative external interpreter (Marshall 2003: 39). The main actors themselves act as ongoing authoritative interpreters, although courts and commissions of inquiry may, on occasions, rule on legality.[9] In all jurisdictions (but most noticeably in South Africa since 1996),[10] some of the roles and conventions of chief ministers and their ministers have been formally codified even if they have no force in law.

The power of prime ministers is thus contingent, open to interpretation and manipulation. It is largely left to the incumbents to decide how and where they wish to exercise authority guided by variable principles of constitutional practice. And much the same is true for cabinet; it does what the head of government asks of it. Take the views of three senior public servants accustomed to working in and around cabinet.

- 'Cabinet government is the arrangement the prime minister makes to ensure that decisions are made in the interests of the general, rather than the individual minister, with a view to presenting a unified programme for legislation and supply' (former Canadian Privy Council Office official).

- 'Cabinet government is a shorthand term for the process by which government determines its policy and ensures the political will to implement it' (former British Cabinet Secretary and Head of the Home Civil Service).

- 'Cabinet has two main functions: policy coherence and political support' (former Secretary, Department of Prime Minister and Cabinet, Australia).[11]

Prime ministers would, implicitly at least, emphasize cabinet as a source of control, power, and leadership. In the relative absence of formal-legal constraints, the analysis then must focus on what capacities, institutional or individual, prime ministers have to drive cabinet.

The Centralization of Policy-Making

In the UK, structural changes at No. 10 and the Cabinet Office allowed Blair to strengthen the centre of government. Like Canada, the cabinet is allegedly in desuetude. The frequency and content of cabinet meetings are said to have diminished significantly under Blair. Bilateral agreements have replaced collective government, and Blair is the coordinating nodal point. Robin Butler, former Cabinet Secretary and Head of the Home Civil Service, reported that 'during the late 1940s, cabinet met for an average of 87 times a year, with 340 papers being circulated; in the 1970s, 60 times a year, with 140 papers; and by the late 1990s, no more than 40 times a year, with only 20 papers' (cited in Hennessy 2000*b*: 5).

In place of cabinet the prime minister found support by building his own resources. First, there was the Policy Unit, which mutated into the Policy Directorate when it merged with the Prime Minister's Private Office. Initially the focus was on improving communications with Alistair Campbell heading the Strategic Communications Unit (SCU). Latterly the emphasis fell on policy advice. The Cabinet Office was reformed to improve central coordination and it now serves the prime minister rather than the cabinet. The Cabinet Office has 1,620 permanent employees excluding its agencies and 2,440 in total. Several new units were created: for example, initially, the Social Exclusion Unit and the Performance and Innovation Unit, latterly the Strategy Unit, the Office of Public Services Reform, and, most important, the Delivery Unit (Barber 2007). As Hennessy (2002: 20) observed, Blair set out to create 'the department that-will-not-speak-its-name'. Blair sought to control government functions without bothering himself with too many operational details. As Anthony Seldon (2004: 630 citing officials) observed: 'however distracted Blair might be by other events, domestic and international, the work of monitoring...went on regardless ("The [Delivery] Unit never sleeps", Blair was told)'.

Whether this nameless monitoring department was effective remains a matter of dispute. Seldon (2004: 692) noted Blair's mercurial nature and 'lack of policy making and management skills'. In the words of one official:

> What he wants is results. He has a feel for policies but not how the results come. He finds it hard to understand why things can't happen immediately. There is a frustration in waiting for the pay-off and he doesn't have time. He comes back to this when one or other of the policy areas gets hot: education, then transport and now health (cited in Hennessy 2000*c*: 10. See also, Fawcett and Rhodes 2007).

So, officials say:

> 'Tell me what *you* want and *we'll* do it'. But he keeps saying different things. Richard Wilson [Cabinet Secretary and Head of the Home Civil Service] finds it very difficult the way the Prime Minister jumps around. It's a succession of knee jerks (cited in Hennessy 2000*b*: 9).

Blair was also the first prime minister since Ramsay MacDonald not previously to have been a minister. Although 'the machinery of government was in a state of permanent revolution at the centre after 1997 . . . he never succeeded in finding a structure that suited him'. In effect, the reforms were a sign of weakness not strength (Seldon 2004: 694). So, Riddell (2001: 38–9) talks of a 'beleaguered centre' and a prime minister weak on detailed policies.

Hence, the demise of cabinet government though long predicted is yet to occur.[12] As Rentoul (2001: 544) observed: 'a lot of the business of government continued to be done in cabinet committees'. So, during the second term of government (2001–5), there were some 66 cabinet committees and Blair chaired 10 of them. After the 2005 election, Blair reduced the number of cabinet committees to 44, with 25 new committees, mostly mergers of existing ones. Blair then chaired 15 committees. The rationalization was accompanied by the statement that 'government is a collective exercise and what you need to do is harness the collective responsibilities that different ministers have and also the collective experience they bring with them' (*The Guardian*, 24 May 2005). Like Margaret Thatcher before him, Tony Blair discovered that collective government was a useful security blanket. It would seem that Blair's first term was the apogee of 'sofa government', consisting of bilateral discussions with ministers, and that it supplemented rather than supplanted cabinet government in his second term (see Prescott 2008: 205–8).

To avoid political isolation, Canadian prime ministers have tended to establish an 'informal partial Cabinet' through which to build coalitions of influence and test ideas (Jackson and Jackson 2006: 270). These informal inner cabinets have consisted of select cabinet committees or groups of core ministers who assist in deliberation, coordination, and agreement-forging. They serve as concentric spheres of political influence to pluralize advice at the centre and temper prime ministerial authority. For instance, most of Pierre Trudeau's major initiatives towards the end of his third term (1974–9) came from outside his formal cabinet processes (such as his energy initiatives). Jean Chrétien and Paul Martin (his Minister of Finance) determined spending on new policy proposals, often mercurially and without reference to their cabinet colleagues.

John Howard's approach to strengthening the centre in Australia could not be more different from Blair's because the cabinet was at the heart of his efforts to strengthen central capacity.[13] Kelly (2005: 4) concluded that 'Howard uses the cabinet as an instrument of his authority, of ministerial consultation, obedience and unity'. Prime Minister Malcolm Fraser (1975–83) commented on his own style with his cabinet, saying: 'Just because I consulted, it doesn't mean I didn't dominate' (Weller 1989*b*: 147).

Cabinet now meets less frequently than in previous eras. Prime Minister Gough Whitlam's cabinet (1972–5) met 160 times a year and dealt with more than 850 papers and made 1,390 decisions a year. Fraser ran an exhausted cabinet with around 345 meetings of cabinet or cabinet committees each year (peaking at 436 in 1979); dealing with 1,430 papers a year. In seven years it made almost 20,000 recorded decisions. In 2002–3 the Howard cabinet met just 30 times with a further 37 cabinet committees (plus 15 meetings of senior officials on the secretaries committee on national security).[14] Superficially this trend parallels that in the UK but the figures obscure the centrality of the cabinet. Howard introduced several key reforms of central agencies to support his conception of prime ministerial leadership.

The Department of the Prime Minster and Cabinet (PM&C), with 350 staff, has taken an active role as adviser and crisis manager for the last 40 years. It was a department that assisted Fraser and Hawke to drive cabinet debate and policy development. Howard added to his capacity. In 1996, the Cabinet Policy Unit (CPU) was transferred from PM&C to the Prime Minister's Office (PMO). Since its inception, the CPU has been headed by a political adviser overseeing a small political staff. According to the *Cabinet Handbook* (August 2004: 2), the CPU is 'accountable directly to the Prime Minister as Chairman of Cabinet'. The most controversial aspect of this augmentation of political and policy advice to cabinet was the decision to make the cabinet secretary the head of the CPU. In effect, this politicized the post of cabinet secretary, a position staffed from 1949 to 1996 solely by officials. According to PM&C, 'the new arrangements allow the Cabinet Secretary and CPU to become involved in preparatory work that addresses the political and other aspects of Cabinet business where public servants could not appropriately do so' (PM&C 2004: 7).

According to its second head, Paul McClintock (2003: 15–17), the CPU was established 'to really strengthen the capacity of cabinet to identify where the long-term strategic challenges were for Australia, and where were the areas where we wanted to really focus our top effort'. He insisted that 'if you do not have a very structured, formal, organised system for looking at long-term issues, they get lost in the mess of the day-to-day tactics'. This focus on big, long-term issues was reinforced by Howard's insistence that cabinet 'focus on sensitive and strategic issues' (Shergold 2004*a*: 5). Fixed, regular times were set aside for strategic deliberations by cabinet; for example, senior ministers' retreats. From July 2002, cabinet also held separate one- or two-full-day strategic cabinet meetings 'to consider the major strategic issues facing the government in a medium and longer term context' (Howard 2002: 1). In 2003, Howard approved a new unit, the Cabinet Implementation Unit (CIU), staffed by around 10 public servants. The unit was charged with providing the prime minister with information on the progress of implementing cabinet decisions.

The PMO became larger than ever before with between 40 and 50 staff. Howard controlled around one-tenth of the almost 400 ministerial staff (political advisers) employed by the coalition government but, when electoral and other staff were excluded, retained around one-quarter of ministerial staff designated as advisers. Although not formally involved in cabinet meetings, the Office was crucially involved in preparing the prime minister for cabinet and in working through the policy and political aspects of concern to the leader.

In sum, Howard's practice was designed to give cabinet a strategic role, enabling him to work through cabinet, not to bypass it. At the heart of Howard's domination of Australian government was the time he devoted to political management, in cabinet, in the party room, and in parliament; 'it is the hallmark of his time' and it 'circulates like gas through the air-conditioning, invisible yet intoxicating' (Kelly 2005: 3). No one would accuse him of lacking policy-making and management skills. Westminster systems are hierarchical with prime minister and cabinet at the apex. Howard worked with the grain.

The Pluralization of Advice

In some conceptions of the Westminster model, the public service has a monopoly of advice and this advice is weighed, assessed, and then collated for cabinet through departments, ministerial and official committees, and the Cabinet Office. This neat and tidy picture has given way to one of competing centres of advice and coordination for which, allegedly, Blair was the only nodal point. He was supported in this role not only by the new machinery of the centre but also by sources of advice other than the civil service. The civil service dominance of information and advice was broken under Thatcher. Blair took it further. He knew the general direction in which he wanted government to move, but not how to get there.

From the beginning, Blair surrounded himself with a network of special advisers. Their numbers rose from just 8 under John Major to 27 under Blair (Blick 2004: appendix). The total staff employed at No. 10 rose from 71 in 1970 under Edward Heath, to a 107 under Major to over 200 under Blair. However, it is important to put this increase in perspective. Most ministers have just one or two advisers. The total number of political and policy advisers remains small compared with some 3,500 members of the Senior Civil Service.

It is unclear whether this trend led to any significant improvement in policy-making. In the eyes of some ministers, it led to an 'informal decision-making style' centred on 'his personal entourage of advisers' that 'enhances the personal power of the Prime Minister and reduces the quality of decision-making' (Short 2004: 272, 278). In the departments, political advisers are often seen as an asset. The civil service is adept at adapting. They do not fear competing advice, only being left out of the loop. Advisers may create few problems. One permanent secretary pointed out that his minister's advisers were located next to his private office; there was no intention of burying them away in obscure rooms. He wanted them where he could see them. The two offices mingled. Relations were amicable. Everyone was kept informed. Indeed, their help on relations with the media and the party was actively sought. As Sir Richard Wilson (2003: 373–5), a former Head of the Home Civil Service, observed, special advisers (or Spads) are a 'proper and legitimate feature of the constitutional framework within which Cabinet Ministers work'. He preferred to talk about what Spads must not do. For example, they must not do anything that undermines the political impartiality of civil servants, or play any role in their recruitment, promotion, and line management. However, phrases in the Code like 'give assistance on any aspect of departmental business' open the grey area of whether Spads can give 'instructions' to civil servants or simply make 'requests'.

Yet even within No. 10, influence is not guaranteed. Derek Scott, Blair's economic adviser at No. 10, was clearly frustrated by what he saw as Blair's limited grasp of economics (Scott 2004: 14, 17, 206). He argued that Blair paid less attention to his policy advisers and civil servants than to 'the occasional outsider or those members of his inner circle who had little grasp or real interest in policy'.

Moreover, Blair's circle was not the only, or even the most important, source of advice on social and economic policy. Gordon Brown had his own coterie, and his pre-eminent consigliere was Ed Balls, chief economic adviser to the Treasury and a key Brown supporter. So, pluralization of advice also meant competing centres of advice and power. Competition between the various teams was intense.

When compared to Australia, Britain has barely dabbled in the use of advisers. The use of political advisers began with the Whitlam government (Walter 1986) and has grown progressively ever since. They are employed under the *Members of Parliament (Staff) Act 1984*. Tiernan (2007) estimated that, between 1983 and 2004, the numbers so employed rose from 684 to 1,173. Most assist members of parliament. The minority are ministerial staffers and their numbers increased from just over 200 to 391 in the same period. This compares with 81 in the UK, 201 in Canada, and 74 in New

Zealand (see also Eichbaum and Shaw 2007). Cabinet ministers were entitled to nine staff compared to two in the UK.

For our purposes, the most significant growth is in the PMO, which has seen a 'continued growth' in recent decades, 'sometimes independently of broader trends' in ministerial staffers (Holland 2004: 15). During Howard's third term, Holland found that:

> Whitlam's office had 21, while Fraser's office had 23, despite his overall reduction in the number of ministerial staff. Hawke's office ranged from 16 shortly after the election that brought Labor to power, up to 24 by 1990. Under Keating the office had 30 staff, while under Howard it grew to 37, although Howard's ministry had only a marginally larger staff profile overall.

By the end of the Howard government in November 2007, the prime minister had 49 in total (Tiernan 2007: 8). As in the UK, views differ on their effects and effectiveness. Howard stated publicly that he regards as 'both inevitable and desirable' the growth of ministerial advisers at the centre of government (Maley 2003: 1). The official view is that the staffer has 'different responsibilities' but shares a 'common commitment to serve the minister' and those responsibilities are partisan and tied to the political career of the minister (Shergold 2003: 4). Allegedly, they protect the public service from politicization. The critics argue that staffers are powerful, interventionist, and unaccountable (SSCCMI 2002). They have been implicated in cover-ups and for acting as firewalls protecting the ministers from the consequences of their actions (see Marr and Wilkinson 2003; Tiernan 2007). So far, the call for greater accountability and a code of conduct for advisers has been resisted (Tiernan 2007).

The Personalization of Party Leadership

Prime ministers personify their governments. Few other ministers are recognized by the general public. What prime ministers say is always seen as significant. Technological and media developments have led to, in the jargon, '24/7' coverage. A major theme in the 'tales of the Blair presidency' is their professional management of media relations and the use of spin doctors to manage this media-saturated environment (see Jones 1999; Foley 2000; Seymour-Ure 2003). Such professionalization is harnessed to two bigger purposes: continuous electioneering and personalizing the campaign with an exclusive focus on the leader. The consequence is that the prime minister has an independent effect on electoral outcomes (Mughan 2000).

Blair did not invent media management as a way of sustaining the pre-eminence of the prime minister. However, his 'public communications, from the designer leisure wear to the designer accent and the designer press conferences, probably attracted more public interest than those of any previous British government' (Seymour-Ure 2003: 7). Managing the media, or 'spin', is a game of chance and Blair's gambler-in-chief, his 'spin doctor' managing the media, was Alastair Campbell, Director of Communications and Strategy (Oborne and Walters 2004). He was the prime minister's voice. His job was to ensure that the prime minister's voice was also that of the government. Managing the media was a central element in policy formulation. The strategy is called 'triangulation'. It involves packaging policies so they conflict with the left wing of the Labour Party, thus winning support from the right-wing press.

Blair personalized policies with a public mix of sincerity and personal experience. As Seldon (2004: 432–6) documented, whenever Blair thought he was not getting the results he wanted, he took personal charge. He identified himself personally with policy initiatives in, for example, crime, education, health, immigration, and transport (Barber 2007). In the vivid phrase of a former Leader of the Opposition, Michael Howard, when he took charge he had 'more summits than the Himalayas'.

Australian electoral politics is also locked in 'the permanent campaign' mode, with John Howard 'fighting the 24-hours political cycle for the 1,000 days in each three year term' (Kelly 2005: 10) and, to this extent, the comparison with Blair is exact. There are local variations. Howard liked to appear as the Australian everyman, son of the service station owner who talks to average citizens rather than the unrepresentative elite. Shock-jocks and talk-back radio are prominent in Australia, so Howard's day usually started with the breakfast radio interview. He was assiduous in cultivating voters through regular media appearances not confined to politics. Sporting events were also a favourite. He also took the place of the head of state (governor-general) at ceremonials such as when sending troops overseas.[15]

Bean (1993: 129) argued that such personalization means the Australian prime minister has an important, independent effect on electoral outcomes, although McAllister (2006: 3) pointed out that the effects are small. Indeed, in his authoritative review of the evidence, McAllister (2006: 3) concluded that 'in shaping electoral outcomes, leaders clearly matter, though by a much lesser margin than is often supposed'. Consequently, the effects can be marginal. Similarly, for Canada, although there is a certain leadership effect in elections, these effects, according to Blais et al. (2002: 166), 'are not usually overwhelming' and do not change the outcome of the election. Indeed, despite the focus on the leader, the electoral effect of personalization has arguably been declining and regionalization is the most prominent single factor explaining electoral outcomes.

DRAWING THE EVIDENCE TOGETHER

What do the recent changes add up to? Clearly some of the claims about the changing pattern of political leadership are accurate. It helps to distinguish between the electoral, policy-making, and implementation arenas.

First, in the *electoral arena*, personalization is a prominent feature of media management in all countries and has a significant if small electoral effect in most. It is here in the electoral and party arena that the presidential argument is most apt. Spatial leadership has arrived.

In the *policy-making arena*, there is some truth to the claim of a centralization of policy-making around the prime minister. However, this claim applies to selected policy areas only, with the equally important proviso that the prime minister's attention is also selective. Thus, the continuous reform of the British centre paradoxically speaks of the failure, not success, of coordination; while in Australia and Canada constitutional limitations and federal pressures must be accommodated (Keating and Wanna 2000; Bakvis 2001).

The prime minister's influence is most constrained in the *policy implementation arena*, so it is conspicuous for its absence in most accounts of presidentialism. Here, other senior government figures, ministers and their departments, and other agencies are key actors. Prime ministers are just one actor among many interdependent ones in the webs of organizations and governments, national and international, in which they are embedded.

In sum, the fortunes of 'presidential' prime ministers vary markedly between arenas and during their period of office. It is misleading to focus only on the prime minister and cabinet because political power is not concentrated in them, but more widely dispersed. It is contested, so the standing of any individual or institution is contingent: prime minister or chancellor; cabinet or Treasury. As Helms (2005: 259) concluded from his comparison of American, British, and German core executives, 'there is rather limited evidence of presidentialisation', although Poguntke and Webb (2005*b*: 347) disagreed, arguing that the various shifts 'generate *a greater potential for, and likelihood of,* this "presidential" working-mode' irrespective of regime [emphasis added]. In Australia and the UK, 60 years after the Second World War, we are not there yet! Fear not, the debate will go on, and on.

ALTERNATIVE EXPLANATIONS

In this final section we look at four alternative explanations for differences between executive politics in the 'great dominions': court politics; leadership traditions; cabinet as decision-maker; and territorial interdependence.

The Contingent Nature of 'Court Politics'

Cabinet is not only about policy or presentation. It is also about ambition, rivalry, infighting, and despair. If stories of presidentialism are riven with contradictions, part of the answer lies in the contingent nature of court politics. At any given point in time the prime minister may dominate his or her colleagues; for example, after a major election victory. But core executive politics comes in many guises and pre-eminence comes before a fall. There are rivals, factions, and 'events, dear boy, events' lying in wait. Sitting around the cabinet table could be the prime minister's potential assassins and successors. There may be one, there may be several; even more have illusions that they will one day lead their party and government. The politics of succession permeates all cabinet activity.

When there is an obvious heir, cabinet politics provides glimpses of the Hanoverian era, when the kings and the princes were never on speaking terms and maintained rival courts. Gordon Brown was 'a great crag standing in the way of a thoroughly monocratic government' by Blair (Hennessy 2002: 21). Recognition of Brown's authority required a shift from tales of a Blair presidency to stories of at least a dual monarchy: 'Brown conceived of the new government as a dual monarchy, each with its own court' (Rawnsley 2001: 20). White concluded that 'Blair had effectively ceded sovereignty to Brown in the economics sphere' (cited in Seldon 2004: 66; see also Rawnsley 2001: 143; Naughtie 2002: 7; *The Guardian* 6 June 2003; Peston 2005: 67).

There have been several occasions on which Blair has found his authority checked by Brown. Such checks have occurred most often and dramatically over Blair's European ambitions and the budget. Hence, Brown frustrated Blair's wish to join the euro (Keegan 2003: chapter 12; Seldon 2004: 682–3; Peston 2005: chapter 6). Brown also controlled the budget by withholding information. As Scott (2004: 24) commented, 'getting information about the contents of Gordon Brown's budget was like drawing teeth' (Seldon 2004: 674; Peston 2005: 99 and 226–7).

In the second term, 'while Blair aimed . . . to limit Brown's authority over domestic policy, Brown fought to increase it' (Seldon 2004: 627). 'They were not interested in submerging their differences in outlook, but in making an exhibition of them' (Naughtie 2002: 352). It is a fine example of the politics of political space. Brown commanded most of the domestic political space, forcing Blair almost by default into overseas adventures simply because of his inability to make a mark domestically. By 2005, their relationship had deteriorated to an all-time low. Brown was reported as saying to Blair that 'There is nothing you could ever say to me now that I could ever believe.' He had become 'the official opposition to Blair within the very heart of the Cabinet' (Peston 2005: 349, 13 also 353; Fawcett and Rhodes 2007).

A key characteristic of the Blair decade is this shifting of fortunes, the contingency of the court politics and the combative duumvirate. Hennessy (2000*b*: 493–500) conscientiously mapped Blair's inner circle and its changing membership. Beckett and Hencke (2004: chapter 14) describe the 'oestrogen-fuelled', '*Girl's Own*, comic book' view of life at the Number 10 court (see also Oborne and Walters 2004; Campbell 2007; Blair C. 2008). It is not necessary to accept any particular account of life at No. 10 to make the observation that court politics are an important feature of the British executive. They are not confined to the Blair and Brown years (see, for example, Donoughue 2003). Rival barons continue to compete (Norton 2000: 116–17). We saw major running conflicts between Brown and the Health Minister, Alan Milburn, over foundation hospitals. Other ministers struggled to become heavy hitters. David Blunkett's frank if injudicious comments on the abilities and progress of his cabinet colleagues provided examples of conversations that Westminster and Whitehall conduct all the time in private. Thus, Alan Milburn, Health, had 'grown in competence and ability'; Margaret Beckett, Environment and Agriculture, was 'just holding the ring'; Charles Clarke, Education, 'has not developed as expected'; Patricia Hewitt, Trade and Industry, did not think strategically; and Gordon Brown threw his weight around (Pollard 2005: 27–8). His colleagues duly reciprocated. The former deputy prime minister, John Prescott, held Blunkett in a mixture of contempt and suspicion while others gritted their teeth over his 'idiotic indiscretion' (*Observer*, 12 December 2004). Gossip is the currency of court politics and the judgements are markers in the endless ministerial jockeying for position and recognition.

To parallel the Blair–Brown tale, we can recount the four-year Hawke–Keating leadership battle.[16] Tensions erupted in 1987 and were partially contained in a formal pact agreed at Kirribilli House (the PM's Sydney residence) in which Prime Minister Bob Hawke agreed to stand down in favour of Treasurer Paul Keating, during Labor's fourth term. This pact fell apart when, first, in a speech at the Press Club in December 1990, Keating described himself as the 'Placido Domingo of Australian politics'. He disparaged Hawke's leadership style 'as tripping over television cables in shopping centres', dismissing most of Australia's previous Labor leaders on the way. For Hawke (1994: 498), Keating was 'vainglorious and arrogant, disloyal and contemptuous'. Although Labor was massively unpopular in the polls, the First Gulf War of January 1991 restored Hawke's fortunes. He believed he could win the next election. So, he reneged on the Kirribilli pact, precipitating a leadership challenge. Keating took him on in a party-room ballot but lost by 66 votes to 44 in June 1991.

Keating was not vanquished. It was a credible challenge but he did not have sufficient votes. He had to stand down as Treasurer, but a second challenge was inevitable. The new Treasurer, John Kerin, floundered, and Labor's budgetary and economic misfortunes eroded Hawke's support. The Leader of the Opposition, John Hewson, launched the Liberal's economic renewal package under the slogan *Fightback!*, which highlighted that the Hawke government was bereft of ideas. The polls were little short of disastrous. Hawke's cabinet allies sought to persuade him to stand down. In December 1991, Keating overthrew Hawke by 61 votes to 56.

Hawke (1994: 558) claims 'it was not a time for grudges or hatreds'. Keating has not written a memoir or autobiography but Watson (2002: 25–9), his speech writer, argued 'he took the leadership from Hawke because it was owed and because it had been promised him'. It is hard to believe that Keating would demur from that judgement. Although their relationship had been 'brotherly', and they 'put together a nice little story' about their 'shared adventures and achievements', at the end, no love was lost between the two men and Keating has 'always denied that the execution of Hawke caused him any grief'. So, a long-running soap opera came to an end with the 'word magician' in power, leaving the 'dinky-di Australian' to write his self-serving memoirs (Hawke 1994: 561). Keating was beloved by the press gallery. The story ran and ran. It was part of the story of Labor's decline, colouring media and public perceptions alike. It was a prism through which all other political events were interpreted. Keating, the magician, the wordsmith, the man who had the measure of Hewson, brought Labor back from the dead with his 'unwinnable election' victory of March 1993, saying: 'this is the sweetest victory of all'. Hawke won four elections in a row. He was Australia's most electorally successful Labor leader ever. But he was undermined by Keating and abandoned by caucus, if only narrowly. The contingency of court politics is too anodyne a phrase to capture his fate.

In Canada, Jean Chrétien was prime minister for a decade. The rival he defeated in the 1990 Liberal leadership convention, Paul Martin, was Minister of Finance for much of his reign and widely regarded as his probable successor. Between them they dominated the cabinet, but theirs was also an uneasy alliance with little trust. Whenever Martin or other aspirants appeared to be garnering political support, Chrétien warned that unless they desisted, he would remain in office; he knew there was no mechanism to drive him unwillingly from office. Eventually, in 2002, a frustrated Martin left the cabinet (by some accounts he was sacked by Chrétien, by others he resigned); it was easier to gather support across the country when Chrétien finally departed the leadership. When the Liberal party convention occurred, Martin won easily, even if by then the aspirant was handed a poisoned chalice, as has occurred with other successors of long-term Canadian incumbents (Trudeau to Turner, and Mulroney to Campbell).

The court strategies available for pretenders to the throne vary from country to country. Brown fumed and stayed in cabinet; he was only a contender if he remained a leading member of cabinet. Keating plotted and assassinated; he had the means and could wield the dagger from the back bench. Martin left and campaigned; he needed the freedom to gather support from those who were to be delegates at the next leadership convention. Strategies were determined by the rules that opened paths to the prime ministership and by party tradition.

The phrase 'the core executive' always sought to broaden the notion of executive power beyond a narrow focus on prime minister and cabinet (Rhodes 1995*a*; Smith 1999). It stresses the interdependence of the *several* actors at the heart of government. The several stories of court politics in Britain and the dominions show how misleading it is to focus only on prime minister and cabinet. Political power is not concentrated in either prime minister or cabinet, but more widely dispersed. It is contested, so the standing of any individual, prime minister or senior minister, is contingent. All governments fail some of the time. All governments are constrained by world events. All prime ministers intervene. Few control, and even then only over some policies, some of the time. The test of success in politics is elusive and shifting. Maybe, as Enoch Powell said, all political careers end in failure. Maybe, as George Orwell (1970*a*: 185) said: 'any life when viewed from the inside is simply a series of defeats'. It is not that the 'presidential' style uniquely fails, but that its failures are no different from those of more collegial styles.

Traditions of Leadership and Cabinet

We have told some stories about the court politics that surround heads of government. How do we explain the similarities and the differences between our several cases? How do local traditions about and understandings of the Westminster model infuse talk of presidentialism, centralization, and other species of prime ministerial dominance? How to explain the differences? We can look back to the traditions that countries develop about the role of cabinet government and of leadership, as we did in Chapters 2 and 3. If cabinet is the supreme committee for political direction and management, then there are at least three competing executive traditions:

- The political tradition that balances the individual leader against the collective wisdom.

- The representative tradition that assumes that cabinet has a role in providing voice for regional or other interests, often as a means of consolidating political support.

- The collective tradition that sees cabinet as a means of drawing together the threads of a coherent government policy.

In debates about these traditions, it is worth remembering the origin of cabinet: ministers meeting in private to agree on a single line that would then be presented to the monarch. As Crown influence receded, prime ministers assumed its authority, being collectively responsible with their ministers to parliament. It was never the case of *primus inter pares* that nostalgia and bad history sometimes wants to recall. There was always a tension between the strength of individual leaders and the group influence of ministers. David Lloyd George, Robert Borden, and Billy Hughes were prime ministers of Britain, Canada, and Australia in the 1914–18 War and afterwards. No prime ministers have been more powerful, more idiosyncratic, more individualistic. That includes Blair, Chrétien, and Howard and other modern successors.

Essentially cabinet is a committee of notables to organize around and respond to political challenges of office, with all the range and complexity that entails. In all Westminster countries, cabinet still exists; it meets more or less regularly; ministers have formal responsibility for their departments. What, then, in the traditions can explain the way that countries have varied?

Leadership in cabinet can be conceived differently. It depends on tradition and local conditions. The question then becomes: Is there a traditional understanding directing how leadership should be exercised? How authoritarian can a prime minister become? Despite the common origins, each country has developed its own interpretations of the roles.

In Britain the position retains more than a whiff of royal prerogative, but even then it can be interpreted through different lens. There are at least three possible versions: Tory, Whig, and Socialist.[17] Philip Norton is a Tory and a combative defender of the UK constitution against all comers (Norton 1982). He believes the Blair presidency is 'dangerous' because it centralizes power in No. 10, adopts a principal–agent relationship with departments 'that is likely to be difficult to sustain', relies on goodwill for implementation 'that may not be forthcoming', and 'ignores parliament'. These problems are compounded by 'the lack of experience and, indeed, understanding of government by the prime minister and many of those around him', coupled with a 'leadership... obsessed with power' and 'no understanding... of relationships within the system' (Norton 2003: 277). He rails against the notion that the leader knows best.

What to do? For Norton (2003: 278) we need to return to the 'party-in-government' as the body 'responsible for public policy' that 'can be held accountable by electors at a subsequent general election'. In other words, Norton believes in decisive, collective party government and urges a return to the eternal verities of the Westminster model. He criticizes the notion of a Blair presidency to resurrect Westminster.

Hennessy (2000*b*: 535) is a Whig. Moreover, 'history is a discipline that sobers up its practitioners'. He rejects the command and control model of the prime minister as chief executive for two reasons. First, 'command models sit ill with open societies'. Second, 'British political culture reflects the compost in which it is grown'. It is a parliamentary not a presidential compost. So he defends the 'deep continuities' of the constitutional side of the job; relations with the monarchy, accountability to parliament, collective government, and a career civil service (Hennessy 2000*b*: 539). However, he too recognizes that Britain must change to meet the challenges of an interdependent world. He foresees prime ministers ever more entangled in international affairs, an expanding 'hybrid arena' where international and domestic mingle, relentless media pressure, 'the avalanche of information', and a reconfigured British state because of, for example, devolution (Hennessy 2000*b*: 538). In sum, he describes a world of complex interdependences.

To meet these demands, he envisages No. 10 distancing itself from the hurly-burly and developing both a plurality of analytical capabilities and a greater capacity to provide risk and strategic assessments. All such changes would be within the context of collective government; or, to rephrase, to meet the challenges posed by the governance narrative, Hennessy envisages a return to cabinet government with reinforced analytical and strategic support. His understanding of the British presidency is less that it is dangerous, although it may well be, than that to institutionalize it is to plant an alien invention in British soil.

The Socialist tradition in the guise of New Labour has its own conception of how British government should be run. In Peter Mandelson and Roger Liddle's 'shadow' manifesto they argued that, to succeed, Blair needed 'personal control of the central government' (1996: chapter 10). They described, with approval, Thatcher's 'focus on a clear set of goals' and 'strength of will', claiming it 'says a lot about leadership in government'. Blair needed to follow her example 'in getting control of the centre of government'. So there should be a 'more formalised strengthening of the centre of government' to 'give much-needed support to the prime minister' and 'provide a means for formulating and driving forward strategy for the government as a whole'. The No. 10 Policy Unit should be 'beefed-up', and the Cabinet Office needed to be more 'pro-active'. When New Labour came to power, therefore, it should have been no surprise that 'there was never any intention of having collective Cabinet government'. Blair was 'going to run a centralized government, with a commanding Policy Unit which was solidly New Labour' (insider cited in Seldon 2004: 437).

There are two features of New Labour's approach worth noting. First, it is strongly influenced by the example of Thatcher's leadership style. Second, it consigned old Labour traditions, many of which are more democratic, to the dustbins of history. The contrast with Jim Callaghan or Harold Wilson is marked:[18]

> from time to time there is discussion about the need for a formal Prime Minister's Department . . . such talk frequently overlooks the instruments he already has. He is able to provide himself with his own sources of information, he can send up a trial balloon or fire a sighting shot across a Ministerial bow without directly involving his own authority or publicly undermining that of the Minister; and has the necessary facilities to take a decisive hand in policy-making at any moment he chooses to intervene (Callaghan 1987: 408).

Deserting Labour traditions for Thatcherite dynamism had its costs. It provoked criticism for eroding the

> traditional norms of democracy and administration in favour of a model that rested more on central diktat. His three predecessors as Prime Ministers, Attlee, Wilson and Callaghan, had governed collectively: no previous Labour leader, from Keir Hardie to John Smith, had adopted such a personal style of control, and in this respect, as in others [Blair] showed himself to be a leader lacking empathy with the traditions of his party (Seldon 2004: 694).

Yet Blair and his entourage consistently denied they abandoned collective government, arguing their reforms were consistent with present-day constitutional conventions. Such a 'Mandy Rice-Davies' defence is predictable. If policy-making is presidential, then only the president is to blame when things go wrong. However, when the government struck problems in policy-making and implementation, it blamed the long-standing whipping boys of the Westminster constitution, the civil service, said to lack both ideas and drive (Seldon 2004: 436). Others saw a problem with Blair's policy-making and management style and the mistaken belief that running the government was like running the Labour Party writ large. Such auto-critique was not on the central agenda.

The Labor tradition in Australia is determinedly collegial. All leaders, including ministers and prime ministers, are elected by the party caucus. The caucus is bound by the decisions of the party conference, itself constituted of delegates of the branches and affiliated unions. Every member is pledged to abide by the party platform, determined in a duly constituted party forum. Labor's line of authority nominally privileges a system of rank-and-file control. Labor ministers are delegates, not representatives. Furthermore, this system was developed prior to 1914, before the British Labour party had made any mark in the British House of Commons. Australian Labor traditions were home-grown and aggressively proposed. Defending the party from accusations that its members were forced by caucus decision to vote against their conscience, the then Labor advocate (and future prime minister) Billy Hughes asked in 1909:

> Will our critics who accuse us of not being free men tell us by what we are bound save our own word, freely given? If we believe in certain principles, ought we not to do what we can to give effect to them? And if we are not ashamed but rather glory in our course, why should we not testify to its virtue and solemnly pledge ourselves to stand by it?

Caucus influence on cabinet was to be a defining principle for Labor, but was often contested by the prime minister. It destroyed two Labor governments (including one led by Hughes) before later leaders learnt how to manage the process.

Labor decided in 1905 that caucus would elect ministers. It exercised that right for the first time in electing a Labor ministry in 1908. The election of ministers changed the dynamic between prime minister and ministers. Even though Labor leaders had extensive power, they often had to coexist with ministers they might not have chosen. They were aware, too, that *they* were elected by the caucus and could at any time be removed by the caucus. Their rivals were sitting around the cabinet table, potentially assessing their chances and looking to gain support. The then Labor opposition leader, Kevin Rudd, announced in 2007 that he would break this convention and select his own cabinet if elected to government (mainly to allay fears that his front bench would be all factional heavyweights). Although he had to accommodate factional leaders, he dumped six time-servers and appointed his own ministry in late 2007. The point remains: Labor prime ministers have to work with and through cabinet, caucus, and ministers to maintain support. They need to. It ensures their continued existence.

Australia's non-Labor parties copied Labor precedents from early in the twentieth century. They also elected leaders, and thus prime ministers, endorsing and on occasions refusing to endorse them by a party-room vote. Although they cede more authority than Labor to the leaders and allow them to select ministers, the final sanction is retained. When John Howard coined the mantra: 'I will stay as prime minister as long as my party wants me', he was both speaking the truth and warning his potential successor, Treasurer Peter Costello, that he needed the numbers in the party room before he could seize the prize. In Australia the collective tradition dictates how prime ministers operate.

Canadian prime ministers are nowhere nearly as sensitive to such party-room pressures. Elected at large has meant that their hand has been strengthened against internal critics in government and parliament. Since 1919, party leaders have been elected by a party convention, creating a participatory tradition in leadership choice that has extensive cabinet impact. As prime ministers remind their cabinets and party rooms, they were not elected by them and cannot be removed by them. While opponents of an Australian prime minister may plot, Canadian pretenders sit it out, or leave. The last three Liberal prime ministers, Turner, Chrétien, and Martin, were not in cabinet (or even in parliament) when they secured the leadership. The Conservative's Brian Mulroney had never been elected to public office when he won the party leadership; he was only in the House of Commons briefly before he became prime minister.

That position gives them authority because they are shielded from internal revolt. Consequently, perhaps they outstay their political welcome. Chrétien ruled through inner cabinets, primarily so that he could decide what decisions were announced and when, but cabinet committees still played deliberative roles. Such committees might approve programmes, but the prime minister and the minister of finance together would agree which would receive funding. That is how the leadership-collective dynamic worked.

Although the new South African regime is in its infancy, its presidents are relatively secure, elected for a fixed five-year period (unless impeached). But there are other avenues to exploit to circumscribe the leader. Its second president, Thabo Mbeki, was challenged for the leadership of the ANC in late 2007 by Jacob Zuma in a public brawl that divided the party. He was then regarded as a 'lame duck' president and several senior members of the ANC joined with the opposition Democratic Alliance in calling for his early resignation. Mbeki faced other challenges to his authority over senior appointments and economic policy. Further challenges have come from the floor of the Assembly when the president has given formal addresses to parliament; ANC members have challenged him with searching questions about policy shortcomings under his rule. He duly resigned.

Cabinet as Authoritative Decision-Maker

Minutes of the British cabinet were first taken in 1916. Hennessy (1989: 65) claims: 'the power and majesty of the Cabinet Minute was established that day and has survived undiminished to the present'. Ministers are 'invited' to take a particular course of action, not instructed. But the import and impact is unmistakable and brooks no argument. As Gerald Kaufman wrote of his experience in the Wilson and Callaghan governments in the 1970s, 'Cabinet minutes are studied in Government departments with the reverence generally reserved for sacred texts and can be triumphantly produced conclusively to settle any argument.'

Cabinet *decisions* remain the currency of government, given weight by the traditions that have been developed over a century of bureaucratization of cabinet and its procedures. They provide the documentation needed to give authority.

That stated, the location for the decision may vary. The cabinet system is a terrain across which prime ministers and ministers may wander. Some advocates will argue that every important decision should be made in meetings of the full cabinet because they claim its authority. In practice, where they are made depends on the need for political support and functional requirements. In some jurisdictions there may be extensive policy debate in full cabinet (Australia, New Zealand, and South Africa), while in others there is less deliberation of specific policy such as in Britain or Canada.[19] Decisions may be delegated to committees with the authority to make decisions, or they may be made bilaterally. Meetings of the full British cabinet have become forums for information exchange and reports; in Canada they act as sounding boards. Yet in Britain and Canada many of the decisions are determined in meetings of cabinet committees and endorsed, without discussion and formal acceptance in cabinet, after discussions between the prime minister and chair of the committee.

Examples are plentiful. In the UK, Attlee ensured that all decisions on the nuclear bomb were made in committee and the rest of cabinet was not informed. Fraser rushed his government's policy on South Africa through the Foreign Affairs and Defence committee and then told ministers the policy was set and not for reopening. Callaghan allowed his full cabinet to debate the IMF loan extensively in 1976, but to contain dissent and gain support, not to alter the decision. Chrétien preferred that policy submissions were debated at cabinet committees with the endorsed ones queued in a potential 'hopper', sometimes for years, until he chose to adopt and resource them. Those he ignored lapsed with the dissolution of parliament. Special war cabinets or national security committees have also been frequently created to deal with serious emergencies (often developing their separate practices).

In New Zealand there is now an additional driver. Governments post-MMP are either coalitions (formally or informally) or minority governments relying on cross-bench support. Cabinet must be cognizant of maintaining the support of other parties and key players in the parliament. Supporting parties or sympathetic dissidents may be included in government, or ad hoc accommodations arrived at (such as in the third Clark government where the minister for foreign affairs, Winston Peters, was in the ministry but not in Labour's cabinet). Cabinet authority is refracted and contested by parliament.

In all jurisdictions, cabinet decision-making can be seen as a set of expanding circles. The prime minister is the core. The prime ministers and relevant senior ministers form the next ring or the next inner sanctum. Commonly it comprises their chancellors of the exchequer, treasurers, or finance ministers for economic issues; foreign affairs and defence ministers for security; or a powerful domestic minister for home affairs. The inner cabinet will form the third ring, followed by full cabinet, the complete ministry, and so on. Authoritative decisions can be made in any part of the system depending on circumstance.

Such phrases as 'the prime minister wants' or 'the PM would like' are a powerful stimulus to action. A cabinet decision adds the authority of the collective; it is government policy, not opinion. In all Westminster systems the decision represents the traditional mode of action. Cabinet may allow for interplay and interpretation, but its authority still carries weight.

Territorial Interdependence

Interdependence between levels of government is a feature of major Westminster systems, including the ostensibly unitary UK. For example, the differentiated polity narrative, discussed in Chapter 3, challenges the Westminster model's account of British government. It argues there has been a shift from government by a unitary state to governance through and by networks. Differentiation increased in recent decades leading to significant changes in the functional and territorial specialization of British government. Many forces propelled this trend. The marketization of public services multiplied delivery networks; the degree of international interdependence became greater; and powers were devolved to Scotland and Wales as the UK 'embarked upon a path of regional devolution' (Hueglin and Fenna 2006: 18). There was an appreciable hollowing out of the core executive's capacity to steer. It has to manage packages of services, packages of organizations, and packages of governments. Command and control has limits when the centre is dependent on a multitude of other bodies.

> The more the prime minister and senior ministers have sought to centralise power in their own hands then, perhaps paradoxically, the more fragmented British government has become. The glue of government has started coming unstuck (Norton 2003: 276).

In other words, there is a countervailing momentum at work, generated by a differentiated polity and territorial interdependence that serves to qualify the traditions of strong executive government.[20]

Cabinet as a geographically representative forum is a strong tradition in Canadian politics. Canada is a fragmented country, geographically, ethnically, and linguistically (one region even has nine official languages). Anglophone leaders will need a Quebec lieutenant (although a Quebec primate may not need an Anglophone equivalent). Each province needs an advocate in cabinet. Ministers represent regions as well as portfolios. Some have been powerful figures, responsible for much of the overt patronage that drives much of Canadian politics: Jimmy Gardiner for the prairie provinces in the 1950s, Lloyd Axworthy for the west in the Trudeau government (1980–4) that had no representation west of Winnipeg.

The imperatives of representation affect the organization of cabinet. Since no province wanted to be left out of decision-making, cabinet could not be divided into a cabinet and an outer ring of junior ministers. When cabinet exceeded 40 in number, cabinet could not act as a decision-making forum. Prime ministers had to resort to committees such as 'priorities and planning' as a means of convening inner groups without upsetting regions that might have felt unrepresented in a formal inner cabinet. Departments were created with a geographical focus to deliver services (pork-barrelling) to Atlantic provinces or to the West. Chrétien on forming office in 1993 adopted a two-tiered ministry with 27 cabinet ministers and nine ministers of state to assist. This experiment proved short-lived as Paul Martin, leading a minority government, subsequently reunited cabinet and nominated 39 ministers, while his successor, Stephen Harper, also leading a minority government, included all ministers in his cabinet but listed only 32.

In South Africa, representation is tribal, racial, and regional combined. The list system for the Assembly forces the ANC to garner suitable candidates from each of the nine provinces and major cities to maximize support. Regionally specific groups such as the Zulu people in Kwa-Zulu Natal are, like Quebecers, hemmed into a single province but remain geographically powerful and often need to be appeased with special deals. Although all MPs are nationally elected, they all represent 'constituency' areas informally. The upper house, the National Council of Provinces, which is composed of provincial representatives (nominated by the provincial governments), *must* approve any legislation that impacts on provincial matters. It also has an equal say in adopting any other legislation not necessarily about provincial matters.

As a more homogeneous polity, the politics of place exist to a lesser extent in Australia. Every state will be represented in the ministry but not necessarily in cabinet itself. When vacancies occur, state and party balance will be a consideration. Senior cabinet ministers may be consulted when appointments from their state are made. Minsters will be aware of the need for adequate services to their states. The constitution guarantees equal representation of the original states in the Senate, which influences the composition and complexion of both caucus and the ministry. But Australia has none of the centrifugal forces that threaten Canada; it has a greater tendency to vote as one nation, although it still has a state-based party structure, not national.

The difference for all three countries is that heads of the national government must deal with state and provincial premiers, each of whom has their own electoral mandate, their own interests, and their own power base. Australia may be one of the most unified of federations, South Africa one of the most federal republics, and Canada may border on confederalism with powerful provinces; yet all prime ministers have to negotiate and compromise to advance their policies. For instance, in 2007 a Liberal prime minister in Canberra was faced by a phalanx of Labor premiers in all six states and two territories. To make progress with his policy priorities, he had to work through them. Shared power and concurrent legitimacy demand negotiation.

In effect, for believers in unfettered national government, territorial interdependence, especially federalism, may appear a historical curio and potential encumbrance (Hueglin and Fenna 2006). But it remains central to the challenge of running a government. Whether a British prime minister will face awkward negotiations with Scotland and Wales may depend how much independence those parliaments manage to achieve, for they will surely seek it, especially nationalist governments in Scotland. The difficulties with the Northern Ireland Assembly are an obvious warning. In short, whether we look at unitary or federal states, territorial traditions shape and constrain cabinet government. They are a source of centripetal and centrifugal forces. They are a cause of differentiation and provide political glue. Interdependence may vary over time and between countries, but cabinet government ignores the constraints and opportunities on offer at its peril.

CONCLUSIONS

Arguments that the Westminster system has been undermined by presidentialism are not persuasive. All the chatter about presidencies is often a counter to the messiness of court politics and wider party politics. The debate is also instrumental. For example, for Blair's supporters, it was a way of promoting his standing in the party and in the country. For opponents inside and outside the Labour Party, it was a way of expressing hostility to Blair in particular and the Labour government in general. But, it matters not that the presidential analogy is misleading because the game is not about empirical accuracy. The critics have several widely varying targets. Foley (2004) argues that the epithet can refer to Blair's personal characteristics, to claims that he is too powerful, to the consequences of Blair's command and control style of government, to his international adventures and attendant disregard of domestic politics, to his flouting of constitutional conventions, to the influence of the United States on British politics. So, when used as a smokescreen for attacks on the prime minister and government, the term is but a flag of convenience.

But there are other specific criticisms. If presidentialization is used as an analogy to identify structural changes to the nature of political leadership, it is potentially misleading because the differences between a parliamentary and a presidential system far outweigh the likenesses by some margin (Rose 2001: 236–44). Better to talk of changing styles of leadership, about centralization, about the search for control or direction as events often get out of hand, or as authority meets its 'consent deficit'.

Second, a focus on presidentialism is too narrow; it diverts attention away from the beliefs and practices of individual prime ministers, ministers, and public servants. Such an approach will necessarily lead us to look at the contingencies of political life and the ways in which individuals modify their inherited beliefs and practices when they confront the dilemmas of governance. If one conclusion is clear it is that different prime ministers think differently about their role and approach to the job, over time and across jurisdictions. The office shapes but does not dictate their practices. Analysis of changing patterns of leadership should start here and not with misleading analogies with polities categorized as presidential. The aphorism that 'the prime minister is first among equals' only needs the addition of, 'but he is often more equal than others', to capture life at the top.

Third, the stage on which prime ministers and cabinets perform is not of their own making or choosing. They are the heirs to governmental traditions that provide the language and conventions that modify their beliefs and provide models for their practices. Ostensibly similar traditions such as 'responsible government' will be understood differently in different settings. Australia has emphasized collegiate cabinet responsibility that underpinned Howard's political-management of cabinet, party, and parliament. In the UK, such constitutional conventions are a contested terrain variously constructed against the backcloth of competing political traditions.

Finally, there are recurring dilemmas running through these stories of presidentialism. On the one hand, the Westminster model is a shell; it is a pliable set of institutional beliefs masking the contested and contingent nature of changing patterns of leadership. On the other hand, many political actors continue to use the language of the traditional Westminster model to comprehend 'their' world and describe the past, present, and future of politics. It is part of their everyday language for coping, employing a handful of recurrent metaphors about the drama of politics, the stage on which politicians appear, the court politics of the centre, and gossip about the games people play. In turn, the story of Westminster as a *shell* or *ideal*, and Westminster as an *unfolding narrative* of everyday political life, has to confront the governance tale with its stress on the prime minister as one actor embedded in, and dependent on, webs of organizations and governments.

The inescapable fact for all governments, unitary or federal, is that they have to work in, with, and through a complex of organizations, governments, and networks with power constrained by ever more pervasive and complex patterns of dependence. Governing was never as neat and hierarchical as the models suggested. The more we look outside the Westminster model, the more we find that centralization, pluralization, and personalization represent not a concentration of power, but an endless search for effective levers of control by core executives less powerful than many commentators and insiders claim. While the core executive thesis can encompass the several varieties of court politics, the presidentialization thesis cannot.

In short, the political executive in a Westminster system is variously constructed by agents situated in competing traditions. Our understanding of the executive in several Westminster systems is shaped by different local traditions that, even if they had shared roots in beliefs about responsible government, begin to understand those common roots differently. The Westminster constitution lives as an emblem of a past age and as a living tradition whose offspring influence the ways things are still done.

NOTES

1 Although at this stage Crossman had not actually had experience of cabinet government.
2 Most of the material on the Australian executive takes the form of secondary texts, so it is of limited use as primary source material. For a select bibliography covering both prime ministerial biographies and research-based studies of cabinet government in Australia see Weller (2005, 2007). For pen portraits of several prime ministers see Brown (2002), Carroll (2004), and Grattan (2000). There are a few diaries, memoirs

and autobiographies of politicians, but many are tendentious, self-serving, and unreliable, although they can be mined for quotes. Among the useful contributions are Blewett (1999), Edwards (1996), Walsh (1995), Watson (2002), and Weller (1989*b*). The best account of Fraser's cabinet is Weller (1989*b*: chapter 4). For Hawke, see Blewett (2003) and the bibliography by Warhurst and Chalmers (2003). For Keating, see Blewett (1999). For a select bibliography on John Howard see note 3 below.

3 John Howard has been ill-served by biographers, journalists, and academics alike. Only two full-length biographies have been written – the first a hagiography by Barnett with Goward (1997), the second a more serious study by van Onselen and Errington (2007). The short essays in Brown (2002), Carroll (2004), and Grattan (2000) are introductory and dated. Splenetic abuse by anarchic journalists such as Kingston (2004) and MacCallum (2004) can bring a smile but little by way of insight or originality. Academics seem more concerned to criticize than to explain how John Howard became the second longest serving prime minister in Australian history, outshone only by Robert Menzies. See, for example, the collections of essays edited by Aulich and Wettenhall (2005), Manne (2004*a*), Singleton (2000), and Warhurst (2007). There are exceptions. We found the following useful: Adams (2000, 2005), Brett (2002, 2005), Kelly (2005), Maddox (2005), Manne (2004*b*), and Marr and Wilkinson (2003), although for the most part they have little to say about cabinet government under Howard.

4 Unlike prime ministers, South African presidents are limited by the Constitution to a maximum of two consecutive terms.

5 Foley is the most prolific academic contributor. He describes the 1993 book as 'an earlier version' of the 2000 edition (p. 24), although it is not designated a second edition. Our summary is based on the latter. Others in the UK who identify a trend to presidentialism even as they criticize it include: Allen (2002), Hennessy (2005), Kavanagh and Seldon (2000), Mughan (2000), Pryce (1997), and Rose (2001). The most coruscating critic of all things presidential is George Jones (1985).

6 Both the office of the president and cabinet are stipulated in the constitution, but their exact roles are largely left open. The president exercises executive authority 'with the other members of the Cabinet' (s. 85 2), but cabinet has no other listed functions although criteria for the selection of cabinets are specified. The president's constitutional powers are predominantly procedural: they may summon parliament, assents to bills, may refer legislation back to the Assembly or to the Constitutional Court, may make appointments, appoint commissions of inquiry, and call national referenda. But, formally, the office is given full powers of a head of state and head of government – 'the executive authority of the Republic is vested in the President' (s. 85 1).

7 The South African Constitution requires that the president be elected from among the members of the Assembly but that once elected the president 'ceases to be a member of the National Assembly'. (The Assembly is chosen from party lists under a proportional representation voting system.) The president may attend and speak in the Assembly (s. 54) but the deputy president must be appointed

from the Assembly and remain a member although another minister of cabinet can be appointed as leader of government business in the Assembly (s. 91). In the other four Westminster cases, conventions dictate that the prime minister should be a serving member of the lower house although, in the three with upper chambers, nothing constitutionally prevents the prime minister from coming from the upper house. From time to time individuals chosen as leader of the opposition in Canada have not been members of the House of Commons and thus needed to find a seat. Likewise, in 1984, John Turner became the prime minister in a Liberal government following the resignation of Pierre Trudeau but at that stage was not a member of the House of Commons and had to find a seat.

 8 These ministerial guides have evolved from internal guidelines, to internal handbooks, to publicly available guides and manuals. These are regularly updated by each prime minister upon taking office; see Baker (2000) and Weller (2001).

 9 In judicial reviews of executive behaviour the courts have tended to accept the sanctity of political conventions and framed their decisions within the framework of convention-led government. The point remains, though, that conventions such as ministerial responsibility and prime ministerial and cabinet powers have not generally been judiciable in the realm of the courts.

10 In South Africa the Constitutional Court – the highest court on constitutional matters – has the power to interpret the Constitution and to rule on the constitutionality of legislation. It does not rule on political conventions.

11 All these quotes are from interviews cited in Weller (2007: 16).

12 The problem for any assessment of the demise of cabinet is to specify what exactly has been lost. Weller (2003: 74–8) distinguishes between the cabinet as the constitutional theory of ministerial and collective responsibility, as a set of rules and routines, as the forum for policy-making and coordination, as a political bargaining arena between central actors, and as a component of the core executive. Those commentators who justify talk of the demise of cabinet by treating policy-making and coordination as the defining functions of cabinet have failed to notice that these functions have been carried out by several central agencies, including but not limited to the cabinet, for over half a century. To suggest that any recent prime minister abandoned the doctrine of collective responsibility is nonsense. Leaks are abhorred. Unity is essential to electoral success, so dissenters go.

13 Australian cabinets are deliberative and decision-making bodies that often get involved in the most detailed of matters. By contrast, the Canadian cabinet is largely peripheral. In Canada, a degree of centralization based on the Privy Council Office and the Prime Minister's Office provides 'the premier's capacity to direct and coordinate the activities of ministers and their portfolios' (Bakvis and Wolinetz 2005: 209).

14 Some of this reduced business is because many of the budget deliberations are not decided in cabinet but are removed and handled by ministers and officials in the expenditure review committee process.

15 The tendency for prime ministers to officiate at ceremonial events in place of the head of state has been something of a secular trend especially in times of war.

Australian prime ministers farewelled troops going to Vietnam and coming back from Iraq. Howard performed at the medal ceremony of the Rugby World Cup.

16 For a more detailed account, see Gordon (1993: chapters 7 and 8). He capture the hurly-burly, all-encompassing nature of events. See Hawke (1994: 437–53, 497–500, 531–6, 551–61) for his version of events. On the Keating side, see Watson (2002: chapter 1). Also useful is Edwards (1996: 388–92 and chapter 14).

17 For a detailed account see Bevir and Rhodes (2003); and on competing interpretations of the constitution see Beer (1965), Birch (1964), Johnson (2004), Loughlin (1992), and Rees (1977).

18 For other sources on this theme, see Morrison (1964 [1959]) on Attlee's views and Wilson (1977: chapter 1).

19 This does not mean that in deliberative cabinets all major decisions go to cabinet for debate and approval. As one former Australian cabinet secretary stated: 'if a decision has not gone to cabinet but the prime minister informs me that the decision *is* a cabinet decision, then it *is* a cabinet decision'.

20 On the differentiated polity argument see Marinetto (2003), Marsh et al. (2003), Norton (2003), Rhodes (1988, 2007), and Rhodes et al. (2003).

5

Ministerial Responsibility

> I had been warned...that it was the Minister who had to caution the Permanent Secretary against irresponsibility and not vice versa and this I very soon found out was a wise warning (Richard Crossman, British Minister of Housing, 1975: 617).

> I, as Minister, must accept full responsibility to Parliament for any mistakes and inefficiency of my officials in my Department, just as, when my officials bring off any success on my behalf, I take full credit for them (Sir Thomas Dugdale, UK Minister of Agriculture, House of Commons Debates, Hansard, June 1954, volume 530, 1178–297).

> I am responsible but I am not to blame (Bob Semple, New Zealand Minister of Works, cited in Mulgan 2004: 153).

> I am not responsible for the shoddy research of my department (Canadian minister cited in Jackson and Jackson 2006: 279).

For ministers in Westminster systems the ultimate sanction is resignation or dismissal. It is an extreme sanction. Ministers often resign over policy disputes, political stand-offs, or over personal issues in which they become embroiled, including indiscretions, scandals, ill-health, tiredness, or change of career (Woodhouse 1994; Dowding 1995; Thompson and Tillotsen 1999; Mulgan 2002; Dowding and Dumont 2008). It is their own fire escape or 'get out of gaol' card when circumstances dictate. Ministers are also expected, in some interpretations of Westminster, to resign because of the failings of their officials. Ministers, it is frequently believed, ought to resign if the actions or inactions of others for which they are responsible have adverse consequences. Resignation cleanses the slate. The Crown is considered to be infallible; so if departments or officials fail, the minister takes the blame and resigns as an act of redress. The Carrington case in the UK is often cited as upholding the principles of ministerial responsibility (Woodhouse 2004: 308–9). We begin this chapter with two contrasting vignettes illustrating the range of practices ministers display when faced with failures or controversies.

In April 1982 the Argentine military invaded the Falklands Islands seizing the islands and replacing the British flag with that of Argentina. Lord Carrington, a Conservative minister who had served six Tory prime ministers, resigned along with two junior ministers, Humphrey Atkins and Richard Luce. There was much media criticism about the lack of government preparedness and whether some of the central agencies of government had the best interests of the UK at heart. In his resignation letter to Margaret Thatcher Carrington argued:

> In my view, much of the criticism is unfounded. But I have been responsible for the conduct of that policy and think it right that I should resign ... the fact remains that the invasion of the Falklands Islands has been a humiliating affront to this country ... I have concluded with regret, that support [for the Falkland Islanders] will more easily be maintained if the Foreign Office is entrusted to someone else.

So, he accepted responsibility for the 'affront' and fell on his sword. Surely, this case provides a clear example of a minister observing the conventions of ministerial responsibility. But does it?

Why did Carrington resign? On closer inspection he had many complex and intertwined motives.[1] Did he resign because Argentina invaded the Falklands – an affront to dignity? Did he resign because government policy failed to prevent it? Did he resign because of flawed government policy or because officials made mistakes? Did he resign because he intended to restore confidence in the government as it prepared to recapture the islands? Did he resign because he wished to defend Thatcher and obviate any risk to her prime ministership? Did he resign to reunite the fractured Conservative party following the policy disputes in the first few years in office and in the context of the commencement of hostilities? Did he resign to enable a new minister to step in and oversee foreign policy to prevent any recriminations over who was to blame? Or, did he resign because of media pressure which was intense on both him and the government? His motives could have been any one of the above or any combination of them.

Carrington later claimed the media hounded him from office. He told parliament that a frenzied press had been calling for his resignation; they were, in his words, 'baying for blood'. He was a victim of media exuberance; a scapegoat or sacrificial offering to a press campaign that was damaging the government. Indeed, he insisted in parliament that, while he would not have done anything differently with hindsight, he had 'not mishandled the situation'. So why did he choose to resign against his prime minister's wish?

The second vignette concerns a New Zealand tragedy at Cave Creek. In April 1995 a large, badly constructed viewing platform collapsed into a deep chasm overlooking Cave Creek – a small stream on the rugged west coast of the south island of New Zealand. Thirteen students and a national parks' officer from the Department of Conservation fell forty metres to their deaths; four others were badly injured at the scene. Volunteer staff from the department erected the cantilevered platform without on-site plans or formal building approval. In the immediate days after the incident neither the responsible minister, Denis Marshall, nor the chief executive of the department offered to resign.

A subsequent Royal Commission of Inquiry (Noble 1995) found not only that the platform had been illegal, inadequately constructed, and was unsafe, but that there were major shortcomings in the department and in its oversight of such projects. Pressure, it transpired, had been put on an environmental and regulatory agency to become more commercial and promote tourism development. Lack of resources, poor supervision, and inadequate training were also blamed and both the minister and the chief executive were accused of negligence in the press and in the parliament.

When the adverse findings were reported by the inquiry, neither opted to resign. Marshall made a speech to parliament defending his decision not to resign. He played the 'I'll fix it' defence, stating:

> I am responsible, and that is why I am standing in the House this afternoon, leading the debate for the Government... As Minister I am responsible for the Department of Conservation, and in that context the buck stops with me... My resignation would not be a remedy. My resignation would not bring these young people back to life. My resignation would not fix things... for all the symbolic power of a resignation, I do not intend to proceed from sorrow to abdication (New Zealand Minister for Conservation, Denis Marshall, 22 November 1995).

He maintained his belief that 'blame can be attached only if the Minister could have prevented the mistake or was aware of a possibility of its occurrence'. Then, citing a former prime minister, Geoff Palmer, he added: 'Ministers should be plainly and clearly accountable for what they do and what they decide, but it is unrealistic for them to take the rap for things they do not know about and did not authorise' (Hansard, 22 November 1995). Marshall toughed it out and did not offer to resign until May 1996, some thirteen months after the incident and six months after the inquiry's report. Similarly, the chief executive of the department, despite expectations he would resign, did not undertake to resign until May 1997, when, in his words, he was confident that an organizational change strategy was 'sufficiently on target' (ANZSOG 2004: 8). Both the political and administrative heads of the department claimed they had discharged their accountability obligations by taking responsibility after the fact to fix the problem (Gregory 1998).

THE EVOLVING TRADITION OF 'NO RULES'

Westminster operates as a committee of ministers led by a prime minister sitting in parliament that works together as a government team until they don't. Prime ministers have confidence in their ministers until they don't. Ministers have confidence in their current leader until they depose them and transfer loyalty to the successor. It is a political arrangement unconstrained by hard constitutional rules. This is the great beauty of Westminster. Its conventions are arbitrary, discretionary, expedient, prudent, temporal, renewable, and ongoing. The political executive is represented and legitimated in the legislature, variously answerable and explicable to the legislature over a wide range of matters, and formally accountable to the legislature for certain responsibilities. It is also accountable to itself and, increasingly, to external scrutiny.

The main debate examined in this chapter is how do the main political actors (ministers and shadow ministers, but also their officials and informed commentators) believe the executive is accountable and held to account. What do they view as satisfying the conventions of collective and individual ministerial responsibility, and how has practice changed over time? If, as often claimed, ministerial responsibility is at the centre of Westminster parliamentary government, we are then investigating the ways these five Westminster systems are able to hold governments 'responsible' and ministers accountable (either singularly or collectively as a team) for their conduct and portfolios. We want to establish whether parliament under tight party discipline is less a forum for accountability in the minds of the political elite. Have extra-parliamentary forces, such as political accountability to the prime minister, the party-room meeting, the media, courts, and tribunals, supplemented and in some ways supplanted its role? In this discussion, we distinguish between *public* accountability and *political* accountability, the former involving the legislature and courts, the latter involving other political actors (see Mulgan 2004: 36–74).

We recognize that ministers fulfil a range of roles: providing legal authority, advisory and policy capacities, administrative oversight, and constituency functions. Their formal responsibilities may be documented in administrative arrangements, orders, or left open within the portfolio. In this chapter, we are concerned primarily with their political roles both in relation to the other members of the collective executive and in relation to their departments and officials. We follow Loughlin (1992) and Birch (1964) by focusing on their functional and 'Whitehall' roles. We are also conscious that Westminster operates from two distinct assumptions about ministers. First, in the abstract, they are considered heroic, almost superhuman. There is a vision of ministers as all-capable to the point of being infallible and omnipotent, at the pinnacle of executive authority, unimpugnable and multi-skilled. Alternatively, ministers in the flesh are fallible beings with bounded capacities. As Gerald Kaufman (1980: 38), himself a minister, indelicately put it:

> the new minister may turn out to be rude, lazy, irascible, dirty, a drunkard or – worst of all – stupid. And they [the public servants] are stuck with him...To begin with, they operate on the safest principle, namely that he is an imbecile.

From this perspective, ministers need protecting from the system and from themselves.

Viewed through the lens of governing traditions, elite actors use an array of concepts associated with the notion of ministers being accountable to parliament. These are: 'responsible government', 'cabinet solidarity' or 'collective responsibility', 'ministerial responsibility', and 'ministerial accountability'. Some actors use them loosely or interchangeably; others attempt to distinguish fine nuances or differences of applicability, believing they are not all inevitably coterminous (Woodhouse 1994). There is also frequently robust debate between governments, oppositions, media commentators, or other actors revealing different orientations on matters of interpretation and emphasis.

Ministers often distinguish between three types of responsibilities they uphold. *Collective responsibility* is the belief that the executive requires a team displaying decisional and political solidarity. In practice, it translates into unity and discipline in the cabinet and is evidenced by the consistency and coherence of policy decisions. Unanimity is required even if governments are choosing to vacillate on issues before them. Occasionally, there are resignations if ministers cannot maintain collective responsibility. Ministers have the option of quitting the ministry if political disagreements with their cabinet colleagues become serious or they have major political disputes with the prime minister. Recent examples include: the former UK Foreign Secretary Robin Cook's policy resignation from the Blair government over the war in Iraq; Paul Keating's resignation as Australia's Treasurer under Bob Hawke over irresolvable leadership aspirations; and, in Canada, Paul Martin's resignation both as Finance Minister and as an MP over leadership frustrations with Prime Minister Jean Chrétien.

Individual responsibility involves ministers being prepared to accept responsibility for actions or inactions they take or officials take in their name. This direct responsibility is a consequence of their official position as a minister of the Crown. It requires them to front up and answer for their areas of responsibility in various forums, including parliament and in the media. Ministers are expected to inform or explain, perhaps apologize, take action to 'fix the problem', or in extreme circumstances resign. Answerability is often expressed narrowly by ministers as, 'I will apologize only for errors for which I am responsible'. New Zealand's environment minister Denis Marshall articulated this sentiment above, as did works minister Bob Semple, quoted in the epigraph at the start of this chapter.

Personal accountability involves the behaviour of ministers as people holding senior positions in government (Woodhouse 2004). It concerns their personal actions and is not necessarily directly related to their official position and duties as ministers. Issues here include personal integrity, sexual peccadilloes, pecuniary interests, and conflicts of interest. Resignations for personal accountability reasons tend to be classified as 'ministerial impropriety'; they are much more expected and accepted among governing parties, and they are not our main concern.

Although such a typology may seem clear, there are inevitable tensions between these three dimensions. Ministers are appointed individually to their commission but then opt to act collectively. They may be appointed as members of Privy Council or Executive Council, but apart from providing them with authority to advise, what does this mean or entail? Ministers are not formally appointed *as a cabinet* or *to cabinet*, yet prime ministers announce their cabinets, and their ministers elect to form a political 'committee of ministers'. Their individual authorities are subordinated to those of the group. Governments spend enormous amounts of time negotiating these tensions but there are few hard rules about how to deal with each and every contingency. The resolutions are invariably contingent and political.

Table 5.1 outlines the various dimensions and interpretations of ministerial responsibility we explore in this chapter.

In the next section of the chapter, we follow the structure of this table to organize our discussion of these conventions. We begin with discussion of the political norms of cabinet solidarity and collective responsibility, followed by a focus on individual responsibility and accountability of ministers. In the collective context we explore the politics of blaming and leaking as ways of evading these conventions. In the individual context we trace both the changing nature of accountabilities and the application of the doctrine of ministerial resignation, arguing that the exception is often used to invent the rule. We conclude with a discussion of the webs of accountabilities in which executive government is embedded.

'RESPONSIBLE GOVERNMENT': THE FORMAL POSITION

As we argued in Chapter 3, responsible government is regarded as one of the main foundations of the Westminster system with its inherent potentiality for a

Table 5.1. Conventions of ministerial responsibility

Conventions	Traditional interpretations	Current interpretations and practice
Responsible government (for legitimacy)	The right to govern originally derives from the Crown but is now mediated through parliament elected according to universal suffrage. Ministers 'serve' the monarch but are in practice held to account by parliament for their actions or inactions. 'Sovereign power' is 'loaned' to an executive for a temporal period and governments require the maintenance of the confidence in a collective executive.	With the arrival of disciplined parties responsible government has given way to responsible party government. Notions of responsibility solely to the institution of parliament have given way to the acceptance of responsibility to multiple principals – the media, citizen rights, public opinion, and election mandates.
Cabinet solidarity (for decisions)	Political convention of expedience and prudence at the centre of government. It involves common commitment and support to the political structure of government. Ministers are not expected to disagree publicly with policy positions. The political principle is: 'hang together or hang separately', which implies ministers share a defensive interpretation of their political obligations.	*Realpolitik* has always tempered the political doctrine; especially if rival factions exist in cabinet. Ministers practice political solidarity in public, unless they choose to break ranks. Dissenting ministers can be accommodated and concessions can be made to key ministers. Policy differences can be tolerated within overall party discipline. Cabinet meets less frequently and makes fewer decisions. So cabinet solidarity is more about strategic direction and political positioning and less about consistency and loyalty.
Collective responsibility (for actions)	Government has a collective or 'corporate identity' responsible for all government policy whether or not brought before cabinet. The executive is collectively responsible and answerable for the actions or inactions of any minister	'Collective responsibility' is often distilled into the prime minister being collectively responsible for the government as a whole. It does not mean that PMs or governments fall because of any specific failings. Any fall rests on general votes of

(Continued)

Table 5.1. (Continued)

Conventions	Traditional interpretations	Current interpretations and practice
	or department. PMs often act as the embodiment of collective responsibility.	'confidence' irrespective of the issue.
Ministerial responsibility and accountability (for individual areas of responsibility)	The exercise of authority subject to the responsibility to parliament and ultimately to the electorate. It covers the ministers' portfolios of responsibilities, and decisions or actions taken in their name. It also covers a minister's personal behaviour.	Responsibility to parliament can be routine or perfunctory; but other forums such as the media gain in significance. There are few situations in which the minister resigns for administrative failures (the 'smoking gun'). Public sector reforms have further eroded direct ministerial responsibility and increased responsibility of CEOs and departmental heads.
Accountability to whom?	The obligation of the government (collective) and minister (individual) to be answerable to parliament for their responsibilities by reporting on all matters in their areas of responsibility and fixing the problem.	Increasingly accountability is to the PM and cabinet. The legislature may constitute only one forum among the webs of accountabilities in which the executive is embedded; for example, the media and courts.

strong executive tempered by formal accountability to the elected legislature (Woodhouse 1994; Laver and Shepsle 1996). Although there were many variations in interpretation, notions such as 'responsible government' and 'ministerial responsibility' were traditionally narrowly focused on the institutions of the core executive. So, for instance, the concept of 'responsible government' was taken to mean the maintenance of the *confidence* of the lower house (in the government, its ministers, its legislative proposals, and authorization of its annual budget) in an adversarial party system. Sometimes it was not much more.

The antecedents of responsible government date from the late seventeenth century, premised on the sovereignty of the assembly and on prudent political conventions to guide appropriate behaviour. Distinguished commentators articulated the main elements of responsible government by the mid-late nineteenth century. But few provided a cogent definition or an agreed set of principles on which the unwritten constitution was premised. Custom and convention determined practice, so describing and illuminating such practice was the task of constitutional lawyers. Their intention was not to present an essentialist model, but to articulate a normative and functional account of practice to provide guidance and wise counsel to contemporary and prospective actors. Commonly, they presented arguments for recognizing a set of political relationships that were changing even while they were writing their accounts. Such informed constitutionalists were often silent on the underlying principles even as they traced the evolution of apparent conventions. Their silence did not prevent them, however, making various assertive claims that were relevant only to their times; for example, the emphasis on 'responsible government' rather than representative government.

Between the late-nineteenth and early to mid-twentieth century, the dominant construction of the tradition of responsible government and its attendant elements belonged first to Dicey and later to Jennings. Dicey presented responsible government as a hierarchical relationship based on power and obligation. Royal Will was at the apex, based on the theory that the Crown 'can do no wrong' and had indissoluble powers. But in practice the power was exercised by others. Hence, the power of the 'Crown can act only through Ministers... who [in taking a decision] thereby becomes not only morally but legally responsible for the legality of the act in which he takes part' (1914 [1885]: 327). Public servants acting in the name of ministers, who in turn acted in the name of the Crown, meant that 'indirectly but surely, the action of every servant of the Crown, and therefore in effect of the Crown itself, is brought under the supremacy of the law of the land' (1914: 327). Hierarchical authority meant it was 'the legal responsibility of every Minister for every act of the Crown' (1914: 325). Although Dicey was interested in the provision of stable government, his account does not develop the conventions of cabinet solidarity or collective responsibility.

In the 1930s, Jennings focused far more on the importance of conventions of cabinet solidarity and collective responsibility. He similarly centred responsible government on the power of the Crown to be infallible and above the law. He argued: 'no sanctions could be applied against the Queen, nor, in most cases, against those "servants of the Queen" who are the principal governors, subject to the Cabinet and to Parliament' (Jennings 1959 [1936]: 4). Responsible government was expedient and efficient, underscoring the legal power to act while being held responsible for those decisions. But political responsibilities required coherence and collectivity at the centre of government for responsible government to operate effectively (Jennings 1962 [1941]: 161–87).

Debates in the colonies emanated from local dissatisfaction with gubernatorial colonial government. Colonial rule *was* fallible *and* unpopular. In these settings, responsible government meant self-government: being *responsible for forming* their own governments. As Todd (1880: 25) recounted, 'complaints of misgovernment' in the colonies led to a search for a 'remedy', and

> This was effected by the wise adaptation of British constitutional principles to colonial polity; and by the gradual introduction into each dependency, according to its political condition and circumstances, of the principle of self-government in all matters of local concern, coupled with the unreserved application, in regard to the same, of the constitutional maxim of ministerial responsibility to the colonial assembly.

For Todd (1880: 26), this was the 'virtual transfer of power from an irresponsible to a responsible executive'.

Notions of responsible government only ever applied to the lower house. They did not apply to parliament as a whole. Although the former colonies did not always know what to make of their upper houses, there was no acceptance that the main conventions of 'responsible government', especially maintaining confidence, applied to the government in the upper chamber (Uhr 2006). This was so, whether the upper chamber was appointed (as in Canada and formerly New Zealand prior to 1950), or elected as in Australia, or a hybrid of elected and appointed as in South Africa now. The many attempts to reform upper houses have largely been oriented towards counterbalancing executive supremacy, rather than aimed at imposing notions of 'responsible government' to be exercised by the upper chamber on the executive. There are, however, some implications for upper houses flowing from the conventions of responsible government; the ministry is required to be represented in the upper chamber, so that individual ministers sitting in the other chamber are still 'represented' by ministerial colleagues to answer questions or provide reports.

The situation is most extreme or volatile in Australia where the Senate enjoys almost equal powers to the House of Representatives. Sometime after the 1975 dismissal of the Whitlam government, a constitutional commission declared that 'the core principle of ministerial responsibility to the lower house of parliament . . . is implied in the Constitution' (Constitutional Commission 1988: 13): implied but not stated explicitly. Yet, for the executive, the Senate can make government 'unworkable' and on one occasion has brought a government down, effectively denying confidence. When not controlled by the government, the Senate can pass motions of no confidence in a minister or government but usually to no effect. Such motions are seen as little more than a political stunt and ignored by the government. Stunts such as these inspired Prime Minister Paul Keating to label the upper chamber 'unrepresentative swill' in 1993 over a scandal involving one of his ministers. So, although the lower house regards itself as the chamber forming the government, it cannot take the Senate for granted. The Senate is able to hold government to account in many more ways than the executive cares to admit. Senate ministers and senior officials appear before Senate estimates hearings, not to lower house ones. Senate inquiries are usually more probing and powerful. The Senate can force the House of Representatives to compromise on legislation or even withdraw proposed bills. It is a constant irritant to executive government. There is no equivalent in the UK, Canada, or South Africa, and of course New Zealand has abolished the institution (see Uhr 2006).

Throughout the twentieth century, the old verities of responsible and representative government were gradually subordinated to two more recent developments: the advent of mass, disciplined political parties, and notions of responsibility that extend beyond parliament.

With the rise of disciplined parties across all our jurisdictions, elections came to play a much more significant role in forming and bringing down governments than did the parliament. However, party allegiance undermined the function of parliament to create governments. In the nineteenth century, parliament could regard itself as self-centred and fluid in its making and bringing down of governments, especially if so-called ministerialists fell out. This power changed once fixed parties predominated. From the early decades of the twentieth century, majority governments were 'unmade' only infrequently by parliament, even if they had become disgraced or lost momentum. As a result, electoral contests have assumed far greater importance as the determining but periodic instrument of 'confidence'. This shift has gradually impacted on how actors understand and practise parliamentary politics. In its recent manifestations some scholars have distinguished 'responsible government' (as a nineteenth-century convention applying to 'ministerial' governments) from its more modern-day variant 'responsible *party* government' (governments sustained by rigid party discipline where the party assumes responsibility and imposes some answerability). The former notion has arguably become an abstract concept whereas the latter empirically describes today's political realities (Lucy 1985; Uhr 1998).

Other constitutional and statutory provisions have also encircled the traditions of responsible government, ranging from formal constitutions to administrative law provisions requiring the executive to submit decisions to external review. Executives are not solely responsible to the elected legislature, but to a network of actors such as the courts, tribunals, complaints procedures, and investigatory bodies such as the ombudsman's office and integrity or privacy commissioners. In addition, the media have become an informal but effective critic of executive abuse, with the power to question and interrogate ministers and embarrass or pour scorn on governments. We return to this web of accountabilities at the end of this chapter.

CABINET SOLIDARITY AND COLLECTIVE RESPONSIBILITY

Cabinet solidarity and collective responsibility are twin dimensions of responsible party government that enjoy constitutionality, albeit informally. They lie at the core of ministerial governance. Cabinet solidarity is purely a political convention designed to maintain or protect the collective good as perceived by a partisan ministry. It rests on the notion that the executive ought to appear a collective entity, able to maintain cohesion and display political strength. Collective responsibility involves the preparedness to accept responsibility as a whole for decisions made by the government or its members and defend them in public. Often, collective responsibility is translated to mean that the prime minister as head of government assumes the full responsibility for government actions or inactions, and has a responsibility to explain the actions of the government as a whole even if the issue principally concerns specific ministers. Mostly the question of responsibility is a tactical matter for government and less a function of the style of a particular prime minister.

Politicians tend to use the more partisan term 'cabinet solidarity' implying political unanimity and mutual political obligation, the need to 'sing from the same hymn-sheet' in parliament and in public. Ministers realize that cabinet solidarity and collective responsibility are not formal constitutional provisions but a political necessity borne of expedience. As Dell (1973) argued, they are rules of political prudence (see also Jaensch 1997; Reid 1981). And the need for prudence tends to be reinforced through the political antonym 'disunity is death', especially in those jurisdictions where cabinets have tended to be smaller as in Australia and New Zealand and thus more susceptible to collapse under division.

Lord Salisbury (British prime minister 1885–86 and 1886–1902) forcefully expressed the need for cabinet solidarity. He insisted ministers were 'absolutely and irretrievably responsible' for anything cabinet decides unless they resign over their differences. Salisbury's edict may have been borne of frustration, but it indicates that even before strong party discipline was prevalent, collective solidarity was the buckle that bound the executive together. It enabled them to stick together to prolong the government, broker political deals, and exert greater policy influences than would otherwise have been possible. But it also required ministers to support collective decisions in public, perhaps with passion and conviction, even if the minister was opposed to the original proposal in cabinet.

Following Salisbury, prime ministers interpret this convention as requiring the support of government policy on all occasions, without exception. This emphasis is usually a function of their own sense of survival and because they tend to take personal responsibility for the government as a whole. Statements on cabinet solidarity made by prime ministers may be code for prime ministerial discretion in policy leadership. Pep talks at cabinet may have the same motive or effect. Government policy is *their* policy and they wish to brook no public opposition from their colleagues. To them, cabinet decisions, over which they have considerable discretion, bind their ministers and prevent discord in public. By contrast, other ministers may be less insistent on unqualified support, and clearly many are skilled at the art of nuance.

So, how do we untangle what cabinet solidarity and collective responsibility mean to today's practitioners in government? They are evolving traditions attracting different emphases in different circumstances with different effects and consequences. There is no hard rule but a strong convention laced with opportunistic connotations and adhocracy.

Collective responsibility provides a sense of protection to ministers and departments. It serves as the 'security blanket of executive government'; their protection against the multitude of risks they face (John Nethercote, personal communication 2006; also Reid 1981). If ministers are unsure of the merits of a policy option or worried over the reception it might attract, then cabinet authorization provides both backbone to their resolve and collective endorsement of the outcome. Decisions of the collective are collective decisions. But collective decisions mean that individuals will not necessarily get their own way. Collective responsibility can mean ministers have to be prepared to compromise when debating issues, to give ground or muffle reservations for the common good of colleagues and the government. On many issues that come before cabinet, ministers feel they have to be prepared to accept second-best solutions to enable a majority or consensus view to emerge or for the prime minister's view to prevail, as was the case for both Blair and Howard over the Iraq invasion. The alternatives are to risk major destabilization or resignation on the grounds of political disagreement.

But conventions can be waived. Prime ministers relax Lord Salisbury's edict to accommodate present-day exigencies. There are many instances of accommodation with prime ministers backing down when unable to impose their authority or reluctant to push the matter. Such examples of accommodation are not new and go back a long way. The important point is that no matter how much politicians insist on the principle, cabinet solidarity incorporates disagreement clauses and let-out provisions. The UK experimented with an 'agreement to differ' option in cabinet over the European referendum in 1976. New Zealand now has formalized 'agree to disagree' clauses incorporated into post-electoral agreements and coalition arrangements (see New Zealand *Cabinet Manual* 2008).[2] This provision has emerged because of the difficulties in sustaining coalition governments that can comprise formal coalition partners, supporting parties that give support on confidence, and communicating parties that do not guarantee support on confidence (see Boston and McLeay 1997; Boston 1998; Mulgan 2004: chapter 4). Thus, Labour and Alliance who formed government with a coalition agreement in late 1999 had 'a novel power-sharing system that will allow them to disagree over some policies' (*Financial Times*, 3 December 1999).

Over the past few decades, Westminster-derived governments have demonstrated different patterns in the way they practise collective responsibility. Some have found it necessary to tighten discipline and the political requirements to conform. This strengthening of control was true of the early years of the Chrétien and Howard governments, when a strong sense of purpose was politically required to enable these governments to make hard decisions and cut spending. Other governments have deliberately and consciously relaxed provisions as a way of accommodating political differences. So, for instance, New Zealand's Prime Ministers Jim Bolger and Jenny Shipley had to indulge the foibles and idiosyncrasies of their Maori Affairs minister Winston Peters. As an outspoken critic of the government, Peters was sacked twice – first by Bolger in 1991, and then by Shipley in 1998. He has subsequently proved troublesome to their Labour successor, Helen Clark, although she invented a precedent of making him a senior minister (Foreign Affairs) while not allowing him into cabinet.

Australia's Prime Minister Bob Hawke also found creative ways to deal with dissident ministers. When one minister and leading left-winger, Stewart West, disagreed with a cabinet decision on uranium mining, he resigned from cabinet in November 1983 but remained a member of the ministry. A new clause was added to the *Cabinet Handbook* to reflect the practice that had been created. In the future he and other ministers were allowed to oppose a cabinet decision in caucus (the regular meeting of the parliamentary party), if the minister had not taken part in the original decision or debate in cabinet. After cabinet decisions were made, they were still constrained from any public expression of dissension, but were granted the right to oppose the decision within the walls of the party room. West's stance was a strange 'half' resignation that has no equivalent since the precedent was created. Hawke had to relax the conventions of collective responsibility to take account of internal tensions. Conciliation in small cabinets and caucuses is necessary where governments cannot afford a revolt.

Elsewhere when prime ministerial authority is in decline or under challenge we have seen a gradual weakening of collective responsibility. This erosion is not through the deliberate choice of the leader to accommodate a dissident but a consequence of political circumstance. The bifurcation of policy-making under Blair when it was split between the Blairites and Brownites provides a case in point. Chrétien's decade in government became paralysed towards the end when the loyalties of cabinet were divided between the prime minister and his Finance Minister Paul Martin. The prime minister circumvented cabinet and the need for collective endorsement of decisions in favour of bilateral deals with individual ministers. It was expediency at its best.

Collective responsibility can also be an effective political device to control, on occasion, the unfettered power of prime ministers or strong ministers. In Australia, Hawke was overruled by his cabinet and caucus colleagues and forced to make a humiliating back-down over his decision to allow the US to test MX missiles within Australian territory (Maddox 1989). The New Zealand Prime Minister David Lange was defeated in cabinet in 1987 when he opposed a radical economic package (including privatization, tariff reduction, public sector reform, flat tax, and a higher GST) by his Finance Minister Roger Douglas. Lange recalled how he considered resignation. He initially accepted the decision, arguing:

> The conventions of cabinet government were simple enough. All members of the cabinet were bound by its decisions. Whatever their view of a matter, ministers had, when a decision was made, to uphold it in caucus; if called on, they had to speak in its support in parliament; they had to act in public as if it had never crossed their mind to disagree with it. The prime minister was bound by that convention as much as was the most junior minister, and that was right, because we were not a dictatorship. Convention demanded that those who disagreed resign their office if they could not submit themselves to the judgement of their colleagues (Lange 2005: 249).

In the end, Lange waited a month before he unilaterally overturned part of the cabinet decision on flat tax; he then contemplated a reshuffle of cabinet before engineering Douglas's resignation in late 1988. Such internal conflict broke Lange's personal resolve and hastened the end of his prime ministership. The incident proves both how flexible the convention of collective responsibility is and also how important it is to the health of a government.

Some jurisdictions have additionally chosen to codify their versions of collective responsibility as a means of clarifying official understandings to actors across the system. This codification has occurred as ministers have sought clarification of their responsibilities, and also as other players have entered the inner sanctums or the core executive, especially the increased number of ministerial minders and lateral entry of public service executives. They are engaging in an imprecise science in codifying such concepts and conventions. Accordingly, the attempt to codify has amounted to no more than listing a limited set of legal–technical requirements. For instance, Britain's *Ministerial Code* (Cabinet Office 1997: para. 16) requires ministers to subscribe to the doctrine of collective cabinet responsibility. It states bluntly: 'decisions reached by the Cabinet or Ministerial Committees are binding on all members of the Government'. Ministers who disagree with cabinet decisions are expected to resign. Some have and some have not. Gordon Brown stayed and bided his time. Robin Cook was demoted by Blair then quit the government over Iraq, but praised Blair's attempts to win the UN's backing. After much dithering and threats of resignation, Clare Short eventually resigned over Iraq and claimed in her resignation that collective responsibility was dead. Like Cook, she had had policy disagreements with Blair for some time.[3] Other ministers also harboured major disagreements with the Blair cabinet but did not resign.

The New Zealand's *Cabinet Manual* (2008) similarly insists:

> Acceptance of ministerial office means accepting collective responsibility...Once Cabinet makes a decision, Ministers must support it regardless of their personal views or whether or not they were at the meeting concerned (para. 5.23). [But conveniently adds]...In coalition government, Ministers are expected to show careful judgement when referring to party policy that differs from government policy (para. 5.24).

The general rule seems unambiguous but the rider allows some room to manoeuvre. The message it sends to ministers, even of the governing party: is we know some of you are going to disagree, but be careful how you express it.

The Australian Prime Minister John Howard endorsed a more extensive provision outlining his government's interpretation of collective responsibility – *A Guide on Key Elements of Ministerial Responsibility* (PM&C 1998*b*). His fourfold criteria were utilitarian and pragmatic, combining both political and administrative imperatives. Ministers were *bound* by decisions, must *support* decisions, they must *await announcement* of decisions until endorsement, and needed to *exercise confidentiality* (1998*b*: 2). His code reads: 'decisions of Cabinet are reached collectively and, other than in exceptional circumstances, bind all ministers as decisions of the government' (1998*b*: 2). Inevitably, some latitude was permitted for exceptional circumstances. Second, 'ministers must give their support in public debate to decisions of the government' (1998*b*: 2), but nothing required them to enter such public debates. Third, 'ministers are expected to refrain from public comment on Cabinet committee decisions which are not operative until endorsed by the full Cabinet' (1998*b*: 2). And, fourth, matters 'discussed in Cabinet and in particular, the views of individual ministers on issues before the Cabinet, are to remain entirely within the confidence of the members of Cabinet' (1998*b*: 4). In Howard's version, the emphasis was entirely on *internal* responsibilities to the executive, to assist cabinet solidarity. There was little emphasis on wider collective responsibility to parliament, other than in the requirement to support cabinet decisions in that forum.

When Howard first introduced his code he did so along with a strict code of ministerial ethics released in 1996. After losing a string of ministers in his first term, mainly over matters relating to personal impropriety, he softened his interpretation. His notion of collective responsibility since 1998 shifted to one of collegial loyalty and about defending the ministry at all costs. The doctrine, thus, became to 'defend the collective' at all costs, so that 'no ministerial resignations occur', which would damage the government more seriously. For a decade after 1998, ministerial resignations for reasons of either individual responsibility or personal impropriety were almost absent.[4] Journalists argued that this sudden pattern of cleanness 'beggared belief', and defied logic. However, Howard had an alternative, quieter way of disposing of ministers at risk. He replaced them before any scandals or crises became public. Quietly, over the annual summer recess, he refreshed the ministry with a partial reshuffle. This annual procedure produced a regular, but sometimes enforced, turnover of senior and junior ministers, many of whom were not performing to expectations or were tired and had outlived their usefulness. Two deputy prime ministers were discarded, and a string of senior ministers walked away from office in each of his four consecutive terms. By the end of his government, after almost 12 years in office, only three of his original cabinet remained: Peter Costello, Alexander Downer, and himself, although Amanda Vanstone, Nick Minchin, and Philip Ruddock served as senior ministers for most of the Howard period.

Blaming and Leaking

There are two common ways of evading collective responsibility that are open to ministers. Blaming others is a tactic perhaps as old as civilization. Leaking gets issues into the public domain that the executive would prefer to remain secret.

Blaming others, especially one's fellow cabinet colleagues, is a way of 'smearing the herd' – hiding behind the collective to exonerate oneself. A recent humorous incident occurred in Australia when the Treasurer, Peter Costello, was inundated with criticism over a controversial appointment to the Reserve Bank. The appointee was a businessman and 'Liberal mate' from South Australia (often underrepresented on national boards) but had ongoing disputes with the Tax Office. When questions of his appropriateness were first raised, Costello first indicated that the appointment had been agreed with the prime minister and then enthusiastically endorsed by cabinet. However, Howard told the media that the idea had been Costello's alone, in what another minister described as 'one of the slickest pieces of "I'll drop you right in it" I've ever seen'. To a question in parliament about whether *he* had come up with the appointee's name and then told the prime minister, Costello 'smeared the herd' while turning the question into a play on his leadership rivalry with the prime minister:

> I probably said, 'Mr Prime Minister, how are you today?' Then, having got on his right side I said, 'You are looking fit and healthy as per normal'. After going through the formalities, since we were looking for somebody who is a manufacturer, preferably from outside Sydney or Melbourne, I think I would have said to him, 'What about Mr Robert Gerard?' And I have never seen such an enthusiastic response in all my life. Having had such an enthusiastic response, the next thing we did was to go into cabinet. We said to the cabinet, 'What about Mr Rob Gerard?' I do not want to gild the lily but all of the South Australian cabinet ministers started swinging from the rafters saying, 'What a wonderful idea it is to have a South Australian on the Reserve Bank board!' Let me let you into a secret: some of those South Australian ministers are very agile and very flexible when they swing from the rafters. There was unanimous support in the cabinet (House of Representatives, 5 December 2005: 26).

Leaking is the flip side of cabinet solidarity. It can have many motivations: for instance, policy disagreements, exposure of alternative options, revenge, getting even, a desire to discredit or embarrass. Leaks are usually an act of last resort; they are abhorred but they persist. They are almost always 'read' as an act of disloyalty against the prime minister. Every prime minister has said words to their cabinets to the effect of: 'I will not tolerate leaks', or 'not tolerate going behind my back'. It goes with the territory.

Leaking can be extensive and pervasive. For example, David Blunkett's diaries (2006) not only have an index entry for leaks but there are 35 entries reported. Sometimes the identity of the leaker is unknown, at other times it is, or the people most likely involved are suspected. Yet circumstances will determine whether action is taken against the culprits. Prime ministers *do* tolerate leaks. They may not like them but they live with them.

Equally, prime ministers can themselves be the source of leaks, designed to undermine cabinet colleagues or shift policy expectations. In New Zealand, 'guerrilla war' broke out in January 1988 when Prime Minister David Lange briefed journalists that the flat tax policy of Roger Douglas would be deferred. Lange implied that the decision was one made by cabinet when in fact he invented it himself. He was guilty of leaking misinformation to change government policy and then authorizing further leaks to try to explain his change of position (Bassett 2008: 345–64).

MINISTERIAL RESPONSIBILITY

The formal position on individual ministerial responsibility was largely codified by commentators summarizing what they saw as contemporary practice. It may be a generalization, but there has been far more said about ministerial responsibility by outsiders than by ministers themselves. Ministers are often shy to venture too far in articulating precepts by which they later may be judged.

Accordingly, we find a multiplicity of accounts of ministerial responsibility in the context of responsible government. For Dicey, the doctrine of ministerial responsibility meant 'two utterly different things'. *Politically*, it meant, 'in ordinary parlance the responsibility of Ministers to Parliament, or, the liability of Ministers to lose their offices if they cannot retain the confidence of the House of Commons' (1914: 325). *Legally*, it meant 'the legal responsibility of every Minister for every act of the Crown' (1914: 325).

Jennings (1959 [1939]: 4) also explained ministerial responsibility as a dual legitimating device for decisions taken in the name of the Crown. First, ministers were responsible to the legislature (a lateral responsibility to their political colleagues and counterparts) and, second, they were responsible to public opinion and the electorate (outwards to the wider polity). In complying with the legitimizing role towards parliament he was most prescriptive in *The British Constitution* (1962 [1941]: 144), adjudicating that:

> The responsibility of ministers to the House of Commons is no fiction, though it is not so simple as it sounds. Ministers take all decisions of any consequence, either as such or as members of the Cabinet. Public servants take decisions on behalf of ministers and remain under ministerial control. If the minister chooses, as in the large Departments inevitably he must, to leave decisions to public servants, then the minister must take the political consequences of any defect of administration, any injustice to an individual, or any policy disapproved by the House of Commons. He cannot defend himself by blaming the public servant. If the public servant could be criticised, he would require the means for defending himself. If the minister could blame the public servant, then the public servant would require the power to blame the minister.

He went on to qualify this edict, identifying an emerging consensus that ministers were not necessarily responsible for everything. With increases in delegation and in the scale of government, first, cabinets did not necessarily take responsibility for every decision of individual ministers, and second, ministers did not take responsibility for every error of judgement or incident of maladministration. Strains and compromises were beginning to be conceded by the absolutist hierarchy.

More importantly, and from a Whitehall perspective, Jennings (1962: 146) added:

> No majority Government in recent years has really had cause to fear a parliamentary defeat. Accordingly, the decision of the Cabinet to support a minister is really based not on possible parliamentary consequences, but on the effect which the decision may have on public opinion . . . what really matters is not the support of the House but the support of the people . . . Ministerial responsibility to the House of Commons is thus the means of assuring that government is in tune with popular opinion (1962: 146).

Accountabilities were supposed to flow not merely upwards to the Crown, but outwards to popular sovereignty and electoral opinion. He was in a sense already recognizing the evolution of the tradition.

There remains some argument as to whether the doctrine of 'ministerial responsibility' has much ancestry in parliamentary history. Despite occasional and self-referential assertions from scholars and practitioners, it was not always considered an essential feature of Westminster systems by some key actors, although maintaining the confidence of the House was considered crucial. For example, a former Clerk of the British House of Commons, Sir Courtney Ilbert (1912: 111), in a classic description of parliament, does not record ministerial accountability as an aspect of Westminster, despite noting that the 'practice of putting questions to ministers developed rapidly during the latter half of the nineteenth century' and that the role of parliament had expanded to 'control the actions of those ministers by means of questions and criticisms' (1912: 111).

Formally, ministers are appointed as *individuals* to carry out their responsibilities. They are appointed by the Crown (or governor-general) on the advice of the prime minister effectively to a specific office. They either occupy various politically chosen portfolio titles, such as Foreign Secretary, or Trade Minister, or to posts such as the Chancellor of the Duchy of Lancaster or Special Minister of State, or Vice-President of Executive Council. These positions may or may not have formal administrative or policy responsibilities. In four of our Westminster systems, but not in republican South Africa, ministers may also be appointed individually to the Privy Council or Executive Council. Hence, ministers usually enjoy a double appointment, as ministers with a particular sphere of responsibilities, such as Minister for Foreign Affairs, and as a member of Executive Council or as Privy Councillors.[5] In two of the settler dominions, Australia and New Zealand, the composition of cabinet conventionally mirrors the exact composition of Executive Council, while members of previous administrations forfeit their appointments. In Britain and Canada former members of Privy Council are allowed to continue to use the honorific although they are not considered current advisers. Hence, the British and Canadian cabinets are political executives constituted at a particular point in time; their respective Privy Councils consist of a much larger group of the political establishment (former prime ministers and ministers, and even ambassadors) appointed for life. Rarely in Westminster jurisdictions does the full Privy or Executive Council ever meet (except to sit perhaps for the occasional photograph for posterity).

The link between ministers and the legislature is supposedly sacrosanct. The conventional accountability of ministers being simultaneously elected (or appointed) to the legislature remains largely intact, even in South Africa. Despite constitutional provisions that do not necessarily require ministers to be appointed from parliament, our Westminster systems have continued to insist ministers should be members of parliament. Canada can appoint ministers from the unelected Senate and occasionally appoints ministers who are not currently in either house of parliament. Ministers can come from outside parliament.[6] But they are quickly found a seat in one of the chambers. In Britain, prime ministers similarly appoint ministers who are not currently parliamentarians, although convention insists it is for a short time while they find a seat, or accept appointment to the Lords. The *New Zealand Constitution Act 1986* requires ministers to be members of parliament, but it is now potentially easier to recruit new ministers under the list system because arranged vacancies can be orchestrated. In Australia, because parliament had not been elected when the constitution was proclaimed, ministers were allowed to serve for up to three months so the original nine appointed ministers could become duly elected. In the event, one died and another did not stand. This section persists and still allows ministers to be appointed for up to three months but this flexibility has been used only once, in 1968. South Africa can also appoint up to two ministers and two junior ministers from outside the Assembly, but they, like their cabinet colleagues, are accountable to parliament and attend debates and Question Time.[7]

The difficulties in understanding ministerial responsibility are that there are no consistent meanings shared among elite actors, and the opposition and media have become fixated on the doctrine of ministerial resignation. There are disagreements of emphasis and intent. Executive views of appropriate behaviour tend to conflict with legislative views. Executive actors tend to emphasize the discharge of functions and responsibilities. Legislative actors tend to emphasize the accountability of ministers and requirements to be answerable to one's political opponents. Such views can change according to the career trajectory pursued by actors; promotion to cabinet mutes legislative enthusiasm for accountability often found in oppositions or on the back bench.

Media views also tend to stress the regular need for a scapegoat or a trophy resignation, demanding ministers be accountable to public opinion and to the media's own pack-hunting mentality. These competing views add to the meanings of the doctrine. They contradict and complement one another and fight to be taken seriously. But they also contribute to the fuzziness of ministerial responsibility, precisely because there is considerable latitude in interpretation and because the concept is elastic.

As disciplined parties took a stranglehold over parliament during the twentieth century, it became clear that political actors in the executive developed different perspectives on the meaning of the doctrine compared with the other actors in the legislature. Ministers tried to contain or minimize the accepted meanings or understandings of the doctrine. For instance, as Treasurer in the early 1980s John Howard described ministerial responsibility as 'some high flutin' notion', more imagined than real. Those in the executive gradually came to regard their responsibilities to the legislature as a necessary chore, a place where they can choose to disseminate 'their' information, whatever and how much they are prepared to volunteer.

Interpretations of the role of legislatures invariably acknowledge there is an asymmetrical division of powers between the executive and parliament. The executive is usually dominant. It has the knowledge and information. It is in charge and in 'the know'. Its opponents are more likely to be fishing for scandals. Yet despite the power imbalance, ministers continually remain cognizant of the potential risks of being caught out in parliament, perhaps looking foolish or badly embarrassed if things occurred 'under their watch' (Woodhouse 2003). They resort to subterfuges and rhetorical devices to insulate themselves from risks and minimize scrutiny or embarrassment, such as stating 'I am advised . . .' or 'I am formally led to believe . . .' (meaning if the statement proffered is erroneous it is not the minister who has committed the mistake but officials). Many of the procedures of parliamentary practice, such as Question Time, are meant to ration the exposure, curtail inquiry, and reduce the windows of accountability. Other conventions also limit ministerial exposure, such as taking questions 'on notice' so they can be answered by officials at their leisure, or the practice of ministers only appearing before committees or estimates hearings of their own chamber, not of the other.

Ministers and Administrative Responsibilities

Most attention to the doctrine of ministerial responsibility focuses on the political responsibilities and obligations usually to parliament alone. Responsibility for administrative functions receives less attention. Yet, while ministerial administrative responsibilities have increased enormously, they have also become more fragmented and refracted. Ministers are now responsible sometimes for hundreds of statutes, administrative orders, and organizational entities. Of course, administrative arrangements may be changed and moved from minister to minister at the prime minister's discretion and without the need for parliamentary approval (or even its knowledge).

Administrative responsibilities involve the minister heading a department or public agency. But the precise nature of their role is unclear. Ministers can act as the political figurehead or administrative head; they could oversee the department or intend to manage actively the department. Moreover, portfolio responsibilities will often require the minister to be responsible for multiple departments and agencies and their associated acts.[8] The introduction of new public management (NPM) in its various forms since the mid-1980s has compounded the complexity of these responsibilities.

After its neo-liberal NPM reforms, New Zealand formally placed individual ministers squarely responsible for all decisions and all administrative activities in their ambit. A previous New Zealand *Cabinet Manual* (2003) stated:

> Individual Ministers are responsible for determining policy and exercising relevant statutory powers and functions within the ambit of their portfolios. Ministers are individually responsible to Parliament for their own activities and the activities of public servants in administering their ministerial portfolios (2.26)...As 'Responsible Ministers' Ministers are responsible for protecting the Crown's interest in the departments within their portfolios, and are responsible to Parliament for ensuring that those departments carry out their functions properly and efficiently (2.30).

A subsequent *Cabinet Manual* (2008) asserted:

> Ministers are accountable to the House for ensuring that the departments for which they are responsible carry out their functions properly and efficiently. On occasion, a Minister may be required to account for the actions of a department when errors are made, even when the Minister had no knowledge of, or involvement in, those actions (3.21).

As formal statements, there would appear little scope for flexibility or discretionary latitude. However, in practice, disputes between ministers and the chief executive officers of their agencies belie such formal clarity (Boston et al. 1996: 9

and 316–32; Norman 2003; Mulgan 2004). Ministers, though, have comforted themselves by resorting to two defences. First, ministers hold agency heads responsible for the performance of their agencies. And, second, ministers have insisted that, rather than be responsible for specific decisions or the 'outputs' delivered, they are ultimately accountable only for the more nebulous 'outcomes', where outcomes mean the broader community objectives.

Although responsibility for policy determination is retained at the centre of government, New Zealand has implemented a formal–legal separation of responsibilities between ministers and their chief executives. This separation was undertaken to clarify and separate the roles of the various actors according to principal–agent theory. Ministers are 'principals', with the delivery and implementation of policy devolved to executive agencies and outsourced delivery providers. The public service is small, while the state sector is fragmented by proliferating agencies. This development has led to criticisms that a silo mentality prevails, with self-absorbed agencies exhibiting a coordination deficit across government. Governments have expressed dissatisfaction with broader performance issues (see State Services Commission 2002: 4–5). Interestingly, in New Zealand where this public choice doctrine has been pushed to its furthest, greater transparency of decision-making has resulted. All cabinet briefing papers and cabinet decisions are publicly available on the web within days of cabinet dealing with them.

By contrast, Australian ministers are constitutionally appointed to 'administer' their departments. Section 64 of the Constitution states that: 'The Governor-General may appoint officers to administer such departments of state of the Commonwealth as the Governor-General in Council may establish'. The Public Service Act 1999 (s. 57(1)) reiterates this point by stating that a departmental secretary 'under the Agency Minister, is responsible for managing the Department'. So, in statutory terms ministers formally administer their departments. But how does this requirement affect practice? It doesn't very much. It did prevent the appointment of junior ministers until 1987 because of fears they were not administering departments; but it did not prevent the appointment of ministers without portfolios. However, the prime minister has taken precautions to qualify such a definitive statement on administrative expectations. According to the Australian *Cabinet Handbook* (1998: 2), 'in the Parliament the portfolio minister is ultimately accountable for the overall operation of his/her portfolio'. The phrase 'overall' and 'ultimate' dissipates the formal wording. In a longer version:

> Under the Australian system of representative government, ministers are responsible to Parliament. This does not involve ministers in individual liability for every action of public servants or even personal staff. It does

however imply that ministers accept two major responsibilities: first for the overall administration of their portfolios, both in terms of policy and management; and secondly for carriage in the Parliament of their accountability obligations to that institution (1998: 1).

Instead of a formal–legal separation of responsibilities evident in New Zealand, Australia has incorporated an informal political separation between the minister and the department based on expediency and pragmatism. Ministers have spoken of their 'arm's length' distance from administrative activities. Some ministers speak of their departments in the third person and pretend they are referring almost to an organization independent of them. Howard's Foreign Minister, Alexander Downer, spoke of his department as if it were a separate entity. His statements, which came in connection with allegations that Australian Wheat Board (AWB) executives had paid bribes to Iraq to secure wheat contracts, caused one paper to editorialize:

> In the course of explaining how nobody, at least nobody he wants to defend, knew AWB was paying off Saddam Hussein's wretched regime, Mr Downer mentioned that the Department of Foreign Affairs and Trade did not know either. The Foreign Minister said he knew this because DFAT had put out a statement denying any knowledge of the bribes being paid. And, Mr Downer went on, 'it's very unusual for a government department to put out a statement'. Well, Earth to Alexander, it would once have been very unusual for a minister to talk about his department as if it were an independent agency (*The Australian*, 9 February 2006).

He later attempted to shore up his position in parliament denying knowledge of what his department or the Wheat Board had been up to.

Other senior ministers have articulated similar sentiments. Immigration minister Amanda Vanstone, herself presiding over a number of personnel scandals and cases of mistreatment by her department, distanced herself from the administrative culture. She stated that she agreed with two independent reports calling for major organization and cultural change, and that the department was in need of major repair. In her press release she argued that the trenchant recommendations were in line with the

> department's move to become more open and accountable, to have a stronger client focus and well trained and supported staff. The Comrie report raises some serious issues, which were anticipated by Mr Comrie and Mr Palmer in the report on the Cornelia Rau matter. The Government accepts Mr Comrie's recommendations. The Secretary of my Department will be responding separately to recommendation 12, regarding specific action he might take under the Public Service Act (Minister of Immigration, Press Release, 2005).

It was a brazen reworking of 'I will take responsibility only for the errors for which I am personally responsible'.

There have also been moves to distinguish two types of appointments to government boards, placing some 'outside' government hands. If ministers wish to accept accountability for decisions and actions of agencies under their portfolio, then the argument states that they should politically appoint their representatives to these boards. If they do not wish to accept responsibility for such matters, then ministers should refrain from making appointments and leave appointments to the board itself (see Uhrig Review 2003). This principle effectively asks ministers what they are prepared to be accountable for, and what they are not prepared to be accountable for.

ACCOUNTABILITY TO WHOM?

In this section we ask to *whom* are ministers primarily accountable (see Dell 1973; Mulgan 2003: 24 and 41)? We need to go beyond the formal position, and establish who can impose some forms of accountability, what opportunities exist in the system, and what responsibilities do ministers find hard to shirk or evade. While parliament provides some formal and informal opportunities, and that forum cannot be ignored, it may not be the principal forum for exercising accountability. The same is true of the courts. Ministers believe they face cascading levels of accountability (political, parliamentary, legal, and public opinion), each of which may hold them partially to account for some aspects of their responsibilities. So, below we examine how ministers are held to account, what practices exist to force them to justify and defend their actions or proposals, and what ministers are required or expected to do to satisfy their accountabilities.

Woodhouse (1994: 3–4) has argued that 'collective responsibility provides Parliament with the means of holding the government as a body accountable, and individual responsibility enables the House to focus on a particular minister and his responsibilities without the need to censure the whole government'. Her distinction is valid up to a point; but these two dimensions intersect and are constantly iterative. The collective doctrine not only is by far the stronger, but also determines how the individual doctrine plays out. Modern Westminster governments have shifted considerable ministerial responsibility and autonomy from individual ministers to the wider collective. In some jurisdictions, such as Australia, Britain, Canada, and South Africa, notions of individual and collective responsibility are conflated deliberately. Such ambivalence provides a source of political comfort to governments (for example, if they need to sacrifice a minister to save the government). But such ambivalence can contradict other former expressions of individual accountability.

Ministers, of course, love to play games with the collective and individual conventions. They can duck from one to another as exigencies dictate. Ministers will often appear less prepared to accept individual accountability for decisions that have gone through cabinet. Hence, how far ministers accept accountability for individual policy decisions may be a function of how much cabinet has deliberated on and determined the final policy decisions. In the UK where the principles of individual and collective responsibility are largely merged, cabinet has become less and less a decision-making body and largely a body of information-sharing, communication, political solidarity, and legitimacy. Ministers may be less constrained by collective responsibilities especially within the parameters of their own portfolios. Variations in the decision-making practices of cabinet are thus important filters overlaying the holding of individual ministers to account.

Such ducking and weaving for political advantage has not prevented outside calls for greater precision or clarity to govern these relationships. In Canada, the Gomery Report (2005) recently made a strong case for formally linking individual ministerial responsibility with the convention of collective responsibility, especially through obligations to inform and consult. Although written from a formal–legal standpoint, Judge Gomery stated:

> Ministerial responsibility has to do with the relationship between a Minister and the public servants working in the departments of which the Minister has charge. Law, tradition and convention dictate that the Minister has sole authority for the management and direction of a department. However, the principle of Cabinet solidarity requires that the Minister seek the approval of or inform other members of the Cabinet regarding policies and decisions that may have relevance to other portfolios and the conduct of government as a whole. In addition, the Minister has an obligation to report to Parliament, which can discharge this obligation only if it is kept informed of the commitment (Gomery 2005: 17; see also Wanna 2006: 16–17).

Gomery's requirements could only work in the context of a transparent and disciplined cabinet process, in which cabinet and its committees met regularly and discharged business, and ministers honestly informed their colleagues about matters in their charge. This notion may be naive, especially since not all of our jurisdictions have maintained effective cabinet systems that encourage ministers to speak. Such was the case in Australia under Keating, Britain in Blair's first term, or Canada under Chrétien.

Accountability to the Prime Minister

Individual ministerial accountability is primarily to the prime minister who manages the dynamics of collective accountability. Prime ministers judge performance, determine whether individual ministers stay or go, whether they are reshuffled, promoted, and demoted. If a scandal targets an individual minister, the prime minister decides for the collective whether it is in their best interests to stand by the individual or sacrifice them. Increasingly, it appears sacrifice is the least preferred option, especially if the attention span of the media is likely to be short.

Ministers have come to believe they are principally responsible to the prime minister and to cabinet; to their colleagues in the political executive. They may not articulate this unambiguously in their statements but their behaviour indicates otherwise. They are held to political account by their superior colleagues and their cabinet colleagues. Moreover, prime ministers have real sanctions at their disposal. If a minister under attack performs badly in parliament, the legislature can effectively do little about it; the prime minister can. If ministers are able to obfuscate or duck accountability in the public setting of parliament, it is far more difficult to do so in front of their own colleagues, especially when competition for cabinet posts may be high and some colleagues may have an interest in combative questioning when they are not individually answerable.

Arguably, cabinet not only serves as the decision-making hub of modern Westminster government, but is also the principal accountability forum, although political and partisan. Usually, outside observers do not perceive cabinet in this role, preferring the formality of parliamentary scrutiny and undertakings on the public record. Cabinet does not perform this role simply because it can impose decisions or grill ministers over specific proposals or events, but because it calculates the interests of the government as a whole and assumes responsibility for a broader view. Ministers have to perform in an inner, closed forum which can determine their fate. They have to perform in front of colleagues who are, at one and the same time, rivals interested in the government's survival, potential beneficiaries of slips or gaffes, and sharers in misery. Only after dealing first with their leader and cabinet colleagues, do ministers face the wider accountabilities of parliament, the media, interest groups, and public opinion.

Accountability to the Party

Beyond the cabinet, the caucus or party room regularly reviews and sometimes judges critically ministerial performance. Caucus holds ministers politically accountable, and in some cases involves the wider, extra-parliamentary party organization. These 'judges' can include party office-holders, opinion leaders, grassroot party members and supporters, and even pollsters. Ministers are expected to speak and defend their actions or proposals at party-room meetings if they are introducing controversial measures, or under attack, or need to explain events or actions. In extreme cases, party rooms can move votes of censure against ministers or send delegations to the prime minister to influence policy directions. In New Zealand, accountability to the party can now include reference to multiparty arrangements and meetings.

Accountability to Parliament

Eventually, ministers are required to acquit themselves in public. So they perform in various forums and in front of the media. They appear in parliament, submit to questioning and some degree of scrutiny, undertake to investigate and explain if things go wrong, and take responsibility to fix problems. They submit to media interviews, grilling, and even harassment.

Ministers are still prepared to answer and explain matters of policy to parliament, if only because not to do so is worse. Ministers regularly appear in parliament and before its various committees, but the executive limits their appearances through time restrictions on questions or debates, controls over procedures, and observed protocols. There are vast differences even in the number of days parliaments sit: from 150 to 160 a year in the UK, to 100 in Canada, around 72 in South Africa, to just 60 or so in Australia and New Zealand.[9] Ministerial statements are important in the UK House of Commons, where the opposition also has the right of reply, and can question ministers on the statement. In Australia and New Zealand such statements have been almost eliminated.

In some jurisdictions senior politicians have 'rostered' themselves to limit their appearance at Question Time. In the UK the prime minister appears once a week for questioning for 30 minutes, while other ministers appear twice-a-week. In Australia, Canada, and New Zealand the prime minister and the full cabinet regularly appear at each Question Time for about an hour. Occasionally, there have been perceptions on an erosion of accountability as when Prime Minister Paul Keating and his deputy Kim Beazley adopted an alternating roster for their appearances at Question Time in Labor's fifth term (1993–6). The tactic backfired and was widely interpreted as an insult to parliament and an erosion of accountability. They cannot push too far.

Question Time may be theatrical and stage-managed but it charts the rise and fall of reputation. Ilbert (1912: 113), a former Clerk of the British House of Commons, described the emerging practice of questioning ministers at Question Time, arguing from his experience that

> there is no more valuable safeguard against maladministration, no more effective method of bringing the searchlight of criticism to bear on the action or inaction of the executive government and its subordinates. A minister has to be constantly asking himself, not merely whether his proceedings and the proceedings of those for whom he is responsible are legally or technically defensible, but what kind of answer he can give if questioned about them in the house, and how that answer will be received.

Ministers believe their accountability obligations have been met if they receive a more or less regular grilling by opponents at Question Time. Ministers think they have observed the doctrine of individual ministerial responsibility if they have subjected themselves to such regular scrutiny from their parliamentary colleagues especially from the opposition, even if they gave as good as they got. That is all. But, it is only a potential to censor. Ministers will be grilled only if the opposition chooses to do so. They often do not. So, in the ministers' minds, the doctrine has been discharged if they have been present in the legislature. It matters not whether they faced a tough barrage of questions or were tested by hostile questioning.

Conversely, ministers and their political advisers have deliberately sought to limit the degree of questioning and negative scrutiny. So questions to ministers do not get out of hand, Question Time is limited, and can be even shorter at the prime minister's discretion. Question Time operates with rules of engagement for government ministers, including the issue of relevance, answering the question, not making speeches. However, these rules are often liberally interpreted by presiding officers. Most jurisdictions use a system of 'questions on notice' with possible supplementary questions or 'questions without notice'. In the UK, questions given on notice are randomly selected before Question Time. In Canada, questions are asked to the entire government and the leader of the house determines *which* minister will provide an answer. In Australia, questions to individual ministers alternate between government and opposition members, which gives a surreal bipolar atmosphere to the event. In Australia, over one-third of questions on notice are never answered. In New Zealand, Question Time is now allocated between the various parties in the House of Representatives according to their proportion of seats.

Strong ministers almost invariably *do not* answer questions but seek to turn them around to criticize or embarrass their opponents. So-called 'Dorothy Dixers' have become a plague in all Australian parliaments. Government back-benchers are primed to ask ministers tame or favourable questions so they can make 'good news' announcements in place of critical scrutiny. Although oppositions regularly complain about such practices, the executive has no incentive to amend the standing orders. Speakers occasionally remind oppositions that while they are at liberty to ask questions, they cannot insist on receiving the sort of answers they might like or expect (House of Representatives, 15 February 2006).

Ministers accept some obligation to investigate and explain when issues are raised. Often it is a simple exercise in finding and providing information. At other times it involves more serious disclosure of information ministers would prefer to keep buried. Publicly ministers are keen to present themselves as anxious to find the truth, get to the bottom of things, and to check on the bureaucrats. However, ministers suppress and prevent access to documents that the opposition or media know exist. There has been a tendency to build 'firewalls' around ministers, providing selective advice, so that ministers are told only what they wish to know; for example, Howard over the 'children overboard' scandal.

As the Cave Creek case demonstrates, ministers *are* prepared to stay and fix problems. Answerability involves seeking to make amends, and ministers regard this as a positive and constructive aspect of their duties. Good ministers attend to such issues as a normal part of their daily routines for their departments. When ministers argue they should remain in office after errors or mistakes have been uncovered, they are exercising a convention of delayed responsibility. In effect, ministers are seeking to substitute conventional understandings of ministerial resignation with the convention that ministers ought to survive to rectify personally mistakes or maladministration.

Ministers have transferred responsibility to their senior executives to fix problems. This development is a function of the increased direct accountabilities being delegated to CEOs after NPM. Executives may be required to fix problems whether the cause is a problem of policy or maladministration. The former head of the Australian public service, Peter Shergold, after a number of celebrated cases of policy deficiencies and maladministration, agreed the scandals were 'failures in public administration', and promised: 'if something comes out . . . which suggests there are failures within the public service, then you can have my absolute commitment we will move to address them with the same vigour [as the government had done with the Palmer Report into the Immigration department]' (*The Australian*, 16 February 2006).

Accountability to the Media

Given the executive's dominance over parliament, the media has emerged as the 'new parliament' for modern government. For decades political leaders have announced more government actions through the media than through parliament. Media conferences have become the preferred mode of communicating government statements, even major statements of policy or great moment. There is instant communication with the populace, and the leader can be heard and seen on screen. The slightest fudge or hesitation, lie or half-truth can be examined and replayed. Media conferences are conducted at the government's choosing: the location, timing, who attends, and the scope for questions. Often there is little scrutiny at these events in terms of forensic questioning. Media people are interested mainly in getting the news out rather than probing for other angles or inconsistencies.

Prime ministers in particular have become media driven and presidential in image. They elect to make announcements from the ubiquitous crested lectern, draped with flag, often placed in front of a doorway to a major public building (Mills 1986; Foley 2000). The main focus is on 'the leader' and 'the government', again merging into collective responsibility. The leader is able to explain but also to 'shield' errors by other ministers.

Through the media, public opinion also imposes real accountabilities on governments. Governments have taken polling to new heights; continuous polling, monitoring of issues, using focus groups, and think-tanks to 'trial' ideas.[10] Focus groups are used to both frame and endorse policy directions. But it is not a one-way street driven by craven populism. Governments believe they can use these techniques to influence and 'educate' public opinion as much as they respond to the findings.

Accountability to Independent Officials, Courts, and Tribunals

Ministers are also increasingly liable to appear before investigatory officers, and can be forced to appear under statutes. Under the new *Auditor-General's Act*, Australian ministers can be called as witnesses before the Auditor-General. In 2000, the Health Minister Michael Wooldridge appeared in person under oath before the Auditor-General over accusations his office had leaked confidential information about pending budgetary measures of benefit to specialist health professionals. No other ministers have yet been summonsed, but the precedent exists; and the fact that one minister has been interrogated is a warning to others. The possibility is enough to shape behaviour.

Ministers are accountable for their decisions to independent tribunals and courts. Judicial review can set aside or overturn ministerial decisions, and in some cases substitute alternative decisions in place of ministerial decisions. Officials in departments know that many of their decisions taken in the name of the minister can be challenged and exposed. This knowledge places active constraints on their performance.

The Fixation with Ministerial Resignation

Conventional understandings of ministerial responsibility assume the notion that ministers were ultimately accountable to parliament for their portfolios. Statements of ministerial responsibility are usually positive: *maintaining* responsibility and answerability to the House and *enjoying* its 'confidence'. The opposite statements would bring down a minister or an entire government. This positive doctrine was the natural state of affairs. So, little was said about what it meant. Indeed, it is largely empty of content. Clearly, unless the government lost its majority, withdrawing confidence in a minister was unlikely. Under the modern party system such cases are rare. Governments may occasionally move 'votes of confidence' in themselves to resolve political difficulties; it is a standard operating procedure to use censure motions to affirm confidence.

However, on the negative side, if ministers transgressed it was unclear what ministers should do when facing censure. There never were, and never could be, a clear set of guidelines under which ministers *should* resign, or a defined set of circumstances *requiring* resignation. Traditional constitutionalists are of little assistance in fleshing out the doctrine. They tend, like Dicey, to believe that ministers are 'good chaps' who will know when to resign. The fig leaf of accountability is nebulous in the extreme. A minister should take 'upon himself the whole and sole responsibility' and will know to resign when 'his credit has thereby been impaired' (Jennings 1959: 497). Such attitudes were laced with class notions about members of parliament, who was likely to be in parliament, and how they would behave, with ideological understandings of the sanctity of the institution. Little was said about the conditions under which resignation ought to occur, except where a minister loses the confidence of the House.

For the executive there are many defences and escape routes to avoid potential censure. Even if ministers mislead the House, conventions are adopted to excuse the circumstance. Apologies can be made and errors 'corrected as soon as the error is found, using the procedures of the chamber concerned' (PM&C 1998*b*: 23). Official statements and press releases can be issued to prosecute the government's case in other forums. Officials can sometimes be blamed or made to accept responsibility.

Yet an obsession with ministerial resignation has become the most visible feature of the supposed doctrine of ministerial responsibility. It is always easy for critics to demand a resignation; it has become a rhetorical device. The exception or aberration has come to be taken as the basic rule. Moreover, it often serves as a distraction from what is going on.

Interest in academic and media circles often focuses solely on 'resignations' and the circumstances under which ministers should resign (Woodhouse 2004). Ministerial responsibility is naively and mistakenly interpreted as the preparedness to walk away from power when misfortune occurs. But this expectation does not fit with practice except in the most exceptional circumstances. However, it does not prevent scholars and editorial writers lamenting the demise of the doctrine, or claiming ministers do not adhere to the principles if they fail to resign. In their minds, the doctrine of resignation can assume a life of its own. A recent editorial complained:

> This government has crippled the concept of ministerial accountability... it would be far preferable if the old ideal of ministerial account-ability still held. In decades past, ministers walked without murmur over errors they had little to do with (*The Australian*, 9 February 2006).

Always the nostalgia! Always the straw man! Where is the evidence?

Notwithstanding attempts to devise precise taxonomies of resignation types (see Woodhouse 1994; Thompson and Tillotsen 1999), ministerial responsibility does not mean ministerial resignation, and certainly not for departmental matters. Thompson and Tillotsen (1999: 57) found resignations occurred in only two specific circumstances: over matters of personal impropriety, and because of party political disagreements. They declared that notions that ministers must resign for 'blunders or for serious errors' were 'dead', implicitly assuming that they were once alive. They found that evidence from three jurisdictions:

> the federal parliament in Australia, as well as from Britain and Canada is that ministerial resignation is not expected for departmental maladministration. However, individual ministerial responsibility is alive in terms of the expectations of parliament that ministers behave with propriety and be answerable to the parliament for policy matters. If the matter is serious enough and if there were direct ministerial involvement (the smoking gun), there is an expectation that resignation will follow, though there are exceptions.

In short, individual ministerial responsibility is not 'dead'; rather the conditions under which it is exercised have changed. It is the prime minister's confidence and the handling of the media that matter, not the exertions of parliament. When resignations occur because the minister's 'credit has been impaired', they occur to save the prime minister and cabinet colleagues embarrassment.

A further problem today with opposition and media expectations of ministerial responsibility is that it has degenerated into a 'gotcha' mentality. The objective is to take scalps. For ministers, their understanding of the doctrine is couched in the politics of advantage and disadvantage, where ministers are pursued by their shadow ministry counterparts or opposition attackers. To them it is a potential lynching. However, it is rarely astute for ministers to articulate publicly this political dimension, even though it shapes their defensive behaviour behind the scenes, especially over the political choice of whether to 'tough it out' or go. In the trinitarian struggle, the government's back bench can remain stoic and not partake in the 'blood sport', yet be keenly observing how ministers handle themselves. The opposition can be relentless in its search for the 'smoking gun' to bring down a minister or compound the embarrassment. The doctrine becomes a political duel in which gladiatorial combat is a form of theatre, and where the challenge is ended by 'toughing it out' or when the opposition is able to claim a victim from the government ranks.

Journalists, who feed on such occurrences, often describe the process in metaphorical but graphic terms: the 'chase' is about separating a minister from the herd then searching for the 'killer political blow' to land a 'political scalp'. As professional watchers of the inner sanctum of 'court politics' they seek the 'smoking gun', some direct evidence that links a minister to a blunder. When a resignation does occur over some misdemeanour it is not only regarded as evidence that the constitutional doctrine lives, but also reported as inflicting pain on the government, as evidence of turmoil in the executive and as a major fillip to the opposition.

Yet, it is obvious why ministers want to hold on to power for as long as possible. To focus only on their resignation or dismissal misunderstands how they routinely discharge their responsibilities. Resignation is but a small and potentially misleading component of the picture. Today, ministerial responsibility is about dealing with a web of accountabilities that are fulfilled during the minister's tenure, not on relinquishing it.

Ministers rarely explain the real reasons why they choose not to resign, or, like Lord Carrington, give different versions of possible reasons. Indeed, the real reasons may not help their case or credibility. Occasionally, as with Denis Marshall over Cave Creek, they offer reasons why they believe they should *not* resign when confronted with a crisis or issue. They ignore calls for their resignation. Occasionally, they will countenance the notion of a 'good resignation', that is, falling on one's sword before there is any serious political damage. In extreme cases, when forced to resign against their will, ministers remain resentful, often holding on to the 'heroic' image of themselves as minister.

RETURNING TO THE HEROIC VISION
OF MINISTERS

Prospero's fatalist musings are an all too appropriate counter to the heroic view of the lives of ministers.

> Our revels now are ended. These our actors,
> As I foretold you, were all spirits, and are melted into air, into thin air;
> And, like the baseless fabric of this vision, the cloud-capp'd towers, the gorgeous palaces, the solemn temples, the great globe itself,
> Yea, all which it inherit, shall dissolve, and, like this insubstantial pageant faded, leave not a rack behind.
> We are such stuff as dreams are made on; and our little life is rounded with a sleep.
>
> Prospero, in William Shakespeare's *The Tempest*, Act 4, Scene 1

Ministerial responsibility is the 'stuff as dreams are made on'. Each of our countries has advanced a commonly heroic notion of ministers and their capabilities. We expect them to be heroic, to be capable, honest and incorruptible, to look after their electorates, facilitate networks, sell ideas, oversee effective implementation, and be good at spin and public relations. It's a tall order to fulfil.

Ministers are trapped in this heroic model of the minister. We expect them to be able to cope with the demands, to take responsibility for things under their charge, to be across everything, and to accept blame for things they cannot necessarily control. We also 'bear-bait' them, set traps, erect standards they cannot live up to, and wait for them to flounder. We become fixated with notions of ministerial resignation and the need for a scapegoat.

Pressures on ministers in our jurisdictions have seen them respond in similar ways to these challenges. Their shared heritage matters in how ministers approach their jobs and how other actors respond to ministers. They have increasingly codified their responsibilities and obligations. We see conventions written into guidelines and codes. All jurisdictions have gradually enhanced the power of the prime minister to take and impose collective responsibility over their executives. Ministers wear the fig leaf of accountability lightly. They have resorted to shields to protect themselves from political risks or potential embarrassments. They inform the prime minister, keep the party onside, work the caucus, and engage the electorate through continuous campaigning. They have taken more staff on board to assist their performance. They increasingly resort to spin to keep critics at bay. As ministers, they also burn out physically and leave office voluntarily, largely as a result of the unrelenting 24/7 media imperatives.

Conventionally, parliaments were expected to play a major role in holding government to account. The appearance of ministers before parliament provides the opportunity to witness the performance of the government; to be informed, hear explanations, and have assurances placed on the public record. But parliament is a theatre of limited transparency with some, but limited, ability to question the government. In theory, parliament provides the opportunity to exercise a check on government and individual ministers, although in practice this function is circumscribed by the executive itself. Parliament was once considered the main institution of accountability. Now the media replaces it.

THE WEB OF MULTIPLE ACCOUNTABILITIES

So, today, ministers are embedded in a web of widening accountabilities and concentric circles of actors able to scrutinize their performances. They are constantly negotiating their way through these overlapping multiple accountabilities. Mulgan (2003: 10) suggests there is a series of institutional accountabilities: from elections to parliament, the courts, investigative and audit bodies, and media scrutiny. However, he adopts an instrumental relationship between these actors and ministers of formal reporting requirements (who, to whom, for what, how, and how effective). He asserts 'the full core sense of accountability thus includes the right of the account-holder to investigate and scrutinise the actions of the agent by seeking information and explanations and the right to impose remedies and sanctions'. He imagines a formal one-to-one set of relationships that monitor formal responsibilities.

But relationships of accountability are far more fluid, subtle, more extemporaneous, and more 'gossamer-like'. Some public accountability relations *are* more formal–legal or procedural, such as parliament or annual reporting. But there are also looser political relationships that comprise a web in which modern politics are played out and which can be active or inactive, aggressive or passive as circumstances unfold. Ministers find they cannot remain aloof from these wider accountabilities; they are trapped within the concentric circles, each with a particular form of scrutiny and sanctions.

So, finally, how do we explain these relatively common responses from executive government? Governments confronted the dilemmas posed by the arrival of responsible party government. The constitutional conventions of individual and collective responsibility creaked and groaned under the impact of party self-interest. There were both shared responses and a common trend. The shared responses were, first, to improvise to meet whatever political exigencies confronted the government. So, notions of cabinet solidarity were relaxed to accommodate dissent, ministerial resignations became prime ministerial tactical calculations of political dispensability, and prime ministers found other ways to renew their ministries to ensure turnover. However, such improvisation prompted outrage and calls for a return to the 'golden era that never was' of responsible government and ministerial responsibility. That prompted governments to seek refuge in new rules and codes. Governments sought a greater separation of ministers from administration by using agencies. Codes fast became the modern-day equivalent of a refuge for scoundrels, and prime ministers found themselves torn between issuing new sets of rules and accommodating exceptions to the previous rules.

The common trend was the all-pervasiveness of the 'electronic glut' (Seymour-Ure 2003: 9). Ministers live in a goldfish bowl of continuous news and media coverage. It exacts a harsh price for personal peccadilloes and it is relentless in its search for a story. The new rules sought to provide ministers with a measure of protection from the new scrutiny, by supposedly clarifying for what ministers were responsible. But, as they learnt all too quickly, the search for the story is no respecter of rules. Hence, we find ministerial accountability today applies, except when it doesn't. Collective responsibility applies, unless decreed to the contrary. And governments continue to wear the fig leaf of accountability, sometimes proudly, sometimes begrudgingly. It was perhaps ever thus.

NOTES

1 This paragraph draws on the House of Commons Research Paper, *Ministerial Responsibility*, HC, London, 04/31.
2 Sections 5.25 and 5.26 of the New Zealand *Cabinet Manual* allow ministers to take different policy positions in public, but once an 'agree to disagree' matter has been determined ministers must implement the decision or legislation. Section 5.24 also warns that 'ministers are expected to show careful judgement when referring to party policy that differs from government policy'.
3 There is another interpretation of these events. Tony Blair took his revenge on Clare Short for her intemperate outburst in public and in cabinet over Iraq by not sacking her. According to the Campbell Diaries (2007: 675 and 681), John Prescott, the Deputy Prime Minister, said it was 'not sensible to turn her into a martyr, which is what she wanted, but instead to leave her hanging in the wind for a while' and Blair 'decided he was not going to sack her'. In March 2003, in the House of Commons the then leader of the Conservative opposition, William Hague, 'was on to it, had an absolutely brilliant line in the debate, how TB had "taken his revenge and kept her"'.
4 Only two ministers resigned over personal indiscretions, both Senators and at the death knell of the Howard government (in March 2007). The Human Services

minister Senator Ian Campbell resigned as collateral damage in a government attack on the opposition (because he had also met a shady former Labor premier), while the Minister for Ageing, Santo Santoro, resigned over the non-disclosure of his pecuniary interests and misleading the chamber.

5 The UK and Canada have both preserved the title 'Privy Councillor' for senior ministers. Australia and New Zealand prefer the title 'Members of Executive Council' to designate this rank.

6 So, Steve Harper appointed a Montreal banker, Michael Fortier, to his cabinet in 2006, a move motivated by territorial considerations as the Conservatives sought to bring in representation from the big cities but had been electorally locked out of Montreal and much of Quebec, as well as Toronto and Vancouver. A number of opposition leaders in Canada have been elected who were not then sitting in the parliament.

7 There have not been many suggestions to change the practice of appointing ministers from the ranks of the parliament. Australia's Prime Minister Bob Hawke, in 1979, before he entered parliament, advocated a hybrid system whereby governments could appoint non-parliamentarians to a cabinet post. His idea attracted debate but has not been seriously entertained either by him in office or by his successors.

8 Ministers can be appointed without portfolio, purely as a title, or as a symbolic reference (Minister Without Portfolio, Vice President of Executive Council or Lord President of the [Privy] Council, or Lord Privy Seal). Ministers of State are usually assisting ministers with or without cabinet rank but with fewer administrative responsibilities than senior ministers. This may restrict the issues on which they can be questioned, but does not exempt them from cross-questioning more generally by members of the legislature, the media, or the public.

9 South Africa has an interesting pattern of sitting-days, with plenary and main debates accounting for around 65 days, and special days set aside for the Women's Parliament and Youth Parliament. Furthermore, additional committee days (around 24 per annum) are scheduled outside plenary sessions so that committees can dedicate themselves to the business before them.

10 The UK government has used Demos for this purpose; in Australia Access Economics and Allen Consulting are often used; in New Zealand, the Institute of Policy Studies has performed this role.

6

The Public Service

The Home Civil Service today is still fundamentally the product of the nineteenth century philosophy of the Northcote–Trevelyan Report. The tasks it faces are those of the second half of the twentieth century. This is what we have found; it is what we seek to remedy (Committee on the Civil Service (Fulton) 1968: 9 para. 1).

What Whitehall does believe in, for better or for worse, is continuity (Gerald Kaufman, former British Minister of State for Industry, 1980: 50).

The values of the Public Service these days are embodied in the Public Service Act. They include both being apolitical and professional and being responsive to the elected government. The tension between these values has always been there, but a series of measures have been taken in the last twenty years to increase the emphasis on responsiveness (Andrew Podger, Australian Public Service Commissioner, 2007: 136).

I didn't have any notion of what might be good partisan or political advice. I mean, it just wasn't my field. But if I'd had the urge to, I would have stamped on it as being improper. And if I had not stamped on it he [the prime minister] would have (Gerard Hensley, Head of the Prime Minister's Department, New Zealand, in Boston, 2001: 220).

The New Zealand Treasury (1987) put a gun to the head the government. It had produced a massive two-volume 'incoming brief' for the re-elected Labour government led by Prime Minister David Lange and Minister of Finance Roger Douglas. The report entitled *Government Management* was 'prepared by the Treasury as a briefing, to outline the nature of the issues and to put forward a framework for their analysis' (NZ Treasury 1987: preface). Without mentioning the terms, it advocated a radical neo-liberal, public choice, new public management agenda of reform. The ideas and the language expressed in the incoming brief were definitive and uncompromising. Bureaucrats were dictating terms to the elected government. They repeatedly stated the government had no alternative but to accede to their model. In the words of David Lange, ministers in cabinet were told there was no alternative; Treasury became an 'intellectual powerhouse of the right' and produced a textbook scheme to reconfigure how government operated.

Over the next two decades New Zealand underwent its 'bureaucratic revolution'. It introduced a series of changes, including adopting principal–agent separation, the abolition of 15 departments, a massive downsizing of the public service, contract employment for public employees in a deregulated market, rampant outsourcing, and ministers purchasing outputs from delivery agencies. The rest of the modern world came to New Zealand to observe the social laboratory in operation. Not content with fermenting a 'revolution', Treasury wanted international approbation and recognition for its success. So, in 1995 the New Zealand State Services Commission (with Treasury) commissioned an international expert, Professor Allen Schick, a public management and budgetary guru, to undertake an independent report of the reforms. After his consultations, Schick wrote that New Zealand had done some pioneering things but significantly no one had copied them. He was more critical than they had expected. The tenor of the draft report did not suit Treasury and a senior official challenged Schick over the arguments and wording of the manuscript. Eventually, Schick agreed to the Treasury's edits, although he retained responsibility for the overall authorship (personal communication 19 August 2008). Not one of the finest moments in the history of agency theory where the principal and agent are separated and independently tasked.

Similar sentiments were expressed by a native New Zealander, David Shand. From his then vantage point at the OECD, he suggested the advanced democracies were interested in what New Zealand is doing, but they were not necessarily aiming to copy it. They were just watching (interview, OECD, Paris, 28 August 1994).

In this chapter, we first explore the way that senior public servants create and reinterpret traditions. These traditions are used to make sense of the world they have inherited, the challenges they face, and their place within it. Their purpose is to identify the profession of public servants as heirs to a long and honourable tradition that provides continuity and gravitas. Westminster and its developing conventions provide a sense of surety through which modern practices are comprehended within that professional world.

Then we show how the public services have sought to absorb and modify the threats to that traditional position posed by the claim it was unresponsive and by the managerial strand of neo-liberalism. More specifically, the public service confronted:

- the growth of ministerial staff;
- the contestability of advice; and
- the introduction of performance management and the outsourcing of service delivery.

We identify local variations to these challenges but there is also a shared response:

- the shift from understood conventions about their behaviour to the professional codification of their roles.

Their message remains constant: 'our circumstances may have changed, but our professional core has been retained. Even as we assimilate reform imperatives and promulgate professional codes, we stand in the shoes of our great predecessors.'

REFRACTED TRADITIONS

Public or civil services in Westminster systems have evolved according to a hybrid set of traditions of governance that are partly inherited from the political and parliamentary realm and partly learnt through administrative practice. On the one hand, public services are not the sole masters of their fates. They are not the autonomous inventors or creators of their own identifiable traditions. They exist in and are subordinate to a legitimate political authority. So, there is a derivative character to their traditions. They work in formalized traditions of governance that are dependent and contingent on the political process and notions of proper decision-making and accountability. These *political traditions*, which we have labelled 'responsible government', frame the dominant narratives in which they construct and make sense of their roles and existence. There are distinct political variations in this broad church of ideas about constitutional bureaucracy – Tory conservatism, Whig liberalism, labourist socialism, and, especially in the former dominions, statist traditions of social liberalism, agrarian socialism, nation-building, and, in South Africa, transformational reconciliation.

The most traditional constitutional view is encapsulated in Parris's description in a survey of the origins of the British civil service. Parris (1969: 49) writes of

> an unpolitical civil service whose primary connection is with the Crown, and which, while subordinated to party governments, is unaffected by their changes: the two permanent elements, the Crown and the civil service, which not by chance together left the political arena, supply the framework for the free play of parliamentary politics and governments.

The public service enjoys some institutional continuity and both retains and refracts these traditions of responsible government while also remaining embedded in it. The formative political legacies of responsible government were created and moulded through the clash of inherited traditions. This clash involved the persistence of royal prerogative, the rise of parliament and cabinet government, the widening electoral process and popular consent, interpretations from constitutionalists and the judiciary, the media, and popular discourse. Nevertheless, the public service is an active conduit, conductor, disseminator, and even inventor of such traditions. Often, incoming governments will turn to the public service for advice about how the system is supposed to work or what are 'proper' conventions. The public service is both its own collective memory and that of the system of governance.

The public service also embodies two related *administrative traditions* – the generalist and specialist traditions – that are couched in the normative aspirations of a constitutional bureaucracy. These, in turn, created professional administrative bureaucracies with strong norms, precepts, and values. Such administrative traditions have organic or discrete roots in the bureaucracy but must coexist with the political traditions. So, evolving conventions of responsible government are complemented by evolving notions of professionalism, degrees of independence, expertise and technical proficiency, management, and preferred patterns of recruitment and workforce composition.

In addition, bureaucratic organizations also develop distinctive agency cultures and organizational traditions based on their internal mores, their collective memories and continuing relationships, their discrete training and types of expertise, and their professional values and codes. Often these cultures are agency-specific, insular, and self-referential (Jennings 1962: 138). These departmental philosophies and cultures interact with the service-wide constitutional bureaucratic or administrative traditions in complex and iterative ways.

Public service traditions represent a plurality of inherited beliefs; sometimes separate and distinct, sometimes coexisting but also competing. Such traditions are not merely passively picked up from the political framework of responsible government. Rather, the public service is an active cultivator and preserver of its traditions. It functions as the repository of government history and institutional practice. Its political and administrative traditions are not mutually exclusive. They provide meaning not in the form of some abstract, external constitutional doctrine but in the intersection of daily practice and reflection, occasionally with tensions but often in harmony.

TRANSMISSION AND RECALIBRATION OF TRADITIONS

Public servants construct their understandings of these complementary and competing traditions through two forms of socialization. First, they imbibe beliefs through on-the-job learning and practitioner mentoring. They work in institutional settings and learn the transmitted belief structures and norms. Career structures are learning apprenticeships. Second, they are informed by a literature that packages dominant ideas or beliefs in the traditions of responsible government. This literature has two strands: 'insiders' and 'outsiders'. The 'insiders' comprise former experienced public servants expounding normative frameworks or explaining changing conventional practice.[1] The 'outsiders' comprise journalist, academic and constitutional writers attempting to describe and make sense of evolving political systems to explain to others (see, for example, Bagehot 1963 [1867]; Dicey 1914 [1885]; Hennessy 1989). There is a tendency with both forms of socialization for anachronistic elements or nostalgia to characterize the narrative structures.

But such socialization is not frozen in time. The public service can be seen to be continually recalibrating its framing traditions. It does so consciously and unconsciously, routinely and episodically, as it confronts new challenges. Intensive episodes of recalibration can be interpreted as attempts to update traditional legacies and beliefs, or as attempts to endorse and legitimize cherished traditions in changed circumstances. Traditions thus evolve, are reconfigured, and even reinvented.

As a focus for our discussion we use three examples of the ways the recent leadership of the public service goes about appropriating and inventing its framing traditions. We are concerned to identify which aspects of its traditions the leadership selects and embraces. Which elements of the broader traditions does it engage with and select for endorsement or dissemination?

In Britain, the touchstone for many practitioners is the principles reflected in the Northcote–Trevelyan *Report on the Organisation of the Permanent Civil Service* (1854), still regarded as the main foundation for the modern civil service. There are no British references to the need to maintain the Westminster *system*. Why would there be any such reference when that would be mere self-description? So, *Northcote–Trevelyan* provides the source of the administrative tradition read against the accepted backdrop of the political tradition of responsible government. It provides an ideal, a related set of ideas, and even a measuring stick against which to judge current practice. Even if not often read or understood by officials today, appeals to the supposed principles of *Northcote–Trevelyan* remain common features of debates about the progress and the behaviour of the modern public services.

Reflecting on a life of public service, the British Cabinet Secretary and head of the Civil Service, Sir Andrew Turnbull (2005: 1), concluded in his valedictory address that

> The British Civil Service enjoys an excellent reputation and it is particularly admired abroad . . . Yet it has its detractors and critics, particularly at home. I have reflected on this and have come to the conclusion that the

Civil Service has been strongly shaped by the Northcote–Trevelyan report and the traditions which have developed from it, but that this has also given rise to many of the features which people find unsatisfactory.

Turnbull argued (2005: 1) that

The Northcote–Trevelyan report grew out of the clash between a growing state and an administration based on nepotism. It recommended a series of changes, which have shaped the organisation even to this day. These were:

- a permanent and impartial civil service;
- accountable to Ministers who are in turn accountable to Parliament;
- recruitment and promotion on merit;
- based on self-sufficiency – that is, largely developing its own talent with a presumption of one employer for a whole career;
- providing services from within with little outsourcing;
- highly federal, organised into departments each of whom has a Secretary of State accountable to Parliament.

Turnbull believed these principles were fundamental to Westminster public services.

Turnbull also noted there was a price to pay. Constitutional bureaucracy produced: a 'closed world' that was 'hierarchical and inflexible'; that was slow to change and draw on external talent or use outsourcing; that gave little priority to the development of leadership; and had few incentives to improve efficiency. The service was also 'too reliant on the skills of those recruited many years earlier, leaving it underpowered when requirements changed' (2005: 2–3).

His direct appeal to, and criticism of, *Northcote–Trevelyan* is interesting because the report was silent on many of the hallowed principles Turnbull advances. Myth becomes synonymous with tradition.[2] For example, apart from the term 'Permanent Civil Service' mentioned in the introduction, the report does not mention permanency or defend the case for it. Nor are key attributes such as anonymity or impartiality discussed. The civil service is valued for having 'sufficient independence' but this is not expressed as demonstrating impartiality or apolitical values. There is no mention of self-sufficiency although the report did countenance recruitment from outside and the dismissal of the indolent (a pious hope perhaps!). Nor is the civil service's accountability to ministers mentioned or explored. The authors content themselves with the comment that officials occupy 'a position duly subordinate to that of the Ministers who are directly responsible to the Crown and to Parliament'.

Turnbull's appeal to *Northcote–Trevelyan* attempts to identify and preserve the virtues of the traditional civil service in the face of recent challenges. His message is code for continuity rather than fundamental change. It represents a reinterpretation of administrative traditions by an administrative elite coping with present-day uncertainties and, in the process, defending *their* understanding of *their* administrative traditions. Put another way, Turnbull was projecting his version of the eternal verities of a constitutional bureaucracy. He was also at times critical of those inside government who did not seem to share his view or his preferred ways of working. For example, he described then Chancellor Gordon Brown's operating style as 'sheer Stalinist ruthlessness' (Timmins 2007). Brown was perceived as challenging the sanctity of the administrative tradition; Turnbull defending it against such attacks.

The views expressed in Turnbull's reinterpretation are not idiosyncratic. Similar statements have been made by previous cabinet secretaries who were themselves coping with earlier bouts of reform. For example, the 1994 White Paper *The Civil Service: Continuity and Change* claims that the *Northcote–Trevelyan* report set out the principles that continue to underlie the civil service. According to the then head of the civil service, Sir Robin Butler, they were 'Integrity, impartiality, objectivity, selection and promotion on merit and accountability through Ministers to Parliament' (1994, para. 2.7, p. 8; see also Wilson 2003: 366–7). So, *Northcote–Trevelyan* is employed as a myth set up as an ideal and used as a defence of the civil service, less to resist change and more to select the parts that fit with existing administrative philosophies.

In the former colonial dominions, the transplanted legacies of the nineteenth-century British parliamentary system were largely taken for granted, as was the immediate need for a 'permanent' staff of officialdom. Nepotism was rife at the outset with governors appointing favourites or friends and in some cases ministers appointing their own senior staff, determining promotions and rates of pay. Gradually, colonial administrators began searching for constitutionally authoritative statements. *Erskine May* became the foundation of parliamentary practice, while *Northcote–Trevelyan* became the administrative precedent. Crown authorities (statutory bodies) were established to help professionalize the public service and separate administration and operational matters from politics. Public service commissioners were established as independent offices to oversee the career public service, to modernize administration and protect it from 'politics', while insisting on merit in appointments and promotions (Australia in 1902 and New Zealand in 1912).

The Westminster notion of a non-partisan bureaucracy subordinate to ministers is a long accepted feature of Australian government. The Report of the Royal Commission on Australian Government Administration (RCAGA), headed by H.C. Coombs, a government official who was nominated as Australian of the Century in 1988, starts by commenting that:

This system has traditionally been identified and described as an example of the Westminster system. The Commission has become increasingly aware of the degree to which the Australian system in fact differs from the Westminster model and of the significance for the administration of such differences (RCAGA 1976: para. 2.1.2).

Its definition was that

The Westminster model envisages a government chosen from elected representatives and responsible and accountable to them. It presents the bureaucracy as simply an extension of the minister's capacity; it exists to inform and advise him; to manage on his behalf programs for which he is responsible. Except where Parliament specifically legislated otherwise, its power to make decisions or to act derives entirely from the minister by his delegation and he remains responsible to his Cabinet colleagues and to Parliament for decisions made and actions performed under that delegation (RCAGA 1976: para. 2.1.4).

The Australian public service accepted this interpretation of their position. Ask departmental secretaries about their relations with ministers and they often say: 'I'm a traditionalist; I believe in the Westminster system', meaning they remain non-partisan but work entirely for the minister (Weller and Grattan 1981: 69; see also Weller 2001). Ministerial supremacy was a given.

After a series of recent scandals in which the professionalism of the public service was called into question, senior officials drew on interpretations of Westminster to defend their position and responsiveness to ministers. So, Peter Shergold (2004*b*), Andrew Turnbull's Australian counterpart, lamented in a speech entitled 'Once was Camelot in Canberra?', that recent critics of public administration in Australia thought Westminster was now dead, and no longer found in the administration. He summarized the critics' case thus:

The current view is that 'accountability and responsibility Westminster-style no longer exist' and that the public service has been tarnished by 'politicisation, intimidation and demoralisation'. The public service, and particularly those who head it, now lack the fearlessness and courage of [their predecessors]. Instead, behind layers of secrecy, has been built a rotten edifice of 'plausible deniability', designed to protect Ministers from unpleasant or inconvenient truths (Shergold 2004*b*: 2).

Shergold referred several times in his speech to the Westminster legacy. Most references (2004*b*: 2, 3 and 7) were used as an anchor for his argument and to dispel contrary views:

It is too often forgotten that a Westminster system depends on expectations of confidentiality.

> Australia may be rightly proud of its Westminster tradition but Canberra is far more open to scrutiny than Whitehall. Over the last generation there has been a profound increase in the extent to which public decision-making can be accessed and examined.
>
> I do not think that the particular and distinctive role of the ministerial staffer will bring about the demise of the independent public service or destroy the Westminster system.

To Shergold, Australia's Westminster system was less precisely defined and was constantly adapting. He talked of Westminster 'systems', 'traditions', and 'styles', all in the same speech. He argued that its past ideals, variously constructed, were still alive and well, and in some cases they were more robust now than previously. He warned against distorting the picture by simplistic or idealized versions drawn from perceptions of previous eras and disputed that only former heads were frank and fearless. His message was that there was never a 'Camelot' in Canberra.

His version of the administrative traditions stressed that Westminster was an evolving system involving relations of trust. It was based on balances and counterbalances of power and position, roles and responsibilities, ideas and advice. To him, the panoply of administrative law and new public management were enhancements to Westminster, not threats to it. While he eschewed the term 'constitutional bureaucracy', his argument for an evolving continuity was a plea to be 'bound . . . by the preservation of a shared tradition' (Shergold 2004b: 9).

Prime Minister John Howard (1998: 4) expressed similar sentiments when he argued:

> There are, of course, those who believe that it is an option for the public service to return to some idealised, comfortable past in which it was quarantined from the winds of change blowing through the rest of Australia. Those who hold out such an option for the public service deny the forces transforming Australia. Let me state at the outset my firm belief that an accountable, non-partisan and professional public service which responds creatively to the changing roles and demands of government is a great national asset.

He suggested that the responsibility of government was to 'pass on to its successors a public service which is better able to meet the challenges of its time than the one it inherited'. Tradition and change were iterative.[3]

In Canada, the Privy Council Office's (PCO) 1977 submission to the Royal Commission on Financial Management and Accountability explained the foundations of Canadian constitutional government. Its submission, entitled *Responsibility in the Constitution*, commenced with the proposition that 'our system of government, deriving from British and pre- and post-federation practice, is ministerial in character' (PCO 1993: 1.1). It traced precedents back to the earliest constitutional developments of the Middle Ages: 'The system faithfully reflects the evolution of constitutional responsibility stretching back to Magna Carta and beyond' (PCO 1993: 1.21). Many of the early references to precedent were to British writers. The PCO drew on British traditions, while delineating Canadian adaptation and practice.

More recently, a commission of inquiry held between 2004 and 2006 into the 'Sponsorships Scandal' and led by Judge John Gomery, examined the behaviour of the public service. Gomery criticized the lack of formal accountability in the system. He disagreed with officials on the meaning of conventions, writing in his final report that the 'government expresses the belief "that the public service has no independent identity, and hence no accountability apart from that of Ministers and the government of the day"' (Gomery 2006: 62). Unconvinced, he agreed with one of his academic advisers, Lorne Sossin (2006: 30), who argued forcefully that

> A range of unwritten constitutional conventions and principles clearly give rise to obligations, responsibilities and constraints on decision-making by members of the public service which arguably together confer constitutional status on the public service as an organ of government.

According to Sossin (2006: 30), the constitutional convention of a non-partisan public service

> should include refusal to follow instructions which are motivated by improper partisan interests...While Ministers are responsible for the decisions of the department, officials alone are responsible for their obligation to remain non-partisan.

The report argues that some legislation, such as the *Financial Administration Act*, provides the Canadian public service with a clear, separate, legal status.

Gomery's interpretation was a response to a host of senior Canadian public service executives appearing before the Commission who used the opportunity to defend their record with a restatement of the traditional verities of their profession. They had evoked the principles of Westminster to explain their behaviour and that of ministers in the scandal. Some used Westminster conventions of anonymity to lay responsibility squarely on the shoulders of ministers, while others wielded their understandings of Westminster to shield themselves from direct accountability.

Unlike in Australia, key actors in the Canadian government do not often explicitly articulate traditions of Westminster, principally because it would imply English cultural dominance over French sensitivities. Canadians talk of 'responsible and representative government' derived from parliamentary practice (Jackson and Jackson 2006: 35–51). However, in the context of the Gomery inquiry, a number of senior officials described the Canadian variant of Westminster as they interpreted it. The former Clerk of the Privy Council, Jocelyne Bourgon, in her testimony to the Commission, spoke of the strength, in her own words, of the 'parliamentary accountability system' in which a minister 'assumes full ministerial responsibility' for everything done in their name (cited in Gomery 2004: 8162 and 8257). Ministers were formally accountable for every decision, while public servants were accountable only for the advice they gave or for 'personal responsibilities'. In her view, 'we're always responsible for advice we may have given, good or bad, for lack of courage in not giving any when it needed to be given. We're responsible for our personal actions' (cited in Gomery 2004: 8257).

Alex Himelfarb, the Clerk of the Privy Council and Secretary to the Cabinet at the time of the inquiry, in his testimony before the Commission, stressed that the Canadian public service was one of the variety of 'Westminster systems' each with slight differences in convention and law:

> The public service has a long tradition of continuity. It precedes and often exists longer than a government of the day. So it brings all of that accumulative knowledge of the processes, of the procedures, of the conventions to bear on its advice. It provides a degree of continuity that political advice doesn't. It also has particular responsibilities by tradition (cited in Gomery 2004: 1835–6).

He argued that the public service had to remain 'non-partisan' in its provision of advice and in implementing policies (cited in Gomery 2004: 1833). Continuity gave the public service specific duties and responsibilities, to advise the minister as best they could independently. But elected officials 'are ultimately responsible for everything that happens in their portfolio or department under mandate' (cited in Gomery 2004: 1905). He defended an aspirational definition of ministerial responsibility by stating:

> The principle of ministerial responsibility in the Westminster system is that a minister would be answerable in parliament for everything in their mandate even for things over which they have no authority; in fact, for decisions that they may be obligated not to interfere with (cited in Gomery 2004: 1889).

Himelfarb contrasted legal responsibility ('to our superiors through the hierarchy of government and, ultimately, to parliament') with ethical responsibility ('to report wrongdoing even if you don't have the authority'). Although he commented that 'every public servant coming across wrongdoing has a larger responsibility', he also admitted there was a 'lacuna' in the system that left 'enormous space for judgment and courage' (cited in Gomery 2004: 1934).

Again, the appeal to notions of Westminster serves more than its ostensible purpose of describing the system. Himelfarb and colleagues were answering from the dock under oath, emphasizing the inherent ambiguity of Westminster administrative traditions, but insisting that lines of accountability and responsibility still exist. They stressed the ambiguities because otherwise they could be accused of reneging on their professional responsibilities. Westminster, thus, is variously an ideal, an explanation, and a defence all rolled into the same expressions of principle and convention.

In New Zealand, public management reforms, delineating the 'proper' roles of ministers and public servants, are more explicit. Yet similar concerns remain, even though the State Services Commissioner has greater statutory independence than the defenders of the public services in the other countries. In reflecting on the relations between the two, Michael Wintringham (2008), a former State Services Commissioner, noted:

> Changes in the public management framework, for laudable objectives as greater efficiency and transparency, can have unlooked for and major consequences. In my view, the public management changes in New Zealand not only weakened an already weak convention of ministerial responsibility – a topic in its own right – but institutionalised responsiveness in a way which can make independence (aka political neutrality), if not more difficult to achieve, certainly something that requires pretty sophisticated management by public servants.

He argued that public servants had to be prepared to stand up to ministers at times. He believed that the transparency required under New Zealand's open information requirements

> has not resulted so much in 'bad behaviour' by public servants – tailoring advice, providing oral rather than written briefings etc. Its biggest perverse effect is that we don't do things that we should do in the interests of better policy outcomes for New Zealanders.

There was a need for constant attention to protect the traditional values. He noted that, although all the attention on issues of advice occurred when issues became public, the seed for a good working relationship lay in its continuity. The way big cases

> pan out is often anchored in the accumulation of small interactions between Ministers and chief executives . . . Unless one continually patrols the boundary – both for responsiveness and for independence – it can be well nigh impossible to get it right when the big one arrives.

The danger is that, when times are stable, it is too easy to become close to ministers. Wintringham agreed with a colleague who argued that: 'during periods of political stability… bonds are forged with an Executive through shared work and constant interaction'. He added:

> This is visible to the Opposition. The comfortable relationship requires careful boundary management – one of the reasons I have never called a Minister by his or her Christian name, invitations to do so notwithstanding. They are not our friends.

His conclusions reflect those of the other countries:

> The boundary where responsiveness and independence rub along together is far from tidy. It is where politics (sometimes pretty raw politics); public law; employment law and process; constitutional conventions; egos; good and bad behaviour; all rub up against one another…

The public service in New Zealand is the creation of past practices and modern management. The maintenance of its qualities requires public servants to respect and defend its virtues.

These national protestations of continuity still resonate with British views. Public service advocates espouse a common heritage and appeal to the same understandings of their roles. Any one of the advocates of the traditional public services would have been comfortable as the author of the famous Armstrong memorandum of 1985 that restates the constitutional platitudes. For Armstrong 'the duty of the individual civil servant is first and foremost to the Minister of the Crown who is in charge of the department in which he or she is serving'.

The resonance is not accidental. These actors in the former colonial dominions believed they were replicating Westminster practice and behaving in ways consistent with its principles whatever local adaptations had been made. Twenty or thirty years ago senior public servants would not have made reference to their lineage from nineteenth-century notions of a professional independent public service. Such references would have sounded anachronistic, self-serving, and reactionary. Shergold (2004*b*) admitted that the recourse to such traditional views would have been regarded as 'inward-looking and defensive, focused on process not outcomes, hierarchical, risk averse, short-term view, predictable, lacking in innovation'. The mood of the day in those decades stressed the need for responsiveness, for the 'can-do manager' motivated by results-based achievement, managerial competence, and performance-driven commitment. When new public management (NPM) arrived and was eventually embraced by a professional public service, talk of Westminster was largely suspended by the architects of reform. It was a 'no–no'.

Today, these same public servants are prepared to discuss how far we have moved from Westminster, or from the *Northcote–Trevelyan* ideals: what aspects we have held on to; how elements of Westminster still apply and enable the system to work; how Westminster still provides a defence from powerful critics; and how to cope with future changes. In the post-NPM state, historical legacies are increasingly seen as important. So, Shergold (2004*b*: 8) was anxious to stress today's continuity with the previous norms of the public service but within different contexts:

> The Westminster tradition today, just as fifty years ago, refers to a complex
> set of balanced relationships, marked by subtleties and nuances.

While the core relationships at the top have changed considerably over past decades, this was not always perceived by the key actors themselves. There remains a certain nostalgia for the days when the civil services were reputedly at their most effective, when they were regarded as doing the greatest good. Mostly this golden era tends to refer to the mid-twentieth century. Then there were giants of the profession: Sir Warren Fisher, Sir Edward Bridges, and Sir Norman Brook, Heads of the Home Civil Service in Britain in the 1930s, 1940s, and 1950s, educated, urbane, and effective, and regarded as the archetypal mandarins. In Canada, the senior officials of a similar era became the subject of a collective portrait, *The Ottawa Men* (Granatstein 1982). It charted their considerable impact on post-war Canada. In Australia, a group known collectively as the Seven Dwarfs ruled for decades at the top of the Australian public service. They were scarcely a united team, but they were able to dominate the provision of advice in an environment where there was little intellectual or institutional challenge to their authority.

It is difficult to determine precisely why this particular era of civil servants has attracted such hallowed status. It was that period sandwiched between the mass mobilization of society required for the pursuit of total war together with the belief in the efficacy of state action, and the decline of faith in state solutions in the late 1970s. Whether the giants of those periods deserve the plaudits is debatable; it will be the subject of ongoing dispute as administrative historians plumb the archives as records become available.

One consequence of this nostalgia suggests that today's leading public executives are pale by comparison. But, as Shergold (2004*b*: 2) noted recently:

> There is a growing tendency to look back to the Secretaries of the past with
> nostalgia, finding in them qualities that have failed to withstand the passage
> of time and which reflect badly on their contemporary incumbents. The
> past becomes legend, and those who occupy the present are portrayed as
> unworthy to stand in the shoes of those who have gone before.

He later added:

> The perceived decline in the power and status of the public service often
> seems to coincide with the departure of the perceiving public servant.

There is a remarkable conjunction of personal and administrative history. Whether individually, or in collective groups... retired diplomats, military brass and mandarins have a disarming tendency to see their successors as failing to live up to their own high standards of truth, ethics and integrity (Shergold 2005: 2).

We would expect no less than this defence of the modern bureaucrat.

CHALLENGES AND DILEMMAS: WHY AND WHY NOW?

The main challenges faced by the Westminster-derived public services over the past twenty years came from two sources: the claim that it was unresponsive to political demands and from the neo-liberals that it was not sufficiently skilled in management. Governments came to believe that the public service was impervious to political rule (see Aucoin 1995; Lange 1998; Savoie 2003) and had become too powerful and obstructionist. It was accused of having invested too much in its own independence and permanency. It was accused of being insular, self-referential, and unresponsive; and accused of being an 'entrenched aristocracy within a democracy' and seeking to be above governments (Savoie 2003: 12).[4]

In the UK, Prime Minister Margaret Thatcher (1979–90) was out of sympathy with the ethos of a 'permanent' civil service she thought too risk averse. Prime Minister Tony Blair (1997–2007) extended rather than reversed this trend and sought to make public agencies more responsive, contestable, and focused on delivery.

The Lange government in New Zealand was concerned by the excessive centralization under Muldoon. Lange argued that 'the public sector had grown incrementally. It had become passive. It was taken for granted. It took itself for granted. Its achievements were in the past. The intellectual drive which had created it came from the left of politics but now the intellectual impetus was on the right' (1998: 13). And 'like almost every modern government we were preoccupied with efficiency and getting value for money. Against those imperatives, the public service did not mount a particularly effective defence of itself' (1998: 13).

In Australia, successive governments eroded tenure in the public service, expanded contractual employment and introduced performance regimes. They also used various mechanisms for exerting political control over agencies and their agendas (such as the growth of political advisers as policy managers). The story is similar in Canada, where deputy ministers are personally exposed to public accountability, employed on short-term contracts, and are more open to political pressure. Their ministries are run on results-based business lines.

The public service now deals with a different set of politicians. Compared with the nineteenth century, when many parts of the Westminster system came into being, politicians are now full-time career politicians, highly educated, reflexive, and spin-conscious. Ministers are more interested in immediate impact and effectiveness. They invest in driving change, and intensive media exposure makes them more directly accountable in the community for the performance of their agencies. Many ministers are not prepared to accept conventional ways of doing things but are interested in having choices, in alternative solutions, comparative experiences, and transforming the incentive structures within policy frameworks (for instance, greater citizen-choice models of delivery).

In New Zealand and Australia, ministers were not alone in the demands for change. The reforms were adopted and pushed with enthusiasm by senior officials, often without much detailed interest from ministers. In New Zealand the real drivers were a group of public servants in the Treasury, led by Graham Scott. They were advocates of rational choice and argued for the efficacy of contracts, purchaser–provider arrangements as a means of improving the performance of the public service. In a small public service community, such a strategically placed and motivated group was able to evangelize their beliefs and turn around the workings of the public service.

The roles and responsibilities of governments in Westminster systems have expanded (for a more detailed account see Rhodes and Weller 2001). Initially, government played largely a regulatory role and had limited responsibilities. In the twentieth century governments created the welfare state but that era of big government gave way to the new public management and outsourced services. Today, improving service delivery has become a key priority for government policy-making. Government responsibilities are still increasing although with far more discretion in policy choice and delivery instruments.

Most important for the public service, there is far more contestability in policy advice, research, and information. Much of the contestable advice is from outside the public sector: from think-tanks, consultancy firms, management consultants, academic centres, and peak bodies and their research arms. The public services no longer hold a monopoly on advice to ministers. Mostly the policy units of departments play a lesser role in original policy formulation, but instead 'add value' by collating, arbitrating, and recommending between contestable options circulating the minister. The picture is further complicated by ministerial advisers and minders. They not only mediate and liaise between the department and the minister but also give the minister more capacity to become involved and have an impact.

So, public services have changed substantially. We can debate why they changed. As the Australian minister quoted earlier (above p. 66) suggests, it was in part because of the struggle between the elected ministers and the appointed officials for greater responsiveness. Or as in the case of the Treasury in New Zealand, it was because public servants believed they needed to do things differently. What is not in question is that public services now work in a more contested environment and many of the old certainties have vanished.

So we have a conundrum: the so-called golden era of the public service was regarded by ministers as a period when officials were too powerful and there was a need to reassert political leadership. Now, in a period of enhanced political control, the senior echelons of the public service are regarded as 'lacking the fearlessness and courage' of their predecessors, open to politicization and partisanship, and ready to adopt a willingness-to-please mentality (Shergold 2004*b*: 2).

We will explore how these traditions interact with the development of the public services by examining four debates: on the claims of politicized appointments, on the contestability of advice, on the delivery of services, and on the codification of conventions and professionalism.

Appointment, Removal, and Politicization of Department Heads

Formally public servants are appointed on the basis of merit and are considered to have no allegiance to any political party. They are meant to serve any elected government with the same zeal and zest. That is the meaning of the term 'political neutrality': it is not neutrality between government and opposition. Public servants serve the elected government. Neutrality implies that they serve any elected government with equal dedication and vigour. The Gomery Report (2005: 64) even suggested: 'the principle of the rule of law requires the neutrality and impartiality of the public service'.

Appointment to the top echelons is normally by prime ministers. In Britain they are advised by a senior cohort of permanent secretaries, but the final choice remains theirs. Nevertheless they have not always understood well the choices they made. When Thatcher said that she wanted secretaries who were 'one of us', she referred more to a propensity for action than any necessary ideological closeness. Most of those appointed were from the expected cohort of high achievers and they were appointed until retirement. The senior civil service in Britain has largely maintained its monopoly of the senior positions, with external selections after advertisement still rare (Richards 2007).

Nor is it common to see secretaries removed for any arbitrary reason, even if there may be occasions when they are pushed into retirement. 'Permanent' effectively still means permanent in Britain. On this criterion the civil service in Britain has not moved far from its halcyon days. There are, however, ways by which some secretaries could be moved on.

In Australia, there have been changes in the position of departmental heads. The term 'permanent head' was dispensed with in 1984 when legislation began the process of removing security. Before then the only way that a government was able to remove a departmental head was to abolish the department the person headed. That requirement was seen as cumbersome and excessive. So, legislation retained their permanence but proposed that after five years they could be rotated to another department. Thus the earlier tradition of career silos (or stove-pipes in Canada) was undermined as the idea of a generic and generalist manager grew. These provisions did not make them secure, but invariably they remained within the Australian public service. After 1994, however, the incumbent secretaries were offered a pay rise in exchange for being placed on fixed-term contracts of up to five years. Strictly speaking, it was not a contract because there were no terms of employment or performance expectations, just a generic set of conditions. The difference was that, if the government did not want to rotate the incumbent and find another job when the secretary reached the end of the term, their employment in the public service abruptly ended. The principal advantage was that, if the contract was ended early, they at last had an agreed payout. All but two secretaries accepted the pay rise and the option was not given to any new appointees.

Secretaries were appointed by the prime minister. Formally, before 1999, it was an executive council appointment, but the prime ministers chose. Sometimes ministers were consulted, at other times they were not. After an election at which the government was returned, a reshuffle of ministers would often be followed by a reshuffle of secretaries. As one noted when told that he did not want to move, his opinion was of no relevance. When he asked who his new minister might be, he was told to read the paper the next day. In another case, when a minister of agriculture inquired about the identity of his new secretary, he asked whether she was a farmer. The reply was, 'I'm not sure, but I will inquire, Minister.' In fact, she came from a background in overseas trade. In mid-term ministers would sometimes ask to see a shortlist of candidates and even interview the possible candidates. If they were senior enough their opinion might matter in the final choice. But they knew that the final decision rested with the prime minister who might want to mix ministerial and secretarial strengths or bring new managerial skills to a department to fix problems without actually shifting the minister.

After 1999, with the introduction of the new Public Service Act, prime ministerial power became more explicit. Secretaries were appointed on such terms and conditions as the prime minister should decide. The prime minister could choose the term of years and whether or not there would be an extension. Indeed, the length of the contract was seen as an indication of the level of trust the prime minister had in the candidate. In making choices, the prime minister acted on a report from the secretary for the Department of the Prime Minister and Cabinet. Prime ministers do not necessarily know all those who could be considered, and those who have worked in their department have a distinct advantage. Their departmental secretary can bring other names forward, a power that makes all other secretaries conscious of his significance for their future. Secretaries retain their positions at the pleasure of the prime minister.

New Zealand has also used contracts but more creatively, with more traditional protection for their senior public servants. All appointments are on contract and that contract may vary from months to years. In addition, the contract has individual conditions in terms of the inputs that will be provided and the outputs that will be delivered for the minister. In exchange the minister has little say in the management of the department as that would create limitations on how the officials could deliver the contracted services. Departmental heads may be appointed for short periods as management change agents; and periods as short as three months have been known. Under New Zealand's fragmented agencification, there are always far more departments and ministries than ministers, so the latter will often be responsible for several entities and will therefore have to develop a working relationship with a number of agency heads.

Appointment, however, is effectively vested in the State Services Commission (SSC). Its chair will draw up a list of potential appointees and will talk to the minister and others. The views of ministers are significant but not necessarily crucial. The Commission will then make a recommendation for appointment. The prime minister and cabinet do not have to accept the proposal, but they almost always do. Only on one occasion have they chosen not to accept the recommendation and asked for another name. They have never usurped the authority in the Act to try to substitute another name or appoint a secretary independently. There is thus no evidence that the public service has been politicized in terms of appointments.

The SSC is also responsible for the assessment of performance. Again the ministers' views form part of that assessment but not the only part. The decision to end contracts does not lie in political hands, although there is a need to ensure that relations between minister and public servants work smoothly.

In Canada, deputy ministers are appointed by the prime minister. They once were able to tell their ministers that, as they did not appoint them, they could not remove them. They were unlikely to be fired, but if there was a falling-out, they might be quietly moved on (Savoie 2003: 141). Others appreciated their dual allegiance. They may be 'accountable to their minister on a daily basis but they were accountable to the Prime Minister in the last resort' (Osbaldeston 1989: 54; see also Aucoin 2006; Bourgault 2006).

In a situation of potential conflict between a minister and a prime minister in Canada, the departmental head is bound to the prime minister. One head remembered:

> I had a chance to talk to the Prime Minister at a social function. He asked me how it was going. I told him that I was having problems with my minister and said: 'I have no time for this minister, I don't like him, please give me a new job'. The Prime Minister said: 'I've no time for your minister either, that's why you're there'. That is the best guidance I had ever been given, it kept me going for eighteen months (Osbaldeston 1989: 59).

The pool from which the secretaries are drawn remains the same in all countries. Despite rhetoric to the contrary, most top officials are appointed from within the public services, usually without advertisement. They are predominately male and reach the top in their 50s. Increasingly they have experience in more than one department, bringing management skill rather than subject expertise to their task. A period in a central agency seems likely to assist a career.[5]

Of course this assumes that the government is prepared to trust those senior officials on whom it must rely. When governments change, new ministers are often suspicious of the incumbent heads of their inherited departments. If they were appointed by their political enemies, they wonder how they can serve the new regime, even if theories of constitutional bureaucracy argue they should. Changes of government, though, may be rarer than this might suggest. Since 1950, changes of government have only occurred six times in Britain, five in Australia, seven in Canada and New Zealand, and once in South Africa, but these ruptures are the occasions when the traditions are put to the test.

In New Zealand no chief executives have been removed when governments changed; indeed, contracts were usually extended when they expired (Boston 2001; Gregory 2004). In Britain, too, there is no expectation that new ministers, however suspicious they may be of the civil service, will be permitted to move on their permanent secretaries. The traditional safeguards have been retained.

In Canada there is a concern about the frequent churning of deputy ministers, so that their time in any position has become short. The Gomery Report proposes three- to five-year terms as a means of lengthening their time in the one office (while the Australian term contracts were designed to shorten those periods if desired).

By contrast, in Australia, the comparative fragility of their position was illustrated at the change of government in 1996. Political recognition of the ability to serve different masters was often limited. One long-term secretary recalled a 1983 conversation with a former Coalition minister over dinner:

> He could not understand how public servants of the calibre of Geoffrey Yeend and Michael Codd, who had served the Fraser government so admirably, could possibly serve those dreadful socialists. My reaction was to point out that he obviously did not understand the fundamental principles of the Westminster system (Ayers 1996: 6).

Suspicion was ingrained. In 1996, the incoming Liberal government sacked six secretaries, around a third of the total. Even if one or two of them were regarded, rightly or not, as too close to the defeated government, the suddenness and extent of the executions staggered the public service. The concern was exacerbated over the next few years. One secretary was removed when the department was blamed for lax administration of ministerial expenses, when it was ministers who were largely at fault. Another was suddenly shifted to an overseas post. The climax came in 1999 when a difficult minister of defence, John Moore, wanted his secretary, Paul Barratt, removed. Ironically, the secretary was one of two former public servants who had been brought back to government by the prime minister when the Liberals won and had later been promoted to Defence. He chose to fight rather than accept his dismissal submissively. When the secretary of the Department of Prime Minister and Cabinet, effectively if not officially the head of the public service, rang to tell him he was fired, he demanded to know why. When not satisfied with the result, he took the government to court (Weller 2001).

In the case it was acknowledged by both sides that nothing he had done was responsible for his dismissal. It was simply that the minister did not trust him and could not work with him. As the judge said, in the finding that the dismissal was lawful, the Public Service Act was passed to allow for the effective administration of the country. If a minister did not trust a secretary, whether or not the distrust was justified, or whether the secretary had done anything to deserve it, the system could not work. So, the prime minister had the right to terminate the appointment. Many of the other secretaries were unhappy with Barratt's decision to test their position in court. They knew they could no longer survive poor relations with their ministers but preferred it was not so bluntly expressed in law. The case changed nothing; it spelt out the reality.

There may well be detrimental consequences, albeit difficult to prove. Tony Ayers, a long-term secretary, commented:

> I have no argument if they got the sack for non-performance. My worry at
> the moment is that people get sacked because someone doesn't like the
> colour of their hair or whatever... This business now of half the depart-
> mental secretaries under threat because their ministers are not getting
> political outcomes. Since when has it been the public servants' job to
> achieve a political outcome. That's bloody nonsense... I wonder if you are
> going to get as frank and fearless advice as you once would (cited in Weller
> 2001: 193).

Yet in all systems, senior officials acknowledge that the senior officials must
amend their style of work to suit that of their ministers, not the other way
around. In the Antipodes the push for responsiveness, and the potential
vulnerability of secretaries that accompanies that shift, has changed the
circumstances in which they work. Some incumbents will play down the
changes and emphasize the continuities, arguing that their job remains
essentially the same (Shergold 2004b).

COMPETITION FOR POLICY ADVICE

Officials used to have the advantage that they could develop a monopoly on
the advice given to ministers. The Treasuries would be the only ones with
models of the economy and the ability to forecast economic trends. Social
services were delivered through large government agencies. Government
utilities provided post, electricity, and water. There were extensive education
and health systems within government hands, even if they were supplemented
by smaller, elitist private sector. These services were all the responsibility of
public servants who could advise ministers on what was possible, what had
been tried, and what should be done. If weak ministers lack expertise, officials
have power because ministers had no means of challenging their assumptions
or their proposals. With strong ministers they were still likely to be influential.
They had the principal, and the last, word in the ministers' ear.

What has changed? Ministers now have the capacity to receive advice from
a wider range of established sources and no longer depend almost exclusively
on the officials. Outside government, banks, accounting firms, and NGOs
have developed the capacity to react as fast to any economic news with
forecasts and analyses as persuasive and legitimate as those of government
departments. They can develop alternative policy prescriptions, some of
which may be more ideologically attractive to ministers than those from
more traditional official sources. In opposition they can assist in developing
a platform that ministers can push once elected. Some think-tanks may be

aligned with political parties, others more dedicated to a set of ideas and open to all who are interested.

In addition, the set of ideas and myths surrounding, for example, *Northcote–Trevelyan*, are called upon as a means of legitimizing change and defending practices. For instance, all three heads of the civil service, Turnbull, Shergold, and Himelfarb, defended the confluence of political and non-partisan advice to ministers. There was benefit in having separate 'political' advice at the centre while preserving the expertise of bureaucratic advisers. Himelfarb stated that 'good policy' emerged from the combination of political advice from the Prime Minister's Office (PMO) and a non-partisan source of advice from the Privy Council Office (PCO). He argued that the PMO

> has a Policy Research Unit where they assess a range of issues that come to their attention from departments or from the outside in terms of their constituency with the government's overall agenda, and they provide advice independently of the Public Service to the Prime Minister on a range of policy issues that they themselves have researched and assessed, generally in close communication with departments and the PCO...PCO provides non-partisan advice, that is, advice that – well, non-partisan policy advice. PMO provides a political lens on policy advice. It is not duplicative. It often converges as good policy is often good politics. But the Prime Minister has access to both a political lens, in particular, a partisan political lens, and a non-partisan source of advice often on the same issues (Gomery 2004: 1833).

Equally, Turnbull (2005: 3) welcomed 'the fact that we are much more open to ideas from think-tanks, consultancies, governments abroad, special advisers, and front-line practitioners'. He ventured: 'in developing policy we not only consult more widely than we used to but involve outsiders to a far greater degree in the policy making process'. He then quoted Shergold approvingly:

> Let me make it clear that I extol the fact that the public service policy advice is increasingly contested. I welcome it intellectually: our perspectives and strategies benefit from challenge. I also welcome it professionally, as a public servant. In my view, more Ministerial advisers does not represent the 'politicisation of the APS' [Australian public service], still less the demise of an independent public service or undermining of the Westminster tradition.

For public servants the challenge now is to know whom the minister has consulted and from what direction they approach the problem (see Savoie 2003). Public servants now have to justify their place at the table, argue for their expertise, and prove their worth to their political bosses. They are not accepted as merely part of the infrastructure.

A second issue is raised by the advent in all countries of ministerial staff. Whether in origin public servants or political operatives, ministerial staffers are appointed to further the political future and aims of ministers. They are often seen as explicit counterpoints to the non-partisan public service. As a Clerk of the Privy Council noted, in the Trudeau years the PMO was partisan, politically active, and operationally sensitive. The PCO was non-partisan, politically sensitive, and operationally active. The intention was to provide an additional perspective and greater assistance to ministers, and particularly to the prime minister.

There was opposition to ministerial staff from public services. Mulroney allowed each minister to appoint a chief of staff. These posts were later abolished by Chrétien, but without an extensive reduction in staff numbers. Initially ministerial staff were concentrated in the offices of senior ministers, particularly the prime minister. Whitlam, Fraser, and Trudeau relied on their staff, but primarily as an addition to the public servants, not as a replacement. Then the staff expanded to all ministers who, comfortable with their partisanship, began to rely on them for a second opinion on the advice they were getting. Indeed, to an extent the staff themselves became a management problem, as some of them developed an unofficial capacity to direct public servants and occasionally got their ministers into trouble (Tiernan 2007).

If the staff were seen as an extension of the minister, there could be a cooperative approach. A Canadian minister argued:

> I gave clear instructions to my political staff that if they lorded over the public servants in the department they would be out. At the same time I made it clear to the senior executives in the department that my staff should be treated as an extension of me in my political role as a minister. I explained that the chief political aide should be the alter ego of the minister. The workload in the department is so large that it is necessary for my staff to work with the department just to keep the work moving (Osbaldeston 1989: 39).

But it did not always work smoothly. Indeed, one Canadian political chief of staff challenged the right of bureaucrats to be there at all, arguing they 'should get back to their real job – to implement decisions and see to it that government operations run smoothly and leave policy to us' (Savoie 2003: 124).

Ministerial staff were appointed by the ministers, survived only as long as the ministers retained office and could be dismissed without warning or reason. They consequently had a high turnover and to a degree oversensitive antennae. In theory there were two conventional understandings: the staff acted in the minister's name, and telling the staff was the equivalent of telling the minister. Neither is still true; staff may choose not to pass on information and papers might come back to the department with the notation 'Not seen by the minister'. Staff may seek out information in anticipation of ministerial wishes and then provide the minister with plausible deniability by only passing on those parts they think the minister has to know.

Public servants have learnt to live with the advent of ministerial staff. Those advisers that are overweening or over-mighty, such as the No. 10 staff under Blair were seen to be, still cause tension. Many work comfortably with senior departmental officers. The number of staff is most extensive in Australia, although the chiefs of staff in Canadian ministers' offices may have caused more comment. Yet, as an Australian secretary noted, the growth in ministerial offices

> has fundamentally transformed the role of a secretary. I constantly have to compete for the policy attention of the minister with those in the minister's office. No two ways about it. I have to fight for my position at the table (Weller 2001: 103).

There are dangers too. As Mike Codd, a former head of PM&C, noted:

> Power has become more centralised around the private office. That's really a fundamental change. It means departments are having views, robust views, filtered and the frustrations creep in. It has the potential to damage the quality and fabric of the public service in the end. Because people who are very good and who want to have a chance of influence, will not stay... if their influence is being muddied and their views filtered, by some people who are very able but others who are frankly not (cited in Weller 2001: 198).

The public servants had to adjust to the new requirements of their ministerial masters and the spirit of the time favoured neo-liberalism and the call for a new public management.

MANAGERIALISM

Governments were the great service providers. They ran the post office, the telegraph, customs and, later, social security. In Australia and Canada, the federal system spread responsibility across different levels of government. Education, health, and police might be run by state or provincial government, or by localities. In unitary systems county police forces and education authorities operated within national legislation. Commercial activities, including airlines, coal mines, airports, prisons, shopping malls, and butcher shops, were often established by government. It was assumed that governments could run them well, and in some core areas that only governments should be able to run them, particularly where they entailed the legitimate use of coercion: areas such as police, prisons, taxation, and the military. They should be beyond commercial interests, although Britain has maintained regiments of mercenaries for the last 50 years without comment or complaint. These activities covered much of what civil servants did.

Few of these activities were unequivocally governmental. Over the last 30 years, the public services faced a challenge to both what functions they carried and how they carried them out. This public management narrative, also referred to as managerialism or NPM, is about introducing private sector management into the public sector. It comes in various guises. Initially it stressed: hands-on, professional management; explicit standards and measures of performance; managing by results; value for money; and, more recently, closeness to the customer. Subsequently, it also embraced competition and markets. This neo-liberal agenda stressed or introduced incentive structures into public service provision through contracting out, quasi-markets, and consumer choice.

So, the notion that government organizations delivered services best was up for debate and several services were privatized or outsourced. The way to promotion used always to be seen as through service to ministers and the provision and development of policy advice. Management was for lesser mortals. No longer. It was now a case of can-do managerialism.

So several options were available to deliver and improve service delivery. Governments can:

- continue to run it though a department;
- identify it as a unit within a department with targets and incentives (Next Steps Agencies or executive agencies);
- create a separate statutory authority (state-owned enterprises);
- outsource the activity to provide regulated competition by market pressure (employment services, prisons) while maintaining control;
- commercialize and force it to act as a private sector unit within regulations (corporatization); or
- sell it through privatization (airlines, banks).

Commercial activities were simple: airports, banks, and airlines could be sold off. Others could be market tested, with government agencies that could not compete being wound back and closed. Public services now come in different guises, even though the most discussed, and the most eagerly sought, positions are those that provide policy advice to ministers.

New Zealand has gone the furthest in explicitly seeking to outsource the provision of policy advice. Policy is seen as just another service or output to be provided to government; and in the marketplace of ideas public servants may or may not be regarded as the best source.

Canada experimented the least. As Savoie (2003: 61) observed:

> Canada has hunkered down and stood by the Westminster–Whitehall model
> more devoutly than even Westminster and Whitehall have ... Canada chose
> not to experiment with the agency model to the same extent as Britain,
> New Zealand and Australia.

However, several Crown agencies with substantial budgets and some distance
from the normal rules of government were created; the Canadian Foundation
for Innovation, with a budget of C$3.15 billion, and the Canada Millennium
Scholarship Foundation (C$2.5 billion) are examples (Savoie 2003: 219).

Britain privatized and then collected service delivery within departments in
the Next Steps Agencies that were provided with targets and a degree of
management initiatives. But they were still part of the department, reporting
to the minister through the permanent secretary.

Australia, under governments of different persuasions, sold banks, airlines
and telecommunications, and outsourced the management of prisons and the
provision of employment services (Davis and Rhodes 2001). Although it
would not be possible to identify a clear strategy that applied throughout
the period – several strategies were adopted and quietly dropped – there was
an underlying logic of seeking to use regulated markets where possible
(Keating 2004). A wide range of activities were gathered in Centrelink so
recipients could get all their benefits from a single source, but after some years
Centrelink was rolled back under the auspices of a department.

New Zealand was more explicit in its managerial reform. Driven by a
coherent philosophy determined by the Treasury, it sought to introduce
purchaser–provider principles into all elements of government activity, including accountability regimes (see Boston et al. 1996). It wanted to decide
exactly what the minister or the government was buying, whether it was
policy advice or a service, what it would cost, and what effect it might have.
It sought to distinguish between those areas for which the public servants
should take responsibility (the agreed policy outputs) and the policy outcomes which the minister sought and for which they in turn were responsible.
The departmental heads signed performance agreements with the ministers to
specify what they would deliver and what outputs would be achieved. The
distinction between outputs and outcomes was easier to isolate in theory than
in practice. As one department head explained:

> I've had performance agreements with four [ministers] and I've so far yet
> to have one that showed the least interest in it. I mean, a more typical
> thing is you send over the draft and nothing happens, and you ring up
> and the minister says 'I think I must have lost it somewhere could you
> send another'... they're not really interested, practically in the year's
> performance agreement. They're interested in issues, how you're going

> to handle them, and whether the issue is in the performance agreement
> or not is totally irrelevant to them (cited in Boston 2001: 214).

The New Zealand experiment may be brave in its conception, but some of the
stark realities of serving ministers remain ever-present.

Whatever the strategy, new skills are required; in an old system the requirement was to manage a large hierarchical agency, with multiple offices and a
range of benefits. Some of the front counters were tough places to work. But
all were part of the same outfit, and eventually responsible to the minister
and, in theory at least, it was more possible to apply principles of accountability. Now the links are less certain.

> Deputy ministers readily acknowledge that the nature of their jobs has
> changed in recent years and that today they are mainly negotiators and
> networkers...Deputy ministers 'will look for quick fixers and sound
> risk-takers who are capable of negotiating agreements that can be appre-
> ciated in terms of results and impact rather than in the usual vague terms'
> (Savoie 2003: 139).

As it was put for British civil servants, they need to learn the art of diplomacy.
So contract management, network management, dealing with the suppliers of
services while keeping citizens satisfied and ministers protected when the
contract fails to live up to anyone's expectations: these are the new requirements. They do not exist in splendid isolation. They must be read within
those refracted traditions; new demands can be absorbed within the over-
arching practices.

The Codification of Professionalism

Public services were traditionally hierarchies, with command structures.
They relied on rules and conventions of behaviour. Ideals could be derived
from practice. The challenge of responsiveness and managerialism, the changing practices, prompted a common response from the public services.
Conventions and shared understandings were weak foundations. So, gradually these conventions have been written down. Just as the guides for
ministers started as one page of good practice and morphed into ministerial
codes, so the rules and conventions of the public services became explicit.
They tell how a good public servant should behave and react. They also tell
ministers what they can expect. They provide not only a standard of behaviour but also protection from the behaviour of others.

The several codes have much in common, illustrating that even if their
institutional structures are different the public services are of common

lineage. For instance, in Australia they were expressed in the new 1999 *Public Service Act* as the 'values' of the Australian public service. They included statements to the effect that the Australian public service:

- is apolitical, performing its functions in an impartial and professional manner;
- is a public service in which employment decisions are based on merit;
- is openly accountable for its actions, within the framework of ministerial responsibility to the government, the parliament and the Australian public;
- is responsive to the government in providing frank, honest, comprehensive, accurate, and timely advice and in implementing the government's policies and programmes; and
- is a career-based service to enhance the effectiveness and cohesion of Australia's democratic system of government.

These values are not necessarily consistent. Does 'accountable' trump 'responsiveness', or 'impartial' override 'transparent' if the two collide? Yet they are familiar in their presentation, even if some favoured phrases, such as the demand to be 'frank and fearless', were not reproduced. The list of values provides a snapshot of the way that public service professionalism under Westminster is interpreted in Australia.

In New Zealand, the attributes of a professional public servant were declared by the State Services Commission to include:

- obeying and upholding the law;
- discharging obligations to the elected government of the day in a politically impartial way;
- displaying a high level of knowledge and competence;
- preparing advice, delivering services, and making decisions reached by using analytically sound, well-rounded, informed, and inclusive approaches;
- tendering advice with courage, tenacity, and independence; and
- promoting and advocating the core values of the organization (quoted in Boston et al. 1996: 329).

In the UK Sir Robert Armstrong's memorandum (1985) on civil servants and ministers grew into the larger if, by international standards, still terse, *Civil Service Code* (2006) that demands that civil servants 'conduct themselves with integrity, impartiality and honesty. They should give honest and impartial advice to the minister' (para. 4). In Canada, the Privy Council Office's *Guidance for Deputy Ministers* (2003) is more demanding. Deputy Ministers should give 'sound public service advice on policy development and implementation' (s. 2.1). They also had to support ministers in their individual and collective responsibilities. Therefore:

advice must be timely, candid, presented fearlessly, and provide the best policy options based on impartial review of the public good and the declared objectives of the Minister and the government.

Policy, the *Guide* required, perhaps hopefully, had to be coherent and improve the life of Canadians.

In Australia the professional code is enshrined in legislation; in other countries these values are included in publicly available guides to conduct. In all these cases these virtues or values are in a sense institutionally neutral; they pronounce the tenets by which good public servants should make judgements. They do not lay down how they should react in a given situation. They inscribe past understandings of how public services should behave. The provisions from the different countries are not the same, but the family resemblances are striking. They are Westminster understandings written down in response to present-day dilemmas, but in essence unchanged.

CONCLUSION

Governments of all political persuasions have railed against bureaucracy and its inefficiency. Staffing cuts recur. The government rids itself of functions by contracting out: the neo-liberal or market strand of managerialism. Governments complain that civil servants are poor managers who fail to deliver: the performance management strand of managerialism. Commentators claim there has been a politicization of civil service, arguing there are more accelerated and outside appointments than previously and too many ministerial advisers. Ministers claim the civil service is not responsive and resists change. The public service confronts two dilemmas: between the generalist tradition and the impact of managerialism, and between constitutional bureaucracy and political responsiveness. These dilemmas drove the changes and motivated the various heads of the public service to recalibrate their traditions.

We have not charted a convergence of traditions in Westminster-derived jurisdictions. We have identified common challenges and divergent responses. The Antipodes have moved much further in altering the conditions of employment for departmental heads than their northern counterparts with the intent of increasing responsiveness. Even so, we show that the heads of the public services have found 'space' or 'voice' to articulate innovative ways of combining past traditions with new organizing principles of governance. In each case, it is not a question of in with the new, out with the old, but of in with the new beside key components of the old. New practices in response to the call for responsiveness and better management are embraced by the public service. Specific activities may change but the essence of the public service is eternal.

National practices may differ as they respond to these challenges. Although each head legitimated Westminster traditions, they fudge the crucial elements they wish to hold on to. Sometimes this is part of the myths and legends associated with Westminster. At other times, they are simply non-specific as to which aspects they continue to consider legitimate. Sometimes they disagree; so while Himelfarb is anxious to hold on to anonymity at all costs, Shergold finds the new requirements holding public servants personally to account as a positive attribute to open scrutiny consistent with the Westminster system. Wintringham worries that public executives may be becoming too subservient and focused on short-term expediency. Turnbull was critical of much of the old trappings of what he saw as the *Northcote–Trevelyan* legacy but he does not want to discard many of the most important attributes. He continues to cherish: the impartiality of the civil service; some degree of permanency (indeed, he prides the UK on having retained more permanency than Australia); on a close accountability between ministers, officials, and parliament; on the promotion of staff by merit; and even on the advantages of departments as non-statutory organizations of state. Australian departmental heads believe that responsiveness is important and they live, reluctantly, with the limited contracts and the knowledge that their careers can be terminated by the prime minister at any time. Our approach may stress local custom and practice but it does not unearth only the differences between the countries. We also identify shared beliefs and a common response to the dilemmas of responsiveness and managerialism. They hold far more beliefs in common with one another than with any other system; for example, they are neutral, expert, and accountable. Most notably, nowadays, all seek to codify their beliefs and practices. The essence of the public service is no longer a shared understanding, it is a written code. As a result, the family of ideas that is Westminster's constitutional bureaucracy persists to this day. To paraphrase Shergold: even if Westminster was never Camelot, its sustaining myths remain germane to the modern public service. They are used to socialize new entrants, to defend the professionalism of the public service, to persuade politicians, to judge peers, and to preserve an ever-mutating ideal. Its myths are real.

NOTES

1 The original source is Northcote–Trevelyan 1854, with Bridges 1950 and 1956 as the subsequent authority. More recently see Wilson 2003.

2 We are indebted to Rodney Lowe for his seminar on 12 October 2005 at the Australian National University on 'Western Public Administration and the Myth of Northcote Trevelyan'. The ideas in this paragraph were developed in his seminar.

3 Howard's successor, Labor Prime Minister Kevin Rudd, appealed to the same source of authority. Speaking to a meeting of departmental heads, he emphasized the need to 'reinvigorate the Westminster tradition of independence and continuity... Westminster by and large has served our system of government well and the time has come to rebuild the Westminster tradition in Australia' (Rudd 2008: 5).

4 A range of academics have recently portrayed the systems as radically changed. Donald Savoie (2003) writes of 'breaking the bargain', the fracturing of the implicit agreement by which politicians and civil servants operated. Colin Campbell and Graham Wilson (1995) write of the 'end of Whitehall'. The picture they paint is apocalyptic; and pre-dates Blair! The old principles have been rejected and the new precepts, according to academic critics, lack accountability and principle. We may venture that what practitioners see as evolutionary and normal adaptation, some academics see as revolutionary and discomfiting.

5 For some comparative figures for Britain, Australia, and New Zealand, see Rhodes and Weller (2001).

7

Parliaments and Representation

There is a myth of a golden age of legislatures when wisdom and oratory and gentlemanly behaviour and public spirit all seemed somehow to flourish and to flourish together (K.C. Wheare 1963: 232).

Reports of my death are greatly exaggerated (Mark Twain, Cable to Associated Press, May 1897).

Parliamentary reform is one of those things, as Mark Twain remarked about the weather, which everybody talks about, but nobody does anything about... The declining effectiveness of the House has been paralleled... by a rising efficiency of the Executive. But there is no necessary contradiction between wanting a strong Executive and wanting a more effective and efficient House of Commons. The more power we entrust to a Government to do things for us, the greater the need for it to operate amid a blaze of publicity and criticism (Bernard Crick 1970 [1964]: preface and p. 12).

There is no single manner in which different countries have been organising the relationship between the legislature and the executive. Although the broad pattern of instituting some separation is apparent in all democracies, the degree of it differs. Unfortunately... we tend to think that the models adopted by Britain, the US and the Netherlands are the only constitutional models which we could conceivably draw from. Yes it is true that in these countries members of the executive do not have shared claim to being members of the legislature. They either resign from those positions, or they never belonged to the legislature. However, for example in the German system, this is not the case. Dual roles of belonging to the Executive and the Legislature are common and it is equally feasible to draw from such examples (Geraldine Fraser-Moleketi, South African Minister for Public Service and Administration, 'Speakers Debate on the Role of the Speaker in Parliament', June 2001).

Like reports of Mark Twain's death, pronouncements about the demise of parliament are not only premature and exaggerated but often mistaken. Those idealists who believe parliament has fallen into decline often look to a 'golden age' of parliament usually dated sometime in the nineteenth century, before the arrival of universal suffrage and the rise of disciplined political parties (Marsh

1995). The reasons for the decline can vary, but, for the idealists, parliament has lost its vibrancy and relevance, and is badly in need of reform (Crick 1970).[1] Yet, such notions that Westminster parliaments are in inevitable decline largely miss the point. They are nostalgic, based on normative notions of open and deliberative legislatures believed to have existed in some mythical age.

As Uhr and Wanna (2000: 11) argue, parliament is evolving and constantly adapting to the pressures it faces. They suggest our 'understanding of parliament would be improved if we adopted a broader idea of "the parliament" and recognised the multi-layered roles performed in and around the institution'. Parliament is better seen as a 'theatre of action' involving a wide variety of actors (not just the elected representatives) who interact around political issues. Understood in this way, 'parliament is an exciting, seething throng of activity, shadowed by uncertainty, out of which political possibilities are continually being framed and reframed' (2000: 12). Especially when the media and other interested actors are included in the parliamentary spectacle, the idea of parliament becomes more vibrant and dynamic. It is not a monumental building housing formalized debates, but a fluid space open to various political actors to engage with the politics of the day (pass laws and make pronouncements, question, lobby, prosecute their cases, answer or explain occurrences). The media's grilling of a minister at a press conference may constitute a far more effective form of scrutiny than the formality of Question Time allows in the legislative chamber, and if the minister 'misleads' the media, the sanctions are likely to be adverse publicity. This understanding of a more complex set of parliamentary-related activities, which we adopt in this chapter, reconnects and reinforces the importance of parliamentary practice to executive politics and ministerial responsibility. It is not a zero-sum game in which parliament 'declines' relative to the executive, but is contingent on political circumstance.

Among our former dominions, the modern-day Union of South Africa has experimented with not one but three distinct parliamentary systems over the past thirty years. Each variant kept some important continuities and resonances with past legacies but each was based on fundamentally different racial conceptions of representation and the associated transitional politics from apartheid and black exclusion to universal inclusion and the movement towards a 'non-racial' 'democratic and open society' (Preamble, The Constitution of the Republic of South Africa, 1996).

From the time when the 'hardline Boers' in the National Party took over the South African state in 1948, the Union's links with the UK (and its political traditions) were progressively weakened while domestic apartheid policies classifying and excluding people based on race became stronger. A new constitution was enacted in 1961 and the unicameral National

Assembly was formed and elected only by whites (excluding Cape 'coloureds' who had voted since 1910). The white unicameral system remained until a revised constitution was unveiled in 1983. Then, from 1984 to 1994, South Africa experimented with a 'Tricameral Parliament' consisting of three separate but unequal chambers representing whites, Indians, and coloureds, respectively. The principal white National Assembly was the supreme legislature, with the other two able to have a say on 'general' government policies and debate issues relevant to their 'own race'. The tricameral model was implemented to offer limited political concessions to some racial minorities while still excluding the majority black population.

After the 'unbanning' of the African National Congress (ANC) in 1991, a third parliamentary system was adopted. After the democratic interim constitution of 1993, a democratically elected National Assembly was elected in 1994 representing all South African citizens over 18 years old. With the 1996 Constitution, the 'post-liberation' National Assembly was deliberately inclusive and formally elected 'to represent the people and to ensure government by the people' (Chapter 4, section 42.3). Following German practice, the Assembly was elected according to a bifurcated or double list system contested by the various parties, with half the MPs coming from the national lists and half from regional lists nominated by the party machines. To ensure adequate regional (and tribal) representation, alongside adult suffrage, this third parliamentary model again drew on German experience and introduced a bicameral structure with an upper chamber called the National Council of Provinces (NCP). The NCP consisted of 10 delegates from each of the 9 provinces and from local government, each comprising a mixture of 'special' appointed delegates and elected representatives. They were selected to represent the interests of their respective provinces.

The South African case is the least similar of all our Westminster-derived systems. It reminds us graphically that full representative democracy is a late characteristic of Westminster, dating back a little over a century at most and a mere decade in South Africa. It also reminds us there is enormous variety in the ways representative democracy is practised in the institutions of parliamentary democracy across these Westminster systems. Full adult suffrage was partially and begrudgingly adopted as representation was gradually extended. Until recently, there were significant gender, racial, and age exclusions. Gradually, women initially, younger adults and, significantly, indigenous peoples in the colonies were enfranchised. In this trajectory of widening democracy, Britain alone preserved customary 'elite notions' of governance where the government through parliament could decide to abolish or suspend elections, an event that last occurred between 1940 and 1945. In short, Westminster parliaments embraced waves of representation, keeping some older traditions of government but changing the ways politics and the relations between core institutions were conducted.

This chapter explores the challenges and dilemmas facing parliaments understood through this wider lens, especially the relations with their executives, and their changing patterns of representation. We pose the following five questions:

1. What are the limits of parliament, and if parliaments are not sovereign and cannot exert control over the executive, what do they do?
2. How does parliament sustain government while containing the politics of the executive?
3. To what extent is the idea of an 'alternative government' or loyal opposition important to political practice and understanding of traditions?
4. How are parliaments made up and how do they combine forms of representation?
5. How has territory been formally and practically incorporated or 'written' into these polities and how does this affect what the executive can do?

In brief, our arguments are that although parliaments have been shaped by party discipline and had their unqualified sovereignty challenged by rival sources of power, they remain central to responsible and representative government in Westminster, and have been periodically strengthened to better reflect societal expectations. This sets up a tension explored in this chapter, which we discuss under the themes of 'elective dictatorship' versus 'theatre of action'. Within this tension, parliaments remain a crucial institution in the web of political institutions shaping responsible government.

Beliefs about 'parliamentary sovereignty' remain strong and have important effects, and though many key actors admit there are limits to sovereignty, there is no 'elective dictatorship'. Forming a centralized and unified executive still relies heavily on the constant control of parliament and parliamentary agendas. Disorderly legislatures can weaken the executive and undermine the government's credibility. Sometimes this disorder can be a problem; for example, when the government's own back bench becomes unruly, or it faces a strident opposition, or exists in minority government. However, the executive has to manage the legislature through the prism of its own party or parties, ceding greater influence to party factions and brokers rather than to parliament. The legitimacy of the political opposition, ostensibly an alternative executive enjoying representation and a platform in parliament, has gradually become more institutionalized (Maddox 1991: chapter 2). Equally, there is increased controversy about the notion of a 'loyal opposition' in some jurisdictions. The electoral and party composition of parliaments also affects the nature of the executive and legislative–executive relations. There are effects on: the composition of the executive, the beliefs and practices of parliamentarians, and the politics of representation. Finally, the ways in which political structures are geographical and territorially organized in these nation states is a major constraint on executive autonomy.

THE LIMITS OF PARLIAMENTARY SOVEREIGNTY TODAY

Although parliamentarians and constitutional experts following Dicey have embroidered notions of parliamentary sovereignty, these beliefs are more usefully interpreted as a political myth. It provides a continuing cloak for actors and a rationale for behaviour. However, although supposedly sovereign, parliaments face real constraints and limits on their powers. Parliaments cannot 'call themselves' to assemble but rely on the executive to convene or reconvene them and to resume sessions. Parliaments are dependent on the executive for their funding and resources. They may nominally 'vote' their own budgets but do not themselves determine their resource allocations. Parliaments often take no part in external affairs, such as declarations of war or foreign affairs, although there has been a growing demand for a convention in recent years to call for votes supporting military or peacekeeping expeditions. International agreements and constitutional duties also place constraints on sovereign parliaments.

Parliamentarians often complain bitterly when they feel this normative sense of 'sovereignty' is being eroded by international agreements, suprastate membership commitments, and rulings from constitutional courts. British parliamentarians have complained over edicts from the European Union that challenged sovereignty. Australian parliamentarians in a federal system have criticized national legislative initiatives because such proposed legislation often prohibits local amendment and cedes subsequent amendments to the national government eroding the individual sovereignty of subnational parliaments.

In Britain, the notion of parliamentary sovereignty can be suspended or 'broken' by political expediency, which can in turn create new precedents. These decisions are in the hands of the executive ratified by the legislature. Elections for the House of Commons were suspended by parliament during the First and Second World Wars. A coalition National Government was formed to govern Britain in May 1940. Outside Canada, this convenience was not replicated in the other Westminster systems with written constitutions.[2] The minority Callaghan Labour government of the 1970s lost several votes in parliament without bringing down the government or causing the prime minister to think the legality of his government was in doubt. In the future, the *Act of Settlement* could be amended allowing a Catholic to succeed to the throne. Such examples illustrate that the British constitution is pliable and can mean what the prime minister wants it to mean and encompass any action with which they can credibly get away.

The situation is similar in New Zealand. Although some basic attributes of the political system are codified in statute, such as a single House of Representatives and three-year non-fixed parliamentary terms, the main understood principles of government remain political conventions. Before introducing MMP,[3] and to address popular concerns that majoritarian governments were unresponsive to the electorate, both a bill of rights (1990) and a citizen-initiated referenda initiative (1993) were adopted. Characteristically, the latter is non-binding on the executive and legislature. But the Constitution, which frames the formal political institutions, is complicated by the representative structures and identity politics of the Maori people flowing from the Treaty of Waitangi. Known as the 'Maori Magna Carta', the Waitangi treaty has been the object of rival interpretations and changing pressures as the Maori people have expressed their identity and desire for some degree of community self-government. According to a New Zealand Cabinet Office briefing note (2004: 3), the main impact of the treaty is twofold: 'balancing the respective interests' and 'expressing an ongoing relationship' between the Crown and Maori. More recently, the tectonic shift to replace first-past-the-post voting with MMP has fundamentally changed the way almost all political institutions in New Zealand work.

The entrenched written constitutions in Australia, Canada, and South Africa limit what parliament can do. Parliaments in these three cases cannot amend their own constitution without securing popular endorsement (by national referendum requiring 'double majorities' in Australia) or by federal and provincial legislative assent (Canada and South Africa).[4] Canada requires the support of both federal houses and two-thirds of the provinces representing at least 50 per cent of the national electorate. South Africa has also constrained legislative sovereignty by requiring that changes to the constitution must receive 75 per cent support in the Assembly and two-thirds of the provinces (six out of nine).

Formal constitutions further challenge notions of sovereignty by requiring judicial interpretation and rulings on the legality of legislation or executive actions. As a consequence, constitutional courts and judicial decisions frequently determine the latitude granted to executive governments in these jurisdictions. This judicial oversight has contributed significantly to the juridicalizing of politics itself.

When constitutional challenges are made in Australia, the High Court can determine what each tier of government is empowered to do. It can also rule on aspects of the political system such as citizens' implied rights and, more recently, 'native title' for some indigenous peoples. Although judges in the High Court and in other tribunals refrained from making legalistic determinations on the practice of politics (the so-called hidden constitution in Australia), they are often called on to define the scope of ministerial or Crown prerogative and cabinet's authority. Judges rather than politicians have 'read into' the largely institutional constitution a series of implied citizen rights, such as the right of free speech and the right to vote, which are not enumerated in the Constitution itself.

Although federal governments (but not the 'sovereign' parliaments of the states) can legislate to put referenda questions seeking to change the constitution, they have largely refrained from doing so, principally because they have been historically rebuffed by a sceptical electorate. The 'founding fathers' of Australia intentionally erected one of the toughest referendum tests in the democratic world precisely to curb executive excess through the federal parliament. In 108 years of Federation only 44 questions have been put on 19 occasions or about one referendum in every two parliamentary terms. Since the Second World War only three referenda have been successful (social services, recognition of Aborigines for the census and public policy purposes, and casual Senate vacancies). After an extensive constitutional review in the mid-1980s, four innocuous questions were put to the Australian people and all were handsomely defeated.[5] Since then there has been almost no debate over amending the constitution, although a heavily constrained question on Australia becoming a republic was put and lost in 1999. Federal politicians are conscious of the difficulties of changing the constitution and the inevitability of their motives being misunderstood. The Australian republic referendum was defeated by two equal sets of opposing voices: those favouring an elected head of state and those seeking to preserve the monarchy. These forces came together to defeat the proposed parliamentary republic model. The executive finds it more expedient to evade the Constitution by using its superior resources, trade-offs, agreed transfers of power, and occasional reinterpretations of its powers from the High Court (Hollander and Patapan 2007).

The South African Constitutional Court ruled in 1996 on whether the wording in the proposed Constitution, drawn up by the government of national unity and the constitutional assembly, was consistent with the 34 guiding principles laid down in the interim constitutional negotiations by representatives of the different parties and races. The parliament had to accept several amendments to the document before it was promulgated in December 1996.

Across all five countries, two separate and parallel debates emerged about how the system works or should work: one from judges and lawyers and the other from politicians and political scientists. Judges and constitutional lawyers describe the system mainly in legal terms from a 'rights perspective' as if there were no accepted traditions or operating political institutions, such as cabinet, the prime minister, or political parties. Constitutional scholars claim authoritative status for their opinions which are usually juridical and doctrinal. They quote judicial interpretations of the constitution and adopt these as precedents and as the basis of legal opinions. Political conventions can often be dispensed with or sidelined when challenged with legal questions of individual rights. Ever wary of tyranny, their opinions often seek to curtail state power for protecting individuals, but not necessarily collective or substantive rights. So, Sir Anthony Mason, the then Chief Justice of the High Court of Australia, ventured:

> Our evolving concept of the democratic process is moving beyond an exclusive emphasis on parliamentary sovereignty and majority will. It embraces a notion of responsible government which respects the fundamental rights and dignity of the individual and calls for the observance of procedural fairness in matters affecting the individual. The proper function of the courts is to protect and safeguard this vision of the democratic process (Mason 1987: 163).

Notice his conception of 'responsible government' as meaning a government behaving responsibly to the people and to individuals, not the political studies meaning of an executive responsible to parliament for its actions. Words mean different things in the lawyers' lexicon.

By contrast, political actors concentrate on the workings of real power within amorphous constitutional limits, on the power of the executive and its control of parliament. They are concerned principally with the 'elected dictatorship' arguments and how political institutions achieve desired outcomes by getting around, reinterpreting, or ignoring constitutional constraints. Yet, in our countries when the law and conventions collide, the law, not parliament, usually takes precedence. So, for example, the Australian Governor-General legally sacked a legitimately elected prime minister in 1975 under the Constitution, despite votes of confidence from the lower house of parliament. Politicians have come to realize that constitutions have real bite.

Moreover, in these federations the central government cannot abolish the subnational governments or change their formal powers. This limit is markedly different from the UK's granting of home rule to Scotland, Wales, and Northern Ireland. In Britain, subordinate governments are created by the 'sovereign parliament' and, even though elected, could in theory be abolished, as have many local and regional governments over the years. Subnational executives in the UK enjoy their latitude to govern at the eventual discretion of the national government. This situation is not the case in formal federal (or union) compacts, where often the national parliament was created by the subnational units, which agreed to cede certain powers to the centre.

SUSTAINING THE EXECUTIVE

Conventionally, parliament has four main groups of functions: confidence and legitimation; law-making; conflict and conflict resolution; and scrutiny (Norton 2005: 9; see also Uhr and Wanna 2000: 10–17). Confidence and legitimation refers to the ability to govern and make legitimate decisions. Law-making refers to passing bills by steering them through their various parliamentary stages and committees. Conflict resolution refers not to the opposition but mainly to the executive and its back-benchers and the need to manage the party to sustain confidence. Scrutiny encompasses such activities as Question Time and the investigations of parliamentary committees. For ministers and departments, the key functions fall in the scrutiny category but we need to explore all these functions briefly.

Confidence and Legitimacy

The primary historical role of parliament, from the days before adult suffrage to mass democracy and the rise of disciplined, cartelized parties, is to form and sustain governments with 'confidence'. Lower houses express majority support for the ministry of the day. In New Zealand, it is a case of the lower house not expressing majority opposition. Lower houses thus provide legitimacy to executive action. In the nineteenth and early twentieth centuries, confidence issues in the legislature were more pronounced, especially with 'ministerialist governments' before disciplined parties arrived. However, 'confidence' remains relevant to present-day representatives even if elections rather than confidence decide the survival of governments.

Confidence today is not an instrument of accountability used to bring down or reconfigure 'failed' ministries. Rather, it is a strategic calculation in government ranks about their confidence in their present leadership and their estimation of their chances of winning the next election. In many ways, parliamentary 'confidence' is now about both the *leadership of the government* and the *leadership of the opposition*. So, debates in the major parties have displaced formal parliamentary debates in the respective chamber as the influence on the executive (but cf. Crick 1970: 5–6). Parliaments can be accused pejoratively of degenerating into point-scoring. But this, surely, is what they do best; mutual needling to probe and test the prevailing political constellations. And the main audiences are the media and the various party actors on the front and back benches who, in turn, then listen to the various reconstructions of the media.

Parliament is perceived as a particular theatre of action by its participants. So, parliamentary debates have become rehearsed theatre, where adversarial protagonists line up against one another and perform to bolster their own party support (and that of the leadership) and shore up their own political credibility. By contrast, internal party deliberations can be more robust and brutal. These internal party debates occur in closed party or caucus meetings, between party members, through the party whips or factions, and through media comments and presentations by key players. This aspect is not necessarily evidence of parliamentary 'degeneration', as some critics might suppose (see Cowley 2005; Norton 2005). Rather, it reflects a marked shift in the balance of public versus private deliberation caused by the changing nature of parliamentary politics under the influence of disciplined parties.

The institutional essence of the Westminster system is the peculiar relationship of the parliament to the executive. The political balance in the parliament determines *who* can form and hold government. The selection of MPs is largely in party hands, although their grip over these candidates is likely to weaken once they become elected. The political balance also determines *how* long a party can govern whether as a single majority party, a minority government, a multiparty government, or in coalition. The maximum parliamentary term (ranging from three to five years) limits *how long* the executive can expect to survive provided it does not implode or lose the confidence of the legislature. In all five of our nations, parliamentary terms can be foreshortened for political expediency. With five-year terms, the president of South Africa can dissolve the Assembly at any time after it has served three years with a majority vote of the chamber; or an acting president can do so when the presidency is vacant and the Assembly is unable to elect a replacement. The date of the election can be decided by the president but only after consultation with the Electoral Commission. In the UK, Canada, Australia, and New Zealand, prime ministers can foreshorten terms at their own discretion (by advising the head of state, who by convention accedes to the advice). These discretionary powers remain a legacy of the historical asymmetry in power of the government *over* the parliament. It is a power used often and to political effect. Only South Africa has chosen to use fixed terms for its legislature (five years with the election date of 27 April – a symbolic date on which the first non-racial election was held in 1994).

Parliaments therefore serve as political sites of spectacle and protection. They provide high degrees of certainty and reliability for the governing majority and allow some oversight and scrutiny. Majoritarian parliaments provide both the means of support for most of the government's legislation and shield ministers from accountability (see Chapter 5).

Support for Law-Making

Westminster governments normally assume their important legislation will pass parliament. The exception occurs when there is an elected upper house hostile to the government, as can happen with the Australian Senate, which has veto power over all legislation. However, the executive still has to gain the agreement of the party over the need for the legislation and support for the main provisions. Each piece of legislation is a potential quasi-test of confidence in the executive by its own party supporters. It is sometimes called the 'trinitarian struggle' – the battle for dominance and influence between the executive and the members of the upper and lower houses (see Reid 1973). The executive, as Reid (1973: 515), a former parliamentary official, has argued:

> may dominate the Senate less than the House, or *vice versa*; but in every case it has to *fight* for its dominance; it has to make deals, trade benefits for support, and sanctions for neglect, with all manner of individuals and factions. All of this makes a real difference.

Reid also talked about the conspiracy of the front benches against their own back bench to secure latitude for executive action. It is a conspiracy to avoid scrutiny in which the shadow front bench may collude. For example, the front benches of both sides may find it convenient to limit transparency, to limit resources to back-benchers, and to refuse to allow advisers to appear before parliamentary committees.

There are various mechanisms through which back-benchers can express their views to the executive on bills before parliament. Vocal party dissidents on the government's side have far greater ability to win concessions in proposed legislation than the formal opposition parties. The latter usually have to resort to moving formal amendments in the chambers, which are often defeated by government numbers. The government's back bench believes it ought to be taken seriously and can exert much informal, internal influence. It is expressed at regular party meetings, or party policy committees, occasional delegations to ministers, and informal meetings with party leaders or their staff (Cowley 2005). For example, Australian back-benchers talk of the party room needing to endorse policy proposals.

Conflicts and Conflict Resolution

On many occasions, party discord can lead to internal groups or factions orchestrating to discredit, bring down, and remove their leader or a targeted minister. In the most extreme case, individual MPs have the power to vote against their own government or to quit the party and serve as an independent. Often the mere threat is sufficient to win concessions or influence outcomes. Crossing the floor in parliamentary votes remains one of the most extreme forms of public disobedience. It is practised rarely.[6] The main exception is majority party revolts in the UK commonly on policy principles. Cowley (2005) and Norton (2005) have charted back-bench revolts and exercises of dissent in the UK. The equivalent books in Australia, Canada, New Zealand, and South Africa would be slim.

Hence, the executive cannot unilaterally impose its iron will over its own support base. On the contrary, the executive's links with its parliamentary support base are crucial, especially those with the influential opinion-leaders in the party. In smaller polities, such as New Zealand and Australia, prime ministers usually meet with their entire back bench every sitting week and are answerable to the meeting. The practice is well established in Labor administrations but it is also found in conservative governments. Attendance is considered compulsory and these meetings discuss in some detail parliamentary schedules and legislative programmes. In the larger jurisdictions, meetings between the leadership and the full back-bench representation are less frequent and less formal. Yet, prime ministers (or the president in South Africa) cannot ignore the party room for long. Whether they do it in person or through ministers and whips, factional heads, or advisers, they must align their decisions or actions with the parliamentary party. In both Australia and New Zealand, the party room both elects and can remove the leader (by a single vote and without much notice), giving it not only influential power in policy matters but an immediate execution power as well. Parties operate as 'sounding boards' prone to internal rumination, regularly debating and assessing the standing of leaders and occasionally expressing mutterings of dissent. In the UK and Canada, the power of execution is less immediate, although prime ministers remain aware of the need to keep party support, as Chrétien, Martin, Thatcher, and Blair have all found to their cost (see Chapter 4). In these jurisdictions, the demise of prime ministers is usually protracted. So, prime ministers who are being deposed serve out their final months as caretakers until their successor assumes office. South African presidents enjoy securer tenures, and can be removed from office only under exceptional circumstances; for example, illegality, misconduct, and inability to perform the functions. However, as Mbeki found, his party can still rebel and publicly force a president to resign.

Scrutiny

If parliament's evolving role in forming and sustaining the executive remains strong, its other important roles of holding the executive to account and scrutinizing the actions or inactions of the executive have declined over time. Arguably, scrutiny of the executive was the parliament's primary role three centuries ago, but it has now become of secondary importance to the institution. Politicians talk of the difficulties the legislature has in holding governments to account. They complain about the secrecy and lack of transparency overlaying much of the executive's decision-making, the difficulties in getting useful information on policy outcomes, ministers' reluctance to 'answer' questions in Question Time, and spin taking precedence over substance. Because the legislature is on the receiving end of the executive's largesse for meaningful information, the list of woes is endless and the pattern of complaints repeats as governments and oppositions change places. As one Australian minister said about a 'question without notice': 'if I give you the answer to that question, you will know as much as me, so I'm not telling you'. Paul Keating created controversy in his second term by announcing that he would only attend Question Time twice a week. A tradition of attending and answering questions was considered important and Keating's bluff a violation. How far the executive prevaricates and rations information depends on what it considers it can get away with at different times.

Yet, institutional conventions associated with parliament's customary scrutiny function still remain and have effect. In shielding the ministry from accountability, legislatures still expect ministers to attend, be answerable, and to rebuff attacks from opponents and the media. This expectation enables the party room as a whole to evaluate continually its confidence in the performance of ministerial colleagues. Assessments of how well a ministry is performing in the eyes of the back bench are perhaps the most arduous test of the political performance of government. As many ministers have said: 'the opposition is in front of you, the enemy is behind you', meaning the significant opposition comes from the government's own back bench (Daly 1977, but also attributed to John Boyd–Carpenter). The caucus and party room has a continual interest in scrutinizing government performance and refreshing ministries periodically. Renewal of the ministry, involving reshuffles and promotions to better positions, enables the government to

deal with policy or political problems. Such renewals are of continual importance to the party room and for the survival of the government.

All parliamentary debates are stage-managed to a certain extent. In South
Africa, where there is a desire to 'build an African parliament', timed debates
have become sequential speeches essentially non-adversarial and aspirational
(Hahndiek 2006). Speeches are delivered by a list of different party representatives given time according to their party's share of representation in the
Assembly. They are short and formalistic urging unity while citing specific
grievances or issues of concern. In these 'debates' it is not uncommon for
speakers to have just one or two minutes on the central podium. In one
typical debate on social policy about a 'better and safer world for the future of
our children', 14 speakers shared the allotted 71 minutes agreed by the whips.
While the minister and ANC speakers received 52 minutes in total, seven
speakers from smaller parties were granted one minute each. In another
budget debate on the transport departmental vote, the whips had agreed
145 minutes for the speeches while 18 speakers had elected to participate.
The minister received 40 minutes in two blocks of time, but nine speakers
were given two minutes each, and a further three received between six and
eight minutes.

Although these debates do raise criticisms of government policy and implementation, protocol is important. Non-government members feel it necessary
to say 'yes this is going well, but...We have to be seen to be questioning
progress rather than doing a straight-out tackle' (Delport 2006). The main
game for the ANC remains to protect ministers in the formal debates while
suggesting constructive criticism. Ministers are expected to provide disarming
public explanations for poor performance, usually listening and responding to
criticism by apologizing and undertaking to address administrative problems.
Denied deniability, ministers admit *mea culpa* and promise to do better in
future. Their immediate standing rests on their credibility with the cabinet and
rank and file.

It is behind the scenes that parliaments are often considered effective by
practitioners and commentators alike. Much of parliament's scrutiny function
is performed not in the main chambers, but in standing and select parliamentary committees. Cross-party parliamentary committees provide a site for
more formal back-bench scrutiny. In recent decades, they have increasingly
expanded their investigative mandates and policy coverage as well as their
powers to have public servants appear and take questions under oath.

Committee deliberations have two principal functions. First, it is a forum
for debate of the merits of proposed legislation, raising issues, and allowing
the executive to 'revise and resubmit' their legislative proposals. Second, it
legitimizes executive business to multiple audiences: to the parliament as a

whole; to the party caucus and membership; to the media and interest groups; and to the community (Norton 1981). Especially with contentious legislation, committee deliberations and reports are integral to the politics of sustaining government.

Ministers are not normally members of such committees (but in rare instances can be in New Zealand), although shadow ministers as an apprenticed executive can be more active participants on them. Occasionally, committee investigations, such as the UK investigation into Iraq and the 'sexed up' Ministry of Defence claims that it had weapons of mass destruction, or the Australian Senate inquiry into 'children overboard', have held a blowtorch to the executive by exercising the inherent parliamentary powers of investigation and inquiry (SSCCMI 2002). These celebrated forms of committee scrutiny may not be an everyday occurrence but are at the same time not rarities; they find voice when the political landscape permits.

So, contrary to the dominant narrative, Westminster parliaments are not in decline. In the largest parliament, the UK, party revolts against the executive are common but do not necessarily bring down governments. For example, Jim Callaghan faced a series of Labour revolts against his economic and domestic policies. John Major confronted revolts against the Tories' European policy. Tony Blair survived mass revolts over the Iraq war, student fees, the education bill, and sometimes managed to pass his legislation only because the opposition supported it. With such a large governing party back bench relative to the opposition parties, British majority parliamentarians enjoy the luxury of being able to afford to entertain such rebellious votes of consciousness.

South Africa has an equally large governing majority with the ANC holding 279 seats or 70 per cent compared to its closest oppositional rival (50 seats). It has not witnessed mass parliamentary revolts, but its muscles have occasionally been flexed against the executive, most spectacularly in the election of Jacob Zuma to the ANC leadership in December 2007. Even where conventions are still being shaped, most of the serious scrutiny of executive business takes place in the open committee stages of the South African parliament. These committees meet regularly, sitting up to 100 days a year. They are large, with mainly voluntary membership (attracting up to 15–20 members), and anything up to 20 committees can be meeting on any one sitting-day, although 6–10 are more normal. They are often led by non-government members. They are technocratic and forensic in orientation and conciliatory in tone. Many make a significant contribution to government legislation. As well as these influential multiparty committees, the provincial-based upper house, the NCP, comprising premiers and a combination of appointed 'special' and 'permanent' delegates from provincial legislatures, ensures regional and implementation issues are addressed with some vigour.

In smaller parliaments, party members do not have the liberty to 'rebel' by crossing the floor so adopt other means to express their dissent. In Australia, Canada, and New Zealand voting is solid and controlled by rigid party discipline. There is no tradition of government back-benchers voting against the executive in large numbers (although individuals may occasionally dissent).

Australian government back-benchers expect to debate the prime minister sometimes robustly in the sanctity of the party room. Such discussions are not perfunctory. Press releases or announcements of policy changes are frequently made after such meetings. Often the media are briefed on both the debate and the outcome of the meeting, enabling them to cover the event in detail. If such party-wide meetings fail to win concessions, then separate delegations of concerned MPs can meet with the PM privately to seek resolution. In Canada, in periods of minority government (led respectively by Joe Clark, Pierre Trudeau, Paul Martin, and Steve Harper), the executive has been forced to work through parliamentary networks and smaller opposition parties. Parliament is effective as a deliberative body under these conditions, and indeed, the fragmented nature of Canadian party politics across the provinces is likely to make minority government a recurring phenomenon, even 'a permanent condition' (Aucoin 2006). Some governments have been spectacularly ousted from office (in 1979 and again in 2005).

The strongest arguments for parliament's decline emerged in New Zealand in the 1970s when 'inflated' majority governments of both persuasions rammed through less than popular legislation and seemed impervious to defeat at the ballot box. To redress this executive dominance, New Zealand embarked into a 'brave new world' of multiparty parliaments elected under an MMP system designed to empower voters and stymie executive dominance. The irony here was that the electoral commission set up principally to defuse the issue recommended the German-inspired MMP option which, despite the opposition of both major parties, was successfully passed on a referendum in 1993. This electoral reform has subsequently adopted at the composition of parliament for a long time to come, with six to eight parties now common in the House of Representatives. Minority government or coalition arrangements are probably a permanent state under the new election laws. MMP provides existing MPs with incentives to fragment existing parties to gain representation or ministerial appointments, such as the shifting alignments of the Maori MP Winston Peters, or to form new parties to attract disillusioned voters, for example the United Future Party. To date, the changed composition of parliament has not had much impact on the composition of the executive, as minority governments have been preferred to wider formal coalitions. Dissidents such as John Anderton or Winston Peters can be incorporated into ministries,[7] but minority governments have tended to look to support from 'supporting parties' or 'contributing parties' rather than seek full coalition partners. The formation of governments has been long and drawn out sometimes with unpredictable alliances. Within a parliamentary term, most party representatives have considerable latitude to express divergent views and exert influence even on budgetary legislation. New Zealand now has significantly compromised the 'financial initiative' power of the Crown. In her third term as prime minister leading a variety of minority Labour governments (most not formal coalitions), Helen Clark said, 'we have worked well with other parties and been prepared to share power' but she saw it as 'mushy work' (Helen Clark, *The Standard*, 25 April 2006).

FUNCTIONS OF THE UPPER HOUSE

Governments are not formed in upper houses, although their members may usually join governments and become ministers. These second chambers have multiple roles ranging from augmenting diversity of representation and providing more robust deliberation, to imposing veto-points on the legislative process, and providing a set of checks and balances over executive decision-making (Uhr 2006). As upper chambers they scrutinize, monitor, and investigate the policies and behaviour of the executive. As legislative chambers with their own powers and legitimacy, they review, reflect on, and attempt to revise legislation (Shell 2007). Their members are subject to different pressures from those applying to the lower house executive, such as longer parliamentary terms or the lack of individual constituencies. They are also usually elected or selected by different means, representing regions, states, or expertise and experience.

Different political traditions have emerged in dealing with the legacies of bicameralism historically based on estates of the realm. Both New Zealand and the UK adopted the stance of abolition or disempowerment, respectively. New Zealand's upper chamber (the Legislative Council) gradually drifted into irrelevance over the first half of the twentieth century and was abolished in 1950 (Mulgan 2004: 62). Despite claims that the unicameral system fostered 'unbridled power', there have been no serious attempts to re-establish the second chamber, and suggestions to reinstate one were not widely shared or supported in the electoral reviews of the 1980s and 1990s. New Zealand explicitly chose to remain unicameral but to make the single chamber more widely representative. The UK has chosen since 1909–10 to fuse both houses, by gradually removing the obstructionist and review functions from the House of Lords. Yet despite the removal of many of its formal powers, it still remains a review chamber and potentially obstructionist house. Mooted reforms for the 'democratization' of the chamber under Blair were never clear-cut. In office, with other pressing priorities, the zeal for reform gradually dissipated, fuelled by concerns about dual mandates if a largely elected Lords was introduced. As in Canada with its appointed upper house, UK governments have preferred to retain the power to appoint its preferred candidates to the Lords.

Governing traditions in Canada have meant the governing elite was not motivated to seek the abolition of the appointed Senate because of regional sensitivities and historical bargains over the proportion of seats. Rather, governments have circumscribed its role and influence, until it is relatively powerless as an upper chamber. It enjoys only partial roles in budgetary approval. Prime ministers have reserved to themselves the right to make appointments to the chamber, so they are able to 'stack the bases'. As with the British House of Lords, there have been serious attendance problems with some senators previously residing overseas. This situation has led to serious campaigns advocating the reform of the Senate. For instance, the Conservative opposition led by Stephen Harper adopted the '3 Es' (elected, equal, and effective) and included it in its platform for the 2006 election. However, as a new minority government, it chose not to act on these proposals. The prospects for Senate reform in Canada remain dogged by problems because of the historical compromises among provinces with four equal divisions of 24 seats each to Quebec and Ontario, 24 to the Maritime Provinces, and 24 to the now more populous Western provinces. Canada as a nation cannot reopen the debate on Senate reform without riding the maelstrom of territorial traditions and provincialism. Any proposed changes would encounter the wrath of Quebec and the smaller but 'over-represented' Maritime provinces and raise the issue of whether native peoples and other minorities should be represented.

Both the Australian Senate and the new South African Council of Provinces are uniquely federalist and regionalist institutions. Both combine provincial representation into parliament on conditions other than equal democratic representation across the nation. The Australian Senate is directly elected. The South Africa Council of Provinces is partly appointed, partly indirectly elected, according to party representation in the provincial legislature. Both can veto proposed government legislation, and cause the executive grief. But there are differences in their leverage and influence over the executive and its preferences.

The South African upper house is able to block ordinary legislation bills seeking to amend the constitution and other bills affecting the provinces. Different majorities are required for constitutional and provincial issues.

There is also a 'beholden' problem. Provincial premiers, who head the provincial delegation and often have the sole vote on bills, are appointed by the president. There have been claims that these premiers act as beholden to the president and acquiesce over proposed legislation. Provinces and some of the non-government parties have already complained that provincial interests have become subordinate to national intentions, and called for greater direct electoral input to provincial delegations to the NCP.

The Australian Senate is an explicitly federal institution, made up of territorially elected representatives on a modified proportional representation basis. It is an intentionally, that is constitutionally, powerful house, with almost equal powers to the House of Representatives. It has over time increasingly sought to overrule or challenge the executive of the day. Its members have a tendency to seek to embarrass the government by holding selectively targeted inquiries and going on fishing expeditions for potential scandals. The government often cannot control the Senate, so many of its procedures are different from and more powerful than those of the lower house, and senators of all persuasions have more scope to review executive decisions. Senators fiercely defend their prerogative to interrogate government, due in no small part to their independence from the lower house executive. With forensic analysis and questioning, they have used estimates inquiries and functional (policy) committees to good effect, a feature often recognized by public servants commanded to appear before them (Thomas 2009). When the Australian government does not hold a majority in the upper house and relies on minor parties and independents, these senators are able to extract concessions from the executive in exchange for their necessary votes in support of legislation. As a result, the Australian Senate has become the most powerful upper house in the Westminster stable. It has unrivalled importance in its influence over legislation, and has emerged as the stronger of the two houses for executive scrutiny (APSA 1976; Bach 2003).

Australia's Federation debates made clear this balance of power was deliberate. Competing notions of political design and constitutional law were interwoven into the federal compact. Notions of territorial consent ('state approval') and majority rule ('popular approval') run almost equally through the two dimensions of responsible government: executive and legislative action. Quick and Garran (1901: 706) argued that

> the State should not be forced to support Executive policy and Executive acts merely because ministers enjoyed the confidence of the popular Chamber; that the State House [Senate] would be justified in withdrawing its support from a ministry of whose policy and executive acts it disapproved; that the State House could, as effectually as the primary

Chamber, enforce its want of confidence by refusing to provide the necessary supplies... On these grounds it is contended that the introduction of
the Cabinet system of Responsible Government into a Federation, in which
the relations of two branches of the legislature, having equal and coordinate authority, are quite different from those existing in a single
autonomous State, is repugnant to the spirit and intention of a scheme of
Federal Government. In the end it is predicted that either Responsible
Government will kill the Federation and change it into a unified State, or
the Federation will kill Responsible Government and substitute a new form
of Executive more compatible with the Federal theory.

These beliefs meant that the principal role for the 'popular' lower chamber in
responsible government was to form the legitimate government on its numbers
alone. It does not join with whatever Senate numbers the governing parties
might control, even though Senators were always invited to become ministers in
the government established by the Representatives. The Representatives also had
to initiate money bills but these bills had still to pass the Senate before they
became law. However, there was no requirement that the popular chamber had
to be the one that initiated other legislation. Unlike the House of Lords or the
Canadian Senate, the Australian Senate can and does initiate 'backdoor' legislative proposals. So bills are introduced first into the upper chamber to test
whether they have sufficient political support in that chamber before they go to
the lower house. Backdoor legislation can also depend on whether the minister
responsible for the proposed legislation is a minister in the Senate.

A 'LOYAL' OPPOSITION

Westminster traditions expect parliamentary oppositions to materialize. With
plurality voting and two-party systems, oppositions emerge from the losers of
the last general election, and there is no debate about this status. The
Westminster system is unique among political systems in that it seeks to
establish within itself a permanent role for a political 'opposition', based on
historical and hierarchical notions framing the executive's relations with the
constitutional monarch. The monarch has to be given options or an alternative administration in case the incumbents lose favour or confidence.
Oppositions are legitimate elements of the system. Practitioners talk of the
'Loyal Opposition' or 'Her Majesty's Most Loyal Opposition', although in
Canada 'Official Opposition' is preferred. The title and role mean they are
loyal to the regime, are available and ready to govern, and have formed an
executive in waiting, but will in the meantime provide political opposition or

policy alternatives to the present government. Such inbuilt adversarial politics ensure there is a continual 'debate' on the government's performance, on policy options or alternative ideas, and that these alternative views can be widely canvassed. Even if many opposition parties often resort to bickering and constant niggling, it remains the case that public criticism of government is legitimate and expected.

The existence of a formal opposition, with 'opponents' participating in the system of government, reflects a commitment to the customs, institutions, and processes of responsible government. Opposition groupings choose to work *through* the system, learning its norms and conventions, and accepting the outcomes of elections and parliamentary votes. The opposition serves to stabilize the system.

Governments are expected to have learnt how to oppose before they are ready to form government. Notions of political apprenticeship underpin responsible government. Oppositional politicians 'learn the ropes', serve time in responsible positions, and collectively develop a track record to put before the electorate, all of which serve as a form of political indenture. Conventionally, shadow ministries will mirror the portfolios announced by government with a close 'fit' between the responsibilities of ministers and the equivalent shadow spokesperson in the opposition. This mirroring reinforces and institutionalizes a specific one-on-one adversarialism of opposing actors and views. Indeed, in Canada, opposition spokespeople are referred to as 'critics', as in the 'Finance critic' or 'Foreign Affairs critic'; their role is signified in their titles. South Africa alone does not operate with a formalized shadow minister system although some party spokespeople have begun to specialize in particular issues.

Oppositions enjoy formal status within parliament and with the media and wider polity (Maddox 1991). Oppositions will vigorously defend and complain if there is any encroachment on their status. Britain formally identified a Leader of the Opposition from 1807 although in the early days the post was often based in the House of Lords. Only after 1896 did it conventionally reside in the Commons. Canada followed suit in 1869, although in the early years the post was occasionally left vacant. The Australian opposition has been recognized since federation in 1901, with the position of Leader of the Opposition acknowledged in the first national parliament and continuing since then. Interestingly, when the non-Labor parties are in opposition they almost always form a coalition opposition with members of both the Liberal and National parties represented in the shadow ministry. New Zealand identified a Leader of the Opposition between 1889 and 1891 and then again continuously since 1903 with only a few short interludes where the position was vacant. Non-governing parties in post-apartheid South Africa have used the term only since 1999.

In all countries in our study except South Africa, the status, legitimacy, and political standing of the opposition have increased over the twentieth century, underscoring its potential and actual role in the political process. To enable them to 'challenge' and criticize governments, oppositions have gradually acquired important and tangible political advantages. Opposition politicians enjoy paid employment. They receive MPs' salaries and additional salaries for particular positions such as the leaders, whips, or committee chairs. They also have the privileges and rights of parliament and taxpayer-funded financial resources. Examples include election funding, and funding as 'recognized parties' for such items as offices, staff, travel, cars, IT and communication and equipment, and library and research facilities. These benefits allow them to perform their duties more effectively. As a measure of standing, the salary of opposition leaders and their deputies has steadily risen and been pegged against the senior ranks of the ministry. However, there is usually no separate budget for the opposition in parliament from which it might commission independent research. Party funds can provide for such endeavours, and public funds can be made available to allied think-tanks and the research arms of oppositional parties.

As alternative governments, oppositions are fully institutionalized into the policy process through both their ready access to the media for alternative comment, and substantive involvement in key parts of the deliberative and legislative processes of government and parliament. Routinely and without controversy, the opposition is given equal time in parliamentary debates, in Question Time, media coverage of politics, and publicly funded election broadcasts (or party political broadcasts). They are represented at most state functions and commemorations. Oppositions can often establish parliamentary committees (select committees and other investigatory inquiries) and guide their conduct and deliberations, and lodge minority reports on their findings if they choose. Opposition members chair important committees in the UK, such as the public accounts committee, and in New Zealand roughly one-half of the committees now have non-government chairs. In Australia, the opposition is routinely nominated as the deputy chair of committees, but before 2005, opposition politicians chaired parallel 'policy' committees of the Senate, which had notable investigatory powers. Britain alone conducts an independent vote for the speaker. Australia, Canada, New Zealand, and now South Africa have rarely entertained the notion that an opposition member should be in charge of the legislature. Even in the Australian Senate, by convention, the government nominates one of its own members as president even when it does not have a majority of senators. Significantly, oppositions can call on other officials to investigate issues of concern on their behalf. For instance, they can request the auditor-general to investigate a matter involving public resources on compliance, corruption, or performance audit grounds. They can also appeal to ombudsmen, and information or privacy commissioners and, if necessary, the police. If auditors-general are requested to investigate a matter by the opposition they would normally comply with this request as part of the annual schedule of investigations negotiated with the public accounts committee.

The standing of the opposition is also surrounded by formal provisions and conventions; for example, caretaker provisions; equal time with the media; rights to public advertising; administrative briefings from public servants; and red and blue books for incoming governments. Public servants can also brief shadow ministers at their request with the permission of the respective minister. Senior officials will brief parliamentary committees on which the opposition sits, informing them of policy issues and relevant factual material so they can better prepare alternative policy positions. They can also brief party policy committees subject to certain guidelines. The opposition leadership is regularly briefed on matters of national security, military deployment, or foreign affairs; that is, core affairs of state which are not usually the subject of partisan politics. Before elections, the public service produces two separate sets of incoming briefs for whomsoever will form the new government. There is a blue book for conservative parties and a red book for Labor. In caretaker periods, the opposition is formally taken seriously as a viable alternative government with equivalent rights and respect (Tiernan and Menzies 2007).

But oppositions do not automatically materialize and their identity can be a problem. Although Westminster systems are expected to have an opposition, in practice they are contingent. Weak oppositions themselves can become subject of political debate and controversy. Although their basic legitimacy to exist may not be questioned, there may be debate on whether a given opposition is effective and fit to govern; whether it can perform 'as an opposition'. Critics will argue whether it has the appropriate leadership and assembled a shadow team of recognized competence. Often the sternest critics of the opposition's leadership come from within the ranks of the opposition itself (not only from dissidents but also from rival leaders). Prime ministers often face a string of opposition leaders throughout their terms (Blair faced four, Chrétien eight, Howard four, and Clark has faced four). Leaders of the opposition face the 'most difficult job in politics', testing their ability to lead, their mettle, their ability to cut through, and their skill in matching the prime minister in standing and credibility. Against this, there is also the notion shared by many opposition politicians that opposition is perpetual purgatory, a fantasyland, or a 'make-believe' world where nothing tangible flows from any decision. Speaking from years of acrimonious oppositional experience, former Australian Prime Minister John Howard reiterated this point.[8] He said that being in government when there is a 'considerable build-up of people of ability' is 'a nice situation to have. It's better than the alternative and that is you engage in make-believe government in opposition and not the real thing' (Howard 2006).

Some Westminster systems have found it difficult to settle on an agreed opposition. For instance, in New Zealand there has been much debate post-MMP about what constitutes 'an opposition' and whether it ought to be a single entity or pluralist multiparty composite or rotating responsibility. Although New Zealand has persisted with the tradition of identifying and labelling the largest non-government party as the 'opposition', its status has been challenged by other non-governing parties who wish to share the oppositional advantages. Given the legacy of adversarial parliamentary politics, it is of strategic advantage to be the party to lead the debate against the government and to put 'the alternative view'. Lesser parties would receive lesser prominence and attention to their proposals. To date, there has been no agreement among the non-governing parties in Wellington to cooperate as a single opposition. So, in a departure from conventional notions of Westminster, New Zealand may be evolving closer towards a continental European system where coalitional governments are opposed by a diverse array of non-governing parties but without an official opposition. In Clark's third term, the National Party opposition under John Key pulled itself together and increased its standing in opinion polls, so debate about the standing of the opposition waned. But in the future, if non-governing parties are fragmented or about equal size, the debate will surely be reignited.

In Canada, there are three reasons why oppositions can be a problem. First, the Liberals are arguably the only national party that can attract votes across the nation, and as a result enjoy a hegemonic status. Even when they are in opposition, there is no other rival party that can dispute their claim to legitimacy. Against Liberal governments, there is often a fractured array of regional parties not a solidified opposition. Second, there have been times when there was no effective parliamentary opposition. In 1993, the defeated Progressive Conservative party was reduced to just two members in the Commons, and the separatist Bloc Quebecois (with 54 seats) was forced to assume the leadership of the opposition. For three years, a bifurcated opposition was in place with the Bloc occupying the position in the lower house but without representation in the upper house. The Progressive Conservatives formed the opposition in the Senate. With the western Reform Party (with 52 seats) entering parliament at the 1993 election, the antagonistic oppositional parties refused to work together, fractured by political persuasion and geographic representation. Third, when the Bloc Quebecois became the largest non-governing party in parliament, it rejected the title and role of performing the 'loyal opposition'.[9] Between October 1993 and June 1997, the Bloc led the critique of the government in the lower house only but was never likely to be an alternative government. Arguably, this parliamentary 'imbalance' had an effect on executive practice with the Liberals believing they could not be defeated.

South Africa has little tradition of legitimate opposition politics. In the pre-apartheid era, oppositional parties were either discredited and sidelined or outlawed and repressed by the police state. So far, as a transformational regime, the new South African parliament has not settled on the concept of an opposition, and as a former clerk of parliament stated, 'we don't use the term opposition any more in parliament' (Hahndiek 2006). Some smaller non-government parties have toyed with the idea of calling themselves the 'Official Opposition', but interestingly do not use the term 'loyal opposition'. Since 1999, the small Democratic Alliance (with 50 seats) has labelled itself the 'official opposition' on business cards and has had a sign made for its party room. The other parties in parliament do not recognize this title and the ANC expressly rejects the view there is an official opposition or an alternative government in waiting. The standing of Democratic Alliance's claim is further clouded because its present leader, Ms Helen Zille, is not a member of parliament but, since 2007, the elected mayor of Cape Town.

In the present circumstances, it is unclear how far the South African opposition can oppose the executive. The ANC expects 'unity of purpose' across the legislature. It rejects dissenting voices, but listens to constructive criticism. One opposition spokesperson admitted, in the period of transition 'the best role for the opposition is to sit still and say nothing'. Indeed, an interesting ruling to the Assembly was made by the first speaker, Ms Frene Ginwala:

> The procedures and conventions of the parliament are not a series of petty rules designed to impress the uninitiated by complexity. The rules of a parliament besides providing for law-making and oversight of the executive and regulating our debates, serve another, often unspoken, function. That function is a subtle and sensitive one, always important, but in a young democracy such as ours whose wounds of conflict are not yet healed, its importance is crucial. That function is to ensure that the reconciliation among groups which was the great miracle achieved in 1994, our founding year, becomes a strong and enduring relationship with a joint commitment among all political parties to recognise the legitimacy of other parties and to accord to them the dignity, respect and tolerance to which they are entitled. It implies that differences are expressed and resolved by reasoned debate, not by shouting one another down. It implies that, no matter how little one likes what the other has to

say, one shows the respect to listen to what he or she has to say. It is important to bear in mind that each member here speaks for thousands of his or her fellow citizens (21 September 1998, *Annotated Digest of Rulings 1994–99*, National Assembly).

REPRESENTATION OF WHOM?

In Westminster jurisdictions, the legislature determines the composition of the executive. With few opportunities to augment the executive from external sources, the composition of the legislature is fundamental to representation in the ministry. To be a member of the executive, one must be a member of the legislature. While the UK, Canada, and South Africa can technically appoint ministers from outside parliament (and have), they are usually either appointed to the upper house or the party quickly finds a suitable by-election for them to contest, or they are incorporated into the national list. Canada has a strong tradition of including a minister from every province in cabinet, and if the governing party is not represented in that province then a senator from the province is usually appointed. South Africa's constitution allows the president to appoint up to two ministers and two deputy ministers from outside the Assembly, but they are then accountable to the full parliament. In New Zealand and Australia, ministers have to come from parliament, although initially as a transitional measure the Australian Constitution allows an appointed minister three months to take up a position in parliament. This provision has been used only once (in 1968) since the first parliament.

Representation in parliament has three principal effects. First, it predetermines *who* can be considered for executive positions. Second, it requires that, as members of the executive, ministers will spend much time participating in and preparing for the business of the legislature. Third, party representation has curtailed Burkean notions of representative independence, substituting disciplined party voting in parliament. MPs and upper house parliamentarians largely see themselves now as representing *party* interests.

Westminster traditionally relied on two forms of representation: social estates and constituency-based representation. These forms were once regarded as mutually exclusive, although the separations have become more blurred over time. They were bastardized in Canada where the prime minister appoints senators. All five jurisdictions have widened the franchise. Adult suffrage now extends to women, the young, and various indigenous groupings. They also have increasingly addressed the issue of the proportion of women represented in the main political institutions, with various affirmative action policies to encourage participation and improve the gender balances. Three countries have had one female prime minister, while New Zealand has had two. With significant indigenous minorities, Australia and New Zealand (but not Canada) have had lengthy discussions about the rights and forms of indigenous representation, although only New Zealand has a fixed proportion of indigenous representation in parliament.

The UK and Canada retained plurality voting, relying on first-past-the-post voting in individual single-member constituencies with large numbers of seats to fill (646 in the UK and 308 in Canada). In the UK, with sharp socio-economic cleavages, this election system produced a stable, adversarial party system with parties enjoying geographical regions of significant support. In Canada, the election system has produced the reverse, leading to claims the system is 'too competitive' (Lovink 1979). It has produced a volatile and fragmented party system susceptible to minority governments but still distinguished by adversarial politics. While Canadian parties are disciplined, they are prone to the provincial control of party machines, and there is a tradition of parachuting experienced candidates in at the centre (e.g. party leaders, heads of business, and public servants). Parties are closely associated with leadership personalities and, in refreshing leadership, parties can resort to acknowledged non-parliamentary identities. In both these countries, while an MP's primary loyalty will be to the party that has put them there, there is a strong constituency loyalty nevertheless that often causes MPs to take a stand against party policy.

Australia after much experimentation has settled on a hybrid electoral system based on majoritarian and regionalist principles, relying on compulsory voting with constituency representation in the lower house and a territorial form of quasi-proportional representation in the Senate. Voting for the lower house (with 150 seats) is by the alternative voting method (or preferential voting, see Farrell and McAllister 2006), meaning the least disliked candidates win seats and reinforcing the degree to which party cartelization prevails. For the elected upper house, voting is by quasi-proportional representation using the single transferable vote, but since amendments in 1984 the voting system comprises a party list system in each state and territory. Unlike Canada, the Australian hybrid electoral system has produced a remarkably stable party system with integrated parties across the nation. Party loyalists predominate in the two chambers (and in the state legislatures) and most MPs have served some apprenticeship time working their way up through the party before pre-selection. Factions control seats, territories, and pre-selection voting. There is little resort to celebrity candidates or to local branch determinations of their preferred candidates. It is machine politics, but it is under challenge.

The two major outliers in representative politics are New Zealand and South Africa. Because of their recent electoral and constitutional crises, both have adopted list-based forms of proportional representation voting systems for their lower houses, and have multiparty legislatures. South Africa relies exclusively on a dual list proportional system with no formal constituency base for its 400 elected representatives, although informal but weak constituency links are encouraged where members reside. Half the Assembly (200 seats) is elected from a national set of lists submitted by the parties, and the other half from nine provincial sets of lists allocated according to the population size of each provincial region. The lists are 'closed', meaning voters cannot change the order given or vote for one candidate above another; they have to accept the party's rank ordering. This system enshrines party control over listed MPs (and potential candidates) and makes MPs cautious of bucking the system or falling out of favour with the party elite. The ANC, with about 70 per cent of the Assembly seats, has used the list system to recruit and reward an older generation of 'party stalwarts' who were selected mainly because of their local record in the struggle against apartheid. These ANC stalwarts come to parliament as a cheer squad, not intending to engage in debates across the chamber. They sit under the side eaves of the chamber exchanging memories and reminiscing. More activist individual members of the assembly complain that parliamentary politics are dominated by contending party blocs rather than by constituency politics.

New Zealand has now adopted a three-pronged hybrid electoral system, in which voters each have two valid votes to cast. Voters on the general electoral roll can vote for local candidates in one of 63 constituencies and have a separate vote in a national list system and they can switch preferences. There is also a separate Maori roll, and registered indigenous voters are able to vote in the national lists and for their own Maori candidates in seven Maori seats. The number of Maori seats fluctuates slightly depending on the proportion of Maori registration. Around 58 per cent of the 121 MPs have retained a constituency base and win the seat on a plurality basis while the remainder owe their seat to their ranking on national party lists. Parties with constituency members can also gain additional representation or a 'top-up' of seats according to how well they performed in the national vote relative to their representation gained from the constituency vote. Parties without a single constituency member require 5 per cent of the list vote to qualify for a seat in parliament. Because minority governments are now almost inevitable, cabinets have been constructed with ministers from other parties and with non-cabinet ministers from within the parliament. Helen Clark has relied on a Labour dissident, Jim Anderton, and the conservative Maori populist, Winston Peters, at various times during her three terms of office.

CENTRE–PERIPHERY DYNAMICS

One of the most enduring arguments about the Westminster system is that it entrenches a centralist, unitary polity that tolerates no other competing sources of authority. It institutionalizes the tyranny of the centre. We suggest that Westminster is a myth which assumes power, is centralized, and unitary. Behind the screen in our Westminster systems, political power is likely to be either federal, devolved, or deconcentrated on regional grounds. If we take our argument to the extreme, we can entertain the proposition that even in the small territory unitary systems, such as the UK or New Zealand, power is also disaggregated even though the term 'federal' is not used to describe the system. Such disaggregation has real consequences for the political authority of the centre. Some choices still reside with the central executive and national parliament, but others do not. Subnational structures create various 'no go' areas for the central executive where other policy preferences have to be recognized.

In Australia, Canada, and South Africa, centralized power has been circumscribed. Government power is constitutionally disaggregated and the national level government has only limited capacity to impose its own priorities domestically (and legally must attach its decisions to a 'head of power' in the Constitution). While Australia has become one of the more centralized federations in world, as a territorial polity it is riven with inter-jurisdictional politicking. There is constant negotiation and renegotiation with states and territories as the Commonwealth seeks to exert policy influence or gain compliance for its policies. The federal government frequently uses the power of the purse to try to impose its views where it cannot do so constitutionally. States have an incentive to accept such funds but not necessarily to comply dutifully with federal preferences. Over time, the consequence of this division of powers has led to accusations of reduced accountability, reduced transparency, lower than expected performance, and heightened blame shifting. In the post-NPM era, cooperation and coordination difficulties have generated an administrative discourse of 'service delivery across jurisdictional boundaries': effect in networked governance based on service delivery (Rhodes 1997), a concept recognized by governments as well (see ANZSOG 2008). Also there has been an increase in 'national' policy frameworks which are jointly agreed between central and subnational governments but where the implementation 'power' remains held at lower levels.

Canada is even more disaggregated than Australia and the central government has only weak capacities to intervene domestically. Provinces are able to opt in or opt out of federal policy initiatives (for example, pensions, taxes, and policing). There is a far higher tolerance of difference and diversity. Outside a few nation state responsibilities, such as foreign affairs and defence, policy responsibilities are concurrent, shared, or lie with the provinces, which hold the enumerated powers under the Constitution. Canadian federalism en-shrines decentralized competiton between centres of legitimate political power, with the province of Quebec being the most disarticulated. Empirically, there are many policy areas in which the provinces elect not to cooperate with national or central agendas or policy proposals.

By contrast, the South African Constitution lists 48 powers held concur-rently between the national and provincial governments and 35 powers that are exclusively provincial or local. There are few exclusive powers exercised by the National Assembly but it can amend the Constitution if sufficient prov-inces agree. National governments can also intervene in provincial matters in order to maintain 'national security', 'economic unity', 'maintain essential national standards' or 'minimum standards', or 'prevent unreasonable action taken by a province which is prejudicial to the interests of another province or to the country as a whole' (section 44(2)(a)–(e)). Like the German Länder, these provinces exercise considerable direct influence over what the national executive can do, not only as legitimate subnational governments but also through their instrumental role on the NCP.

Britain has established three regional assemblies each elected according to a system of proportional representation rather than first-past-the-post voting. This feature represents a significant break with electoral traditions. Subnational regional assemblies will encourage the establishment and institutionalization of minor parties at the regional level, which can affect national party representa-tion. Both internally with Scotland, Wales, and Northern Ireland, and externally through its membership of the European Union, Britain may be closer to a federal state than its practitioners in Westminster recognize. Moreover, even within England, policy can be much more disaggregated than the conventional wisdom acknowledges. Powerful individual ministers and their departments exercise considerable autonomy, while regional and local authorities retain their own discretion in geographically discrete areas. In policy sectors such as educa-tion, health, and transport, powerful policy networks operate with which national governments have to negotiate and to which they must cede power. So, although Britain has retained a complacent discourse of a strong executive rule, in practice such a strong executive may not exist in domestic public policy.

CONCLUSIONS

I would ask leave to say that for every man who has taken part in the noble conflicts of parliamentary life, the chiefest ambition of all ambitions, whether in the majority or in the minority, must be to stand well with the House of Commons (Sir William Harcourt, former Leader of the House of Commons, 24 June 1895, cited in Morrison 1964: 182).

Contrary to the decline of parliament thesis, we have described a diversification of practice. Some parliaments have abolished or neutered upper houses. Others have not. Some remain adversarial, others more consensual. Some accept revolts on the floor, others do not. Some create minority governments, in others the executive is majoritarian, and in both cases the executive claims dominance. Most have added layers of codification to their constitutions, but most have found ways around the spirit of these codes. There are debates about how parliament should interact with the powerful executives that sit in their midst. We do not see a single response, nor do we see quiescent institutions. Executives have to work, consult, and cajole to keep their legislative majorities. Oppositions can make life difficult, wound ministers, make a case, or change the terms of debate, even if they cannot win a vote on the floor of the house. Territorial representation creates pressure to negotiate, to consider the regional impact of government policies. Conventions remain robust and powerful. These 'theatres of action' are taken seriously by participants. The ministers know their reputation depends on their performance. The opposition realizes its future does too. If parliament has declined so much, why would they worry? But they do.

Responses have ranged across the spectrum. New Zealand moved the furthest. Once the most quiescent of parliaments, its new electoral system has enforced the need to negotiate all legislation, to permit greatest scrutiny. The UK and Canada, with partly tamed upper houses, muddle through, uncertain of where governments will meet networks of opposition. Territory and history may shape the conventions. Nowhere have they made parliament irrelevant. For all the rhetoric of an 'elected dictatorship', the executive cannot ignore the 'theatres of action' that are the parliaments.

NOTES

1 Although Bernard Crick wrote nostalgically about the fundamental decline of parliament, he nevertheless warned: 'it is neither relevant nor helpful to recall or invent some golden age when Parliament "really did" govern the country, or when independent and encyclopaedic back-benchers "really did" make Ministers tremble. Even if the facts were ever so, it is not a sensible intellectual method to compare everything in terms of a falling off from some ideal image of the past' (1970: 3).

2 Canada only allows parliamentary terms under the Constitution to be extended in times of war or insurrection provided no more than one-third of members oppose it.

3 New Zealand's mixed member proportional system combines an individual constituency member form of election with a national proportional 'list' party top-up
   system. In addition, seven Maori seats (individual constituencies overlaid nationally
   across the general electorates) preserve distinct Maori representation elected by
   Maori registered in a separate electoral roll.

4 Double majorities in Australian referenda consist of an overall national majority
   plus a majority in a majority of the states (at least four of the six). In Canada,
   constitutional amendments do not apply to provinces whose legislatures express
   dissent towards (do not pass) the proposed amendment.

5 The referenda questions sought to introduce consistent four-year terms for both
   houses of parliament, fair elections, recognition of local government, and some
   limited rights and freedoms. All failed to secure a majority of votes and win a
   majority of states.

6 For Australian data, see 'Crossing the Floor in the Federal Parliament 1950–2004',
   Research Note No. 11, Australian Parliamentary Library 2005/6.

7 John Anderton was a rebel left Labour MP who quit Labour and established his own
   Progressive Party, subsequently becoming Deputy PM in the first Clark government
   and continuing to hold ministerial positions in her subsequent governments.
   Winston Peters became the 'most obvious contemporary populist' in New Zealand
   politics (Gustafson 2006). He began as a National Party member (1978–81 and
   1984–93, losing his seat in the early 1980s), before becoming an Independent MP in
   1993. He then led the New Zealand First Party (1993–2005) before accepting the job
   of Foreign Affairs minister in the third Clark government in 2005. Peters was not
   afraid to play racial politics, claiming New Zealanders were becoming 'serfs in our
   own country' (Gustafson 2006: 64). Former Prime Minister David Lange called
   Peters a 'political opportunist' who is wont to undertake 'extraordinary pirouettes
   in the spotlight' (Lange 1992: 129).

8 After election to parliament in 1974, John Howard initially spent one year as a back-
   bencher in opposition in 1974–5, followed by seven years in government as a
   minister, then thirteen years in opposition, mostly on the front bench (1983–96),
   serving twice as leader, followed by eleven and a half years in government as prime
   minister.

9 A similar situation occurred in 1920 in the Irish Free State when Sinn Fein refused to
   become the loyal opposition and swear the oath of allegiance (Keith 1928: xxi).

8

The Meanings of Westminster

I wonder if we could contrive...some magnificent myth that would in itself carry conviction to our whole community (Plato, *The Republic*, book 3, line 414).

MYTHOLOGY, n. The body of a primitive people's beliefs concerning its origin, early history, heroes, deities and so forth, as distinguished from the true accounts which it invents later (Bierce 2001 [1967]: 229).

Myths which are believed in tend to become true (Orwell 1970b [1944]: 21).

The Westminster system can mean anything you want it to mean (A mythical Canberra adage attributed to Sir Geoffrey Yeend, secretary of the Department of the Prime Minister and Cabinet, Australia, 1978–86).

Westminster systems have responded in many ways to present-day dilemmas. Sometimes, they react to common challenges and on other occasions they seek to meet local or unique demands. Their responses both diverge and follow the same path. So, we return to those dilemmas we identified in Chapter 3 as the core for discussing Westminster. For convenience, we reproduce Table 8.1, our summary of the common challenges and the shared debates. As a first step, we unpack these debates.

WHERE THE WESTMINSTER DEBATES STAND

In the debates on presidentialization, we argued that the presidential analogy distracts from the varying ways that prime ministers exercise the levers of power. There is clear evidence prime ministers have sought to centralize policy-making but they were restrained by the governmental traditions they inherited, by the organizational context, and by their own capacities. The shape of power is changing. The court politics in each country create their own imperatives. But there is nothing as distinct as a 'trend' towards greater centralization, only a pendulum swinging between differing degrees of centralization and decentralization. The prime ministers' powers are contingent, interdependent, and variable. They may be the most powerful, but they are

Table 8.1. Traditions and dilemmas in executive government

Institutions	Traditions	Dilemmas	Debates
Prime minister and cabinet	Royal prerogative	Centralization vs. decentralization	Presidentialization
Ministers	Responsible government	Party government vs. ministerial responsibility	The smoking gun
Public service	Constitutional bureaucracy	Professionalization vs. politicization	Politicization and managerialism
Parliament	Representative government	Elitism vs. participation	Elective dictatorship vs. theatre of action

not as all-powerful as some accounts propose. They cannot do everything and must rely on their ministers and officials as part of not just cabinet but also the core executive and on other governments, subnational and supranational.

When discussing ministerial responsibility there was the common theme of the smoking gun. Ministers rarely if ever resign for the administrative failures of their departments. It is more likely to happen because of their sexual and financial peccadilloes, and then only if stalked by the media tiger. The unwritten conventions of the early days have been eroded, but to still the clamour for accountability and transparency, we now have guidelines or codes of conduct. Ministers, ministerial staff, and public servants all have their own codes that explain how they should behave. Their publication, often initially reluctant, speaks not of a belief in transparency but of a need to fill the void of conventions invoked only at prime ministerial convenience. Once it was argued that only those who governed needed to know how it was done and they could be trusted to behave well, a view usually asserted on anecdotal rather than systematic evidence. Nowadays, in a media-saturated environment, ministers live in a goldfish bowl where their every word and action is potentially subject to scrutiny. The codes offer a measure of protection. They were published and amended, often from one prime minister to the next. However, the application of the rules remains with the prime ministers. In all systems they are the prime ministers' rules. They decide what they are, alter what they want, and act as judge and executioner. Ministerial responsibility, even with public codes, is a political calculation of personal and governmental advantage. Party interest trumps individual responsibility.

Public services have faced the challenges of increasing their responsiveness while reforming their professionalism to encompass management. Ministers have become better educated and more demanding; media scrutiny is more intensive. Responses have varied; there are common trends but distinct responses. In Britain and Canada, ministers have continued to be distanced from the process of appointment of senior officers and the incidence of terminations of contracts of departmental secretaries is few, although they can be reassigned by the prime ministers. In New Zealand, appointments remain the prerogative of a professional commission, but the demands from ministers and the process of assessment are more direct. In Australia, secretaries of departments can be dismissed at the prime minister's pleasure. That need not make them politically partisan; it may make them all the more aware of the political environment. The Antipodes have moved further and faster than their northern counterparts in making senior public servants more directly accountable and vulnerable and in introducing managerialism. South Africa is still further away from original norms; it expects its public servants to be committed to the ANC while bringing professional expertise to the table. Yet all stress the sense of continuity, the ability of traditional interpretations of their role to incorporate and embrace the new. Westminster is a defence and a justification against intrusive ministers and their call for responsiveness and better management. And, again, as conventions are eroded or amended, as public servants feel vulnerable, so the common response is to promulgate codes.

Parliaments in all countries are not moribund, providing automatic majorities for an elective dictatorship. They are best seen as a 'theatre of action' performing the key functions of law-making (for example, taking a bill through its committee stages); conflict resolution (for example, managing the majority party), and scrutiny (for example, Question Time and the investigations of select committees). In every case the executive predominates as long as it can keep a majority in the lower house. In historical terms, governments are rarely defeated on the floor but that does not mean they can take support for granted. Leaders need the back-benchers and take time and effort ensuring their continuing support. How can the members participate in governing and ensure that it is not entirely dominated by the elites of the core executives? The parliamentary response varies from country to country as members of parliament develop their own means to get their voices heard. In Britain they use early day motions or prepare to cross the floor. In Australia and New Zealand they use the privacy of the party room as a frank forum for a hearing. Some chambers, such as the South African Assembly, take parliamentary committees seriously in the oversight of government; others less so. Institutional design creates opportunities. Parliaments are a terrain across which members can roam. Each provides its members with ways of ensuring they are not taken for granted.

How can we explain these variations? Each country's experience is an amalgam of inheritance, myth, and local tradition. The commonality of the myths is clear. Meeting a scholar or practitioner from another Westminster system is like meeting long-lost cousins. They are eerily familiar yet different; it is an extended family of ideas. We recognize the language, the form, and the assumptions. We can have an easy conversation. But when it comes to detailed applications the practices have moved on from the time they were transplanted; they have to react to specific local challenges. They are shaped by local traditions that mutate from year to year.

There is no other way it could have worked. Institutions cannot be static. Even the British have substantially changed their constitutional architecture in the last decade. As we suggest in the opening to this chapter, on some aspects the former dominions have stayed close together, adopting similar strategies to meet the challenges they face. In other cases they have diverged; it may have been caused by the size of the parliament, the divisions within the society, or the choices of leaders. They must look to the future but will be constrained and shaped by the enduring myths of their past.

BENEFITS OF THE WESTMINSTER MYTHS

Westminster has been relegated to the rubbish dump of history by many an academic, but it refuses to be confined there. They believe the terms 'Westminster model' or 'Westminster system' are outmoded. With ponderous certainty, scholars from across our dominions will assert that their system of government 'is not Westminster' or 'not now Westminster'. They are convinced the system they are examining has long since departed from any basic Westminster principles or a stylized model and that their institutional arrangements have developed their own unique or local traditions. Political systems are defined in different terms: the 'Ottawa model', the 'Washminster mutation', the 'African parliament', or some similar term. The modern polity no longer deserves to be defined as Westminster; the term has lost its analytical rigour.

If the test of Westminster is whether any country (including Britain) fits a prescribed set of institutional characteristics, somehow frozen in the second half of the nineteenth century, the critics have a point, though a trivial one. All countries have changed; all have developed their institutions and traditions in ways that were shaped by local circumstances and the behaviour of actors. The critics' argument rests on the fallacy of ideal–typical comparison, and assumes a historical standard against which comparison can be made. They miss the point.

While academics may bemoan the use of the term, in one form or other it continues to thrive. It is used by prime ministers and leaders of the opposition, by frustrated back-benchers and senior public servants; by judges and constitutional lawyers. References often occur in commissions of inquiry and in newspaper editorials. If they all continue to use the term and regard it as useful, as part of the political dialogue, then the issue for us is not whether they are right or wrong, but why they do so. It is of minor concern whether the term is still used fruitfully by other academics.

Given its regular interment, why does the concept of a Westminster system have such resilience and remain so robust? Its continuance in good currency and the failure of academics to bury the term may be a comment on the irrelevance of academic debate: Who else cares about definitional purity and how they describe the system of government? It also raises the broader question: Why do so many practitioners find it useful as a foundational concept, whether used as a defence or as a justification? The concept of a Westminster system works well for them; we need to understand that utility and longevity. We need to ask why it has survived when it may be near devoid of meaning and where so little agreement exists about what it entails.

We have taken these challenges seriously in this book by seeking to show how different traditions have shaped a common Westminster heritage across five nations. In those places the concept of Westminster still has utility precisely because it is not confined or prescriptive. It satisfies several governmental purposes because its flexibility allows different interpretations and uses. Only if the concept were dead might it be possible to agree on a single interpretation. Because it is alive and useful, because it is common currency, its meanings will always be debated, as part of a vigorous political tradition in each of the countries that we have sought to analyse.

So, we seek here not to define the term in any way that could be regarded as definitive or beyond question. Nor will we try to develop a set of institutions that can be established as an ideal model, against which the degrees of deviance can be calculated for each country, as we depicted in Chapter 1. Both exercises are possible but in our view rather sterile. Rather, we seek to explore the ways the terms have been developed and used by practitioners. That requires us to bring together, not one, but several, meanings of Westminster; not one category of interpretation but several, used by parts of the political system for their own purposes. We collect them here under five general headings, each with their own sub-themes.

- Westminster as inheritance – elite actors' shared governmental narrative understood as both precedents and nostalgia.
- Westminster as political tool – the expedient cloak worn by governments and politicians to defend themselves and criticize opponents.

- Westminster as legitimizing tradition – it provides legitimacy and a context for elite actions, serving as a point of reference to navigate this uncertain world.
- Westminster as institutional category – it remains a useful descriptor of a loose family of governments with shared origins and characteristics.
- Westminster as an effective political system – it is a more effective and efficient political system than consensual parliamentary governments.

WESTMINSTER AS NARRATIVE

As a Common Heritage

Westminster countries are part of a family of nations with a common though differentiated heritage. If these countries were to ask how they arrived at the system they have constructed, then the response would start with the formative influences of Britain. Their government is British in origin, parliamentary in form, responsible and representative in spirit. But it is a family of nations, not a flock of Dolly clones. As children from birth display their own characteristics and grow with their own individuality, so nations are from the beginning different and will develop their own processes and mores. Children will, their parents hope, become independent and self-supporting, but they remain part of the family. Parents, too, will grow old and stately, retiring from the business of further procreation, and looking most unlike the vigorous young adult that begot the young nations a century or more ago. Their interests will change. They too remain part of the family.

It does not matter 'how British' the family of nations now is. It does not even matter whether Britain itself fits some original conception of what Westminster government might mean. How 'British' these nations *are* is less important than how 'British' they once *were*. To understand their political traditions they still of necessity need to combine an understanding of their British legacy with a proximate understanding of how they have amended this according to local conditions and ideas.

Although there is a recognizable British heritage, we cannot study only Britain to comprehend how such systems work. University courses in politics no longer start, as they once did in Australia, with a year on British history as a necessary foundation for understanding the way that politics work in the former dominions. Nevertheless analyses of many of the specific processes of government often refer to British experience, to *Magna Carta* and the *Bill of Rights* of 1689, to parliament and doctrines of ministerial responsibility.

Collective responsibility refers more often *to* Lord Melbourne than to practice *in* Melbourne.

In the present-day, the picture of politics found in each place may be unique, but the historical links remain. Politicians from one Westminster system will often ask whether something is done differently or better in another. There are accepted contours and likenesses. They still have so much tradition in common that they do not need to translate everything to suit local conditions. We know what we see and we appreciate the value of a common heritage. The political systems are more alike than different.

As Precedent

Those common histories are reflected in the precedents they have created. They may be as basic as the members of parliament organized in adversarial seating; to the presence of the mace as a symbol of royal power; to the existence of the Speaker (long departed from its original concept) whether with or without a wig; to the rules of procedure bound in *Erskine May*, and to motions of no confidence. Parliaments in our five Westminster systems are all recognizably similar and work in similar ways. Other precedents can include the principle of a cabinet and some form of 'collective cabinet government', whether that is more rhetoric than reality. These transplanted precedents were accepted without much debate by the newly self-governing colonies and have since been moulded to suit local conditions. The centrality of representation for political sustainability was also accepted as a core precedent, and all our former dominions initially adopted single-member, plurality voting at departure. Some, then, went much further than London in extending the franchise, institutionalizing democracy, or opting for proportionality.

Not only is there a strong likeness across these precedents, but there is also a deliberate awareness that it should remain so, now and into the future. Inter-parliamentary unions and parliamentary delegations keep the connections alive. This is not merely about recalibrating to existing British traditions, rather there is a sense that in the collective Westminster family there are principles and practices that are relevant and transferable to the other members of that family.

As Nostalgic Nirvana

There is a view in some quarters that 'once there was Westminster', and now there is only a pale shadow of that ideal and perfect form of government. But when was that era? Most do not specify any dates for this nirvana, although there is a soft spot for the 'glorious years' between the two major electoral *Reform Bills* (1832 and 1867) of the nineteenth century. Westminster is seen as that era when politicians were principled, where unconstrained debate could examine each piece of legislation on its merits, where the executive behaved itself and kept parliament fully informed, where spin was unknown, and eventually where elections were fairly fought on principle. It is a heady brew, a seductive myth, but one that finds resonances in each jurisdiction we studied.

Nostalgia has the advantage of imprecision; the belief that the standard of politics was better some time in the past may provide solace to those who see only disappointment and distaste in the modern process. Lack of historical detail is an advantage; the myth is sustainable only as long as the advocate knows nothing about that period. For of course there is no evidence there ever was such a 'golden age', except in the frustrated mind of the dreamer. In Britain, during the First World War, Lloyd George invented his own advisory group in the 'Garden Suburb' and ran a personalized government. Canada's Prime Minister John A. Macdonald (1867–73 and 1878–91) was an expert in patronage and pork-barrelling. Colonial politics in Australia were rugged, ruthless, sometimes corrupt, and always as cynical and self-serving as anything today. New Zealand's longest-serving prime minister, Richard Seddon (1893–1906), was nicknamed 'King Dick' for running government as a one-man band, holding personally up to seven portfolios and advocating the abolition of cabinet. He too engaged in patronage and nepotism, but is remembered most of all for his pioneering welfare reforms.

In those times, the levers of power may have been less refined; the rules containing behaviour less complex. The ways prime ministers could impose their authority may have been more personal. But these times saw some dictatorial governments that brooked no opposition or scrutiny. It was arguably a simpler era operating at a slower pace, but not angelic. Since then, many aspects of the political system have changed markedly, which in turn have also changed the ways politics are played out. Parties now exert more influence on executives as the electorate has expanded in size and complexity. Communication is mass and instantaneous. Media coverage is more pervasive and insatiable. Living memory is gone and yesterday's leaders become statesmen, not politicians. Curiously, statesmen are almost always dead before they are awarded that accolade. Ideal worlds appeal to us, invented from a past often some decades or even centuries afterwards.

So nostalgia over a sanctified Westminster system provides a counterpoint to modern practice: an appeal to better times. Vagueness about the period being eulogized is an advantage; detailed knowledge is no benefit.

WESTMINSTER AS POLITICAL ADVANTAGE

Westminster can be used as a political weapon with which to belabour the other side of politics.

> Don't you come in here with your puffed up hubris and start lecturing this side of the House about accountability under the Westminster system (John Howard, House of Representatives, 29 May 2007)

It can act as a bludgeon. The issue is always the same: upholding traditional standards. When the system is so infused with convention and precedent, governments will continually argue that whatever they are proposing upholds the traditional standards. They appeal to Westminster as though it provides the unequivocal standard against which their present behaviour can be assessed. That some proposed change is 'consistent with Westminster' is a far better defence of the action than that it merely conforms to some change the government would like to impose. *We* know about the Westminster system, they imply, because we have been living by it.

Oppositions naturally attempt the opposite. Whenever there is a ministerial crisis, the demands inevitably follow that ministers should take responsibility and resign, as, they argue, is required under the standards of the Westminster system. That they never did is no matter. Nor does anyone expect them to, but the rhetoric has a ring of defiance. Oppositions invariably set standards that they would never be prepared or able to live up to in government themselves.

Of course, whichever side is running the argument, the standards are vague because Westminster systems employ conventions, rather than laws, and those conventions are constantly being reinterpreted politically rather than legally. Conventions are inherently flexible, defined by practice, tradition, and oft-forgotten history. They are concerned with the iterative ways of the political system. They are malleable. Conventions are adopted as long as the benefits from abiding by them outweigh the opprobrium from breaking them. Moreover, because there is no definitive ruling or proof about what is, or is not, Westminster, claims can be used as political tools by actors against their adversaries. It makes good theatre.

So, Westminster remains an important part of the political arsenal of participants. It is a continuing debate. And, as in any political debate, rhetoric and propositions are there for use, for interpretation, for manipulation, and for persuasion. Within this political lexicon, terms and practices are open to debate and redefinition. Why should we be surprised, therefore, that the term 'Westminster system' is too?

WESTMINSTER AS LEGITIMIZING INTERPRETATION

Various actors use Westminster to provide legitimacy and a context for their actions. It provides comfort for actors in a 'boundless and bottomless sea'; it is their surety or keel as they stay afloat. It serves as a point of reference to navigate this uncertain world. So, many politicians seek to measure themselves, for better or worse, against the standards of predecessors. Satisfying precedent both informs their beliefs about what Westminster practice is and provides a cover of legitimacy.

Significantly, beliefs about Westminster provide the greatest support to those actors whose position may be the most uncertain in the political system, namely public servants. These officials occupy an ambivalent position, variously interpreted as an extension of the Crown, an extension of the minister, a defender of the public interest. So, senior public servants refer to the Northcote–Trevelyan report or to the Westminster system as a way of defending their position and providing a firm foundation for their traditional roles. We have shown how recent leaders of the public services appeal to broad concepts and then redefine them in modern terms. They recount what the principal elements of the Westminster system should be and relate existing circumstances to those continuing verities. These claims act as a defence against charges of weak-kneed responsiveness or blatant politicization. They provide a thread of continuity and the overlay of professionalism.

Surely, the imputed notions of an independent and permanent realm for the public service, on which these public service heads draw, may have little in common with the organizations and practices over which they are titular head. The service today is larger, more diverse, technical, intrusive, sophisticated, and educated. Media demands may make the cloak of anonymity difficult to maintain. Professional and educated ministers are far more demanding. Flexibility and responsiveness have taken over from rigid, command-oriented bureaucracies. Careers are more diverse. Competition to give advice is fiercer as the former public service dominance is broken. Can-do managerialism is the prized skill, not policy advice. Yet, with all these challenges, the concept of a Westminster system with its professional bureaucracy provides a defence for the public servants against political and social challenges. 'These are our traditions, too,' they say. 'We have helped codify the conventions and written them down.' 'This was the way we were when the great mandarins brought order and competence to the problems of governing,' they imply. Nostalgia can be as real for public servants as for politicians; they use it explicitly to bolster their current case or status.

Periodic public inquiries into the administration of government will often seek to put current circumstances into historical context. The Coombs commission in the 1970s and the Gomery inquiry of the mid-2000s both tried to determine the continuing histories of the public service before asking whether these histories either have been abandoned or need to be adjusted to meet existing circumstances. Both the commissions and their legion of specialist consultants found the Westminster system to be useful shorthand to provide a context in which to place their subsequent recommendations and an intellectual foundation on which to build. Westminster provides the legitimacy of history, on to which has been grafted the imperatives of local conditions. They often deliberately chose to define it in generic or general terms with the implication that beyond such generalization there was little need to go further. Like the proverbial elephant, observers may not be able to describe it but they 'know it' when they see it.

So we do not agree with the comment attributed to Geoff Yeend that 'Westminster can mean anything you want'. Westminster may not provide guidance about how to act in a particular circumstance. Yet its traditions create the framework of ideas, conventions, and practices within which Yeend's own position as secretary to the cabinet was defined and allowed him to have so distinguished a career.

WESTMINSTER AS INSTITUTIONAL DESCRIPTOR

Accepting our conclusions about the meanings of Westminster so far, the descriptor 'Westminster' remains a useful category in political science but not in the taxonomic or checklist way used by Lijphart. He uses the terms 'Westminster' and 'majoritarian parliamentary systems' interchangeably; they help define a group of countries that have generally adopted British modes of government even if, by his set of criteria, many have since diverged from, or indeed never espoused, the original structures. He is trying to categorize. We are not. The danger with Lijphart's approach is that almost any generalization made about Westminster systems is likely to be empirically wrong in practice; as a result, his category is whittled down to Barbados (see Lijphart 1999)! In contrast to Lijphart, we suggest actors within Westminster countries themselves identify with some shared traditions and beliefs, while accepting the differences and variations. It may mean different things to actors in different countries. But self-identification, at least partially, is an important aspect of using the term as a descriptor. That actors feel motivated to identify with some perceived aspects they associate with Westminster is not analytically insignificant.

Where we find some local identification with Westminster precepts, these countries we suggest appear as a grouping of 'most similar' nations, related by history, belief systems, and inclination. They form a loose family of governments, not clones of one another. Westminster was, and remains, useful shorthand to identify their origins and some of their basic characteristics. We consider it unnecessary to 'box' countries. Instead, we prefer to analyse the family of ideas customarily referred to as 'Westminster' that have been variously constructed against a backdrop of divergent and competing governmental traditions. It is not necessary for there to be an agreed reductionist model for political scientists to take seriously beliefs about Westminster.

This approach does pose problems for comparative research. Positivist and empiricist techniques will not take us far. Indeed, as we suggest with Blondel's study (1985) of ministers working in 50 countries, such an approach may be fundamentally misguided. Our approach suggests the merits of an interpretive lens through which to assemble thick descriptions not only of countries but of institutions and actors too.

WESTMINSTER AS AN EFFECTIVE POLITICAL SYSTEM

Finally, there are arguments that Westminster is an effective and efficient political system. The most wide-ranging attempt to measure, rather than assert, the differences between majoritarian and consensual parliamentary governments is Lijphart (1999 [1984]). Lijphart (1999: chapters 15 and 16) asks whether consensus democracy makes a difference. He challenges the conventional wisdom on the trade-off between quality and effectiveness in which proportional representation and consensus government provide better representation whereas plurality elections and majority government provide more effective policy-making. He concludes that consensus democracies do outperform majoritarian democracies. However, because the statistical results are 'relatively weak and mixed', he phrases his conclusion as a negative. So, 'majoritarian democracies are clearly *not* superior to consensus democracies in managing the economy and in maintaining civil peace' (Lijphart 1999: 274, emphasis in the original). However, consensus democracies combine, on the one hand, better women's representation, great political equality, and higher participation in elections, with 'gentler qualities', such as persuasion, consultation, and 'more generous policies' on, for example, the environment. So, there appears to be no trade-off between effectiveness and democracy. (See also Blondel and Müller-Rommell 1993*b*; Weaver and Rockman 1993; and Strøm et al. 2003.)

Unfortunately, such a straightforward conclusion is not possible. As Lijphart (1999: 305) recognizes, and as we have shown repeatedly, local traditions shape political and administrative practices. So, for example, the belief that 'leaders know best' fits uneasily with the practices of consensual democracy. Moreover, as Peters (1999: 81–2) argues, the advantage of major-itarian government is that the executive can act as it wants; the prime minister can shape policy more effectively. The fact that the policies are ineffective could well be a function of poor policy choices, not of institutional differences. Or, to return to a phrase, 'leaders do not know best'. But, in turn, this argument raises the question of whether policy choices would be better if they were the product of persuasion and consultation rather than of adversary politics. In short, the key point is there can be no easy assumption about the effects of differing institutional arrangements.

The effortless superiority enshrined in the conventional wisdom that attributes decisiveness and effectiveness to the Westminster approach flounders on the sheer variety of political practice within Westminster systems and between regime types. There are no reliable ways to determine the effectiveness of regimes because there are no agreed criteria of effectiveness. They are shaped by local custom and practice. Comparative measures of 'effectiveness' are contingent and country specific. Westminster polities tend to face fewer veto-points and countervailing power structures. They embody a fusion of powers that, in theory, could give their governments greater scope to impose their will. But these strong executives are variously constrained.

First, they are constrained by the need to maintain popular consent. Consent is a continual millstone around their necks, although governments usually do not need cross-party support for daily government. Moreover, as the New Zealand case suggests, if executives push their power too far, the populace can engineer an institutional backlash to contain executive domin-ance. As the protests in Australia and Britain over the Vietnam and Iraq wars show, popular protests against government edicts can effectively disempower governments and lead to regime change. Canadian executives are always conscious of the veto power of the Quebec electorate, and to a lesser extent the Maritime and Western provinces.

Second, as with non-Westminster states, supra-state requirements also constrain national executives. European Union budgetary edicts limit the latitude available to national governments to undertake debt and operate fiscal policy. WTO regulations on trade remove some policy scope from governments.

Third, the beliefs and practices encoded in the several local traditions constrain national executives. We have itemized many examples of the ways in which local custom and practice concerning court politics, leadership, cabinet, ministerial responsibility, constitutional bureaucracy, and territorial interdependence shape executive behaviour.

Finally, effectiveness varies over time. Westminster systems can be ruthlessly efficient at passing legislation through single chambers with large government majorities. It is for good reason they have attracted the epitaph 'the fastest law in the West' when important legislation can be passed in hours and without non-government consultation. They are also the jurisdictions that spend most time amending legislation, correcting drafting problems, incremental tinkering, and consolidating. Up to 90 per cent of bills are amendments to existing legislation. Britain's history of nationalization, de-nationalization, renationalization, and privatization followed by regulatory oversight suggests wastefulness, not efficiency. Westminster may be the most wasteful political system given the political effort expended on issues that can be overturned with equal speed. Examples of excess, reversal, and dashed hopes abound; the UK's infamous poll tax; New Zealand's 'Think Big' projects; and Australia's Medibank Mark I and free universal university education. It is not that consensus democracies enact too slowly but that majoritarian democracies enact too quickly.

CONCLUSION: BEWARE THE SEARCH FOR PRECISION

Westminster is a vague term because it is still in use and because it is useful. It is used by politicians, public servants, and observers, as example, as club, as justification, and as a cloak of legitimacy. Most people listening know what they are talking about, even if they might be unable to define a Westminster system in an agreed way. Indeed, no one can provide such a precise definition, even if they would agree on many common features of the system: a parliament majority that is needed to support a government, a fusion of executive and legislature, collective decision-making through a cabinet, some sense of accountability to parliament, and perhaps a professional career public service. Even within these characteristics there will be disputes on how they should work, what conventions should apply.

That is the inevitable consequence of a concept in use in the daily grind of politics. It will serve many purposes; it will be given many interpretations. Sometimes it will be stretched beyond reasonable meaning. That is not because it has no meaning, but rather because it has several. We can, and do, argue at length over the viability of parliamentary government, over the effectiveness of electoral systems, about the existence of cabinet government. No one argues that they are not useful terms, even if they are in dispute, or that they should be discarded because of the lack of agreement. Likewise, Westminster is useful for many purposes; it survives and sometimes thrives because at the core it means something to those who use it and hear it. It is just that those interpretations are not precise. If we insist on one definite, unchallenged, and agreed meaning, the debate soon disintegrates into meaningless nit-picking. We benefit only when we use the concepts of Westminster flexibly as a family of ideas. Westminster lives because people believe in it, but only on its own terms and in specific political contexts.

Bibliography

Adams, D. (2000). 'John Howard: never great always adequate', in G. Singleton (ed.), *The Howard Government*, Sydney: UNSW Press.

—— (2005). 'John Howard as Prime Minister: the enigma variations', in C. Aulich and R. Wettenhall (eds.), *Howard's Second and Third Governments*, Sydney: UNSW Press.

Allen, G. (2002). *The Last Prime Minister: Being Honest about the UK Presidency*, London: Politico's.

ANZSOG (2004). *Cave Creek: A National Tragedy*, Wellington: ANZSOG Case Program.

—— (2008). *Collaborative Governance: A New Era in Public Policy in Australia*. Canberra: ANU E-Press.

APSA (Australasian Political Studies Association) (1976). 'Australian politics: a new ball game?' *Politics* XI (1): 1–68.

Arklay, T., Nethercote, J., and Wanna, J. (eds.) (2006). *Australian Political Lives: Chronicling Political Careers and Administrative Histories*, Canberra: Australian National University E-Press.

Armstong, Sir Robert (1985). *The Duties and Responsibilities of Civil Servants in Relation to Ministers: Note by the Head of the Civil Service*, London: Cabinet Office, 25 February.

Aucoin, P. (1995). *The New Public Management: Canada in Comparative Perspective*, Montreal: IRPP.

—— (2006). 'The 2006 Canadian election: implications for the public service', seminar to Political Science Department, Research School of Social Sciences, Australian National University, 1 March.

Aulich, C. and Wettenhall, R. (eds.) (2005). *Howard's Second and Third Governments*, Sydney: UNSW Press.

Australian Public Service Commission (APSC) (2001). *The State of the Service*, Canberra: AGPS.

Ayers, A.J. (1996). 'Not like the good old days', *Australian Journal of Public Administration*, 55 (2): 3–11.

Bach, S. (2003). *Platypus and Parliament: The Australian Senate in Theory and Practice*, Canberra: Department of the Senate.

Bagehot, W. (1963 [1867]). *The English Constitution* (with an introduction by R.H.S. Crossman), London: Fontana.

Baker, A. (2000). *Prime Ministers and the Rule Book*, London: Politico's.

Bakvis, H. (2001). 'Prime Minister and Cabinet in Canada: an autocracy in need of reform?', *Journal of Canadian Studies*, 35 (4): 60–79.

Bakvis, H. and Wolinetz, S.B. (2005). 'Canada: executive dominance and presidentialization', in T. Poguntke and P. Webb (eds.), *The Presidentialization of Politics: A Comparative Study of Modern Democracies*, Oxford: Oxford University Press.

236 *Bibliography*

Balfour, Arthur (Earl of Balfour) (1926). *Report of the Inter-Imperial Relations Committee of the Imperial Conference 1926*, Canberra: National Archives of Australia.

Barber, M. (2007). *Instruction to Deliver: Tony Blair, Public Services and the Challenge of Achieving Targets*, London: Politico's Publishing.

Barnett, D. with Goward, P. (1997). *John Howard Prime Minister*, Ringwood, Victoria: Viking.

Bassett, M. (2008). *Working with David: Inside the Lange Cabinet*, Auckland: Hodder Moa.

Bean, C. (1993). 'The electoral influence of party leaders' images in Australia and New Zealand', *Comparative Political Studies*, 26 (1): 111–32.

Beckett, F. and Hencke, D. (2004). *The Blairs and Their Court*, London: Aurum Press.

Beer, S. (1982 [1965]). *Modern British Politics*, London: Faber.

Behn, R.D. (2001). *Rethinking Democratic Accountability*, Washington, DC: The Brookings Institution.

Beloff, M. (1975). 'The Whitehall Factor: the role of the higher civil service 1919–39', in G. Peele and C. Cook (eds.), *The Politics of Reappraisal 1918–1939*, London: Macmillan.

Bevir, M. (1999). *The Logic of the History of Ideas*, Cambridge: Cambridge University Press.

—— (2001). 'Prisoners of professionalism: on the construction and responsibility of political studies', *Public Administration*, 79 (2): 469–509.

—— Rhodes, R.A.W. (2003). *Interpreting British Governance*, London: Routledge.

—— —— (2006). *Governance Stories*, Abingdon: Routledge.

—— —— Weller, P. (2003*a*). 'Traditions and comparative governance: interpreting the changing role of the public sector in comparative and historical perspectives', *Public Administration*, 81 (1): 1–17.

—— —— —— (2003*b*). 'Comparative governance: prospects and lessons', *Public Administration*, 81 (1): 191–210.

Bierce, Ambrose (2001 [1967, 1911]). *The Enlarged Devil's Dictionary*, Harmondsworth: Penguin Books.

Birch, A.H. (1964). *Representative and Responsible Government*, London: George Allen & Unwin.

—— (1967). *The British System of Government*, London: George Allen & Unwin.

Blair, C. (2008). *Speaking for Myself: The Autobiography*, London: Little, Brown.

Blair, T. (1996). *New Britain: My Vision of a Young Country*, London: Fourth Estate.

—— (2004). *Tony Blair: In His Own Words*, P. Richards ed., London: Politico's.

Blais, A., Gidengil, E., Nadeau, R., and Nevitte, N. (2002). *Anatomy of a Liberal Victory*, Peterborough: Broadview.

Blewett, N. (1999). *A Cabinet Diary: A Personal Record of the First Keating Government*, Kent Town, South Australia: Wakefield Press.

—— (2003). 'The Hawke cabinets', in S. Ryan and T. Bramston (eds.), *The Hawke Government: A Critical Retrospective*, North Melbourne, Victoria: Pluto Press.

Blick, A. (2004). *People Who Live in the Dark: The Special Adviser in British Politics*, London: Politico's.

Bliss, M. (1994). *Right Honourable Men*, Toronto: HarperCollins.

Blondel, J. (1980). *World Leaders: Heads of Government in the Post-war Period*, London: Sage.

——(1985). *Government Ministers in the Contemporary World*, London: Sage.

——Müller-Rommell, F. (1993*a*). 'Introduction', in J. Blondel and F. Müller-Rommell (eds.), *Governing Together: The Extent and Limits of Joint Decision-Making in Western European Cabinets*, Houndmills, Basingstoke: Macmillan, pp. 1–19.

—— ——(eds.) (1993*b*). *Governing Together: The Extent and Limits of Joint Decision-Making in Western European Cabinets*, Houndmills, Basingstoke: Macmillan.

—— ——(eds.) (1997 [1988]). *Cabinets in Western Europe*, 2nd edition, London: Macmillan.

——Thiébault, J-L. (eds.) (1991). *The Profession of Government Minister in Western Europe*, Houndmills, Basingstoke: Macmillan.

Blunkett, D. (2006). *The Blunket Tapes. My Life in the Bear Pit*, London: Bloomsbury.

Bogdanor, V. (1991). 'United Kingdom', in D. E. Butler and D. A. Low (eds.), *Sovereigns and Surrogates: Constitutional Heads of State in the Commonwealth*, London: Palgrave Macmillan.

——(1999). 'Comparative politics', in J. Hayward, B. Barry, and A. Brown (eds.), *The British Study of Politics in the Twentieth Century*, Oxford: Oxford University Press for the British Academy.

——(ed.) (2003). *The British Constitution in the Twentieth Century*, Oxford: Oxford University Press for the British Academy.

Boston, J. (ed.) (1995). *The State under Contact*, Wellington: Bridget Williams Books.

——(1998). 'Public sector management, electoral reform and the future of the contract state in New Zealand', *Australian Journal of Public Administration*, 57 (4): 32–43.

——(2001). 'New Zealand: cautionary tale or shining example?', in R.A.W. Rhodes and P. Weller (eds.), *The Changing World of Top Officials: Mandarins or Valets?* Buckingham: Open University Press.

Boston, J. and McLeay, E. (1997). 'Forming the first MMP government: theory, practice and prospects', in J. Boston et al. (eds.), *From Campaign to Coalition: New Zealand's First General Election Under Proportional Representation*, Palmerston North: Dunmore Press.

——Martin, J., Pallot, J., and Walsh, P. (1996). *Public Management: The New Zealand Model*, Auckland: Oxford University Press.

Bourgault, J. (2006). 'The deputy minister's role in the government of Canada: his responsibility and his accountability', in John H. Gomery, *Restoring Accountability: Research Studies, Volume 2: The Public Service and Transparency* (Gomery Commission), Ottawa: Canadian Government Publishing.

Boyce, P. (2008). *The Queen's Other Realms: The Crown and its Legacy in Australia, Canada and New Zealand*, Leichhardt, NSW: Federation Press.

Brennan, G. and Pincus, J. (2002). 'Australia's Economic Institutions', in G. Brennan and F.G. Castles (eds.), *Australia Reshaped*, Cambridge: Cambridge University Press.

Brett, J. (2002). *Robert Menzies' Forgotten People*, Melbourne: Macmillan.

——(2003). *Australian Liberals and the Moral Middle Class*, Melbourne: Cambridge University Press.

Brett, J. (2005). 'Relaxed and comfortable: the Liberal Party's Australia', *Quarterly Essay*, No. 19: 1–79.

Bridges, E. (1950). *Portrait of a Profession*, Cambridge: Cambridge University Press (reprinted in R.A. Chapman and A. Dunsire (eds.), *Style in Administration*, London: Allen & Unwin).

—— (1956). 'Administration: what is it and how can it be learnt?', in A. Dunsire (ed.), *The Making of an Administrator*, Manchester: Manchester University Press.

Bright, J. (1910). *Selected Speeches of the Rt. Hon. John Bright, M.P. on Public Questions*. London: J.M. Dent, Everyman's Library E. Rhys (series ed.).

Brown, A.J. (2003a). 'One nation, two federalisms: rediscovering the origins of Australian federal political ideas', paper to the Australasian Political Studies Association, University of Tasmania, Hobart, 29 September–1 October.

—— (2003b). The frozen continent: the fall and rise of territory in Australian constitutional thought 1815–2003, PhD thesis, Griffith University.

Brown J.M. and Lewis, W.R. (eds.) (1999). *The Oxford History of British Empire, Volume 4: The Twentieth Century*, Oxford: Oxford University Press.

Brown, W. (2002). *Ten Prime Ministers: Life among the Politicians*, Double Bay, NSW: Longueville.

Bryce, J. (1921). *Modern Democracies*, 2 volumes, London: Macmillan.

Bulpitt, J.G. (1983). *Territory and Power in the United Kingdom*, Manchester: Manchester University Press.

Butler, D. (1973). *The Canberra Model*, New York: St Martin's Press.

—— (1991). 'Introduction', in D.E. Butler and D.A. Low (eds.), *Sovereigns and Surrogates: Constitutional Heads of State in the Commonwealth*, London: Macmillan.

—— Adonis, A., and Travers, T. (1994). *Failure in British Government: The Politics of the Poll Tax*, Oxford: Oxford University Press.

Butler, Sir Robin (1992). 'Managing the new public services: towards a new framework?', *Public Policy and Management*, 7 (3): 1–14.

Butler, R. (1993). 'The evolution of the civil service', *Public Administration*, 71 (3): 395–406.

Cabinet Office (New Zealand) (2003). *Cabinet Manual*, Wellington: Cabinet Office.

—— (2004). *New Zealand Constitution: Past, Present and Future*, Briefing Note, Wellington: Cabinet Office, November.

—— (2008). *Cabinet Manual*, Wellington: Cabinet Office.

Cabinet Office (UK) (1994). *Next Steps: Moving On* (Trosa Report), London: Cabinet Office.

—— (1997). *Ministerial Code*, London: Cabinet Office.

—— (2000). *Wiring It Up*, London: Cabinet Office.

Callaghan, J. 1987. *Time and Chance*, London: Collins.

Campbell, A. (2007). *The Blair Years. Extracts from the Alastair Campbell Diaries*, London: Hutchinson.

Campbell, C. and Wilson, G.K. (1995). *The End of Whitehall: Death of a Paradigm?* Oxford: Blackwell.

Carey, B. (1980). 'Executive control in the 1970s', in H. Mayer and H. Nelson (eds.), *Australian Politics: A 5th reader*, Melbourne: Longman Cheshire.

Carrington, Lord Peter (1988). *Reflect on Things Past: The Memoirs of Lord Carrington*, London: Collins.

Carroll, B. (2004). *Australia's Prime Ministers: From Barton to Howard*, Dural Delivery Centre, NSW: Rosenberg.

Castles, F. (1985). *The Working Class and Welfare*, Sydney: Allen & Unwin.

—— (2002). 'Australia's institutions and Australia's welfare', in G. Brennan and F.G. Castles (eds.), *Australia Reshaped*, Cambridge: Cambridge University Press.

Central Office of Information (COI) (1957). *Constitutional Development in the Commonwealth*, London: COI.

Chapman, R. (1988). *Ethics in the British Civil Service*, London: Routledge.

Chapman, R.A. and Greenaway, J.R. (1980). *The Dynamics of Administrative Reform*, London: Croom Helm.

Cm 4310 (1999). *Modernising Government*, London: Stationery Office.

Committee on the Civil Service (Fulton) (1968). *Report*, Cmnd. 3638, London: HMSO.

Coombs, H.C. (1981). *Trial Balance*, Melbourne: Macmillan.

Constitutional Commission (1987). *Report of the Advisory Committee on Executive Government*, Canberra: AGPS.

—— (1988). *Final Report of the Constitutional Commission*, Canberra: AGPS.

Cornish, S. (2002). *Sir Roland Wilson: A Biographical Essay*, Canberra: ANU.

Cowen, Z. (1965). *The British Commonwealth of Nations in a Changing World*, Evanston, Ill.: Northwestern University Press.

Cowley, P. (2005). *The Rebels: How Blair Mislaid His Majority*, London: Politico's.

Cox, G.W. (1987). *The Efficient Secret: The Cabinet and the Development of Political Parties in Victorian England*, Cambridge: Cambridge University Press.

Crawford, J. (1954) 'The role of the permanent head', *Public Administration* (Sydney) 13 (3): 153–64.

Crick, B. (1970 [1964]). *The Reform of Parliament*, London: Weidenfeld & Nicolson.

Crossman, R.H.S. (1963). 'Introduction', in W. Bagehot, *The English Constitution*, London: Collins.

—— (1975). *The Diaries of a Cabinet Minister, Volume 1: Minister of Housing*, London: Jonathan Cape.

Daly, F. (1977). *From Curtin to Kerr*, Melbourne: Sun Books.

Darwin, J. (1989). 'A third British Empire? The dominion idea in imperial politics', in J.M. Brown and W.R. Lewis (eds.), *The Oxford History of British Empire, Volume 4: The Twentieth Century*, Oxford: Oxford University Press.

Davies, A.F. (1958). *Australian Democracy*, Melbourne: Longman.

Davis, G. and Rhodes, R.A.W. (2001). 'From hierarchy to contracts and back again: reforming the Australian public service', in M. Keating, J. Wanna, and P. Weller (eds.), *Institutions on the Edge? Capacity for Governance*, Sydney: Allen & Unwin.

—— Wanna, J., Warhurst, J., and Weller, P. (1993). *Public Policy in Australia*, 2nd edition, Sydney: Allen & Unwin.

Dell, E. (1973). *Political Responsibility and Industry*, London: Allen & Unwin.

Delport, T. (2006). Interview with Democratic Alliance Chairperson of the Federal Legal Commission, and Member of South African National Assembly, Cape Town, 29 May.

De Smith, S.A. (1954). *The Vocabulary of Commonwealth Relations*, London: University of London, The Athlone Press.

—— (1961). 'Westminster's export models: the legal framework of responsible government', *Journal of Commonwealth Studies*, 1 (1): 3–16.

Dicey, A.V. (1914 [1885]). *Lectures on the Relations between Law and Public Opinion during the Nineteenth Century*, London: Macmillan.

Dogan, M. and Pelassy, D. (1990). *How to Compare Nations: Strategies in Comparative Politics*, 2nd edition, Chatham, New Jersey: Chatham House.

Donoughue, B. (2003). *The Heat of the Kitchen*, London: Politico's.

Dowding, K. (1995). *The Civil Service*, London: Routledge.

—— Dumont, P. (2008). *The Selection of Ministers in Europe: Hiring and Firing*, London: Routledge.

Dunleavy, P. and Rhodes, R.A.W. (1990). 'Core executive studies in Britain', *Public Administration* 68 (1): 3–28.

Eckstein, H. (1963). 'A perspective on comparative politics, past and present', in H. Eckstein and D.E. Apter (eds.), *Comparative Politics: A Reader*, London: The Free Press of Glencoe.

Edwards, B. (2002). *Helen Clark: Portrait of a Prime Minister*, London: Politico's.

Edwards, J. (1996). *Keating: The Inside Story*, Ringwood, Victoria: Viking Press.

Edwards, P. (2006). *Arthur Tange: Last of the Mandarins*, Sydney: Allen & Unwin.

Eichbaum, C. and Shaw, R. (2007). 'Ministerial advisers, politicization and the retreat from Westminster: the case of New Zealand', *Public Administration*, 85 (3): 609–40.

Elgie, R. (1995). *Political Leadership in Liberal Democracies*, Houndmills, Basingstoke: Macmillan.

—— (1997). 'Models of executive politics: a framework for the study of executive power relations in parliamentary and semi-presidential regimes', *Political Studies*, 45 (2): 217–31.

—— (1998). 'The classification of democratic regime types: conceptual ambiguity and contestable assumptions', *European Journal of Political Research*, 33 (2): 219–38.

Encel, S. (1962). *Cabinet Government in Australia*, Melbourne: Melbourne University Press.

Farrell, D.M. and McAllister, I. (2006). *The Australian Electoral System: Origins, Variations and Consequences*, Sydney: University of New South Wales Press.

Fawcett, P. and Gay, O. (2005). *The Centre of Government – No. 10, the Cabinet Office and HM Treasury*, London: House of Commons Library, Parliament and Constitution Centre. Research Paper 05/92, December.

—— Rhodes, R.A.W. (2007). 'Central government', in A. Seldon (ed.), *Blair's Britain, 1997–2007*. Cambridge: Cambridge University Press.

Fenna, A. (2007). 'The malaise of federalism: comparative reflections on commonwealth–state relations', *Australian Journal of Public Administration*, 66 (3): 298–306.

Fenno, R.F. (1990). *Watching Politicians: Essays on Participant Observation*, Berkeley: Institute of Governmental Studies, University of California.

Fesler, J.W. (1965). 'Approaches to the understanding of decentralization', *Journal of Politics*, 27 (3): 536–66.

Finn, P. (1987). *Law and Government in Colonial Australia*, Melbourne: Melbourne University Press.

Foley, M. (2000). *The British Presidency*, Manchester: Manchester University Press.

—— (2004). 'Presidential attribution as an agency of prime ministerial critique in a parliamentary democracy: the case of Tony Blair', *British Journal of Politics and International Relations*, 63 (3): 292–311.

Fraser, M. (1975). 'National objectives: social, economic and political goals', *Australian Quarterly*, 47 (1): 25.

Fry, G.K. (1993). *Reforming the Civil Service: The Fulton Committee on the British Civil Service 1966–68*, Edinburgh: Edinburgh University Press.

Galligan, B. (1995). *A Federal Republic*, Cambridge: Cambridge University Press.

—— Hughes, O., and Walsh, C. (eds.) (1991). *Intergovernmental Relations and Public Policy*, Sydney: Allen & Unwin.

Gamble, A. (1990). 'Theories of British politics', *Political Studies*, 38 (3): 404–20.

Garran, R. (1897). *The Coming Commonwealth: An Australian Handbook of Federal Government*, Sydney: Angus & Robertson.

Geertz, C. (1973). *The Interpretation of Cultures*, New York: Basic Books.

Gomery, J. (2004). *Public Hearings before the Commission of Inquiry into the Sponsorship Program and Advertising Activities*, Volume 12 (Himelfarb evidence) and Volumes 47 and 48 (Bourgon evidence), Ottawa: Canadian Government Publishing.

Gomery, J.H. (2005). *Who is Responsible? Fact-Finding Report: Phase 1 of the Report of the Commission of Inquiry into the Sponsorship Program and Advertising Activities* (Gomery Commission), Ottawa: Canadian Government Publishing.

—— (2006). *Restoring Accountability: Phase 2 of the Report of the Commission of Inquiry into the Sponsorship Program and Advertising Activities* (Gomery Commission), Ottawa: Canadian Government Publishing.

Gordon, M. (1993). *Paul Keating: A Question of Leadership*, St Lucia, Queensland: University of Queensland Press.

Granatstein, J.L. (1982). The *Ottawa Men: The Civil Service Mandarins 1935–1957*, Toronto: Oxford University Press.

Grattan, M. (2000). *Australian Prime Ministers*, Frenchs Forest: New Hollands.

Green, D.P. and Shapiro, I. (1994). *Pathologies of Rational Choice*, New Haven: Yale University Press.

Greenleaf, W.H. (1983). *The British Political Tradition, Volume 1: The Rise of Collectivism*, London: Methuen.

Gregory, R. (1998). 'Political responsibility for bureaucratic incompetence: tragedy at Cave Creek', *Public Administration*, 76 (3): 519–38.

—— (2004). 'Dire expectations but subtle transformations? Politicisation and the New Zealand public service', in B.G. Peters and J. Pierre (eds.), *Politicisation of the Civil Service in Comparative Perspectives: The Quest for Control*, London: Routledge.

Gustafson, B. (2006). 'Populist roots of political leadership in New Zealand', in R. Miller and M. Mintrom (eds.), *Political Leadership in New Zealand*, Auckland: Auckland University Press.

Hahndiek, K. (2006). Interview with Secretary of the South African National Assembly, Cape Town, 26 May.

Hailsham, Lord (1978). *The Dilemmas of Democracy*, London: Collins.

Hall, H.D. (1920). *The British Commonwealth of Nations*, London: Methuen.

—— (1927). 'The Balfour Report and its historical background', in A.L. Lowell and H.D. Hall, *The British Commonwealth of Nations*, Boston: World Peace Foundation.

Hammersley, M. and Atkinson, P. (1983). *Ethnography: Principles in Practice*, London: Routledge.

Hancock, W.K. (1930). *Australia*, London: Benn.

Hartz, L. (ed.) (1964). *The Founding of New Societies*, New York: Harcourt Brace.

Hawke, B. (1994). *The Hawke Memoirs*, Port Melbourne, Victoria: William Heinemann.

Hay, C. (2004). 'Theory, stylised heuristic or self-fulfilling prophecy? The status of rational choice theory in public administration', *Public Administration*, 82 (1): 39–62.

Heard, A. (1991). *Canadian Constitutional Conventions: The Marriage of Law and Politics*, Toronto: Oxford University Press.

Helms, L. (2005). *Presidents, Prime Ministers and Chancellors*, Houndmills, Basingstoke: Macmillan.

Hennessy, P. (1986). *The Cabinet*, Oxford: Blackwell.

—— (1989). *Whitehall*, London: Secker & Warburg.

—— (1995). *The Hidden Wiring: Unearthing the British Constitution*, London: Gollancz.

—— (1998). 'The Blair style of government', *Government and Opposition*, 33 (1): 3–20.

—— (2000*a*). 'The Blair style and the requirements of twenty-first century premiership', *Political Quarterly*, 71 (4): 386–95.

—— (2000*b*). *The Prime Ministers*, London: Penguin Press.

—— (2000*c*). *The Blair Revolution in Government*, Leeds: University of Leeds, Institute for Politics and International Studies.

—— (2002). 'The Blair government in historical perspective: an analysis of the power relationships within New Labour', *History Today*, 52 (1): 21–3.

—— (2005). 'Rulers and servants of the state: the Blair style of government 1997–2004', *Parliamentary Affairs*, 58 (1): 6–16.

Heseltine, M. (2000). *Life in the Jungle: My Autobiography*, London: Hodder & Stoughton.

Hewart, Lord (1929). *The New Despotism*, London: Ernest Benn.

Hockin, T.A. (ed.) (1977). *Apex of Power: The Prime Minister and Political Leadership in Canada*, 2nd edition, Scarborough, Ontario: Prentice-Hall.

Hogg, Q. (1947). *The Case for Conservatism*, West Drayton: Penguin Books.

Holland, I. (2004). 'Reforming the conventions regarding parliamentary scrutiny of ministerial actions', *Australian Journal of Public Administration*, 63 (2): 3–15.

Holland, R. (2003). 'Britain, Commonwealth and the end of Empire', in V. Bogdanor (ed.), *The British Constitution in the Twentieth Century*, Oxford: Oxford University Press for the British Academy.

Hollander, R. and Patapan, H. (2007). 'Pragmatic federalism: Australian federalism from Hawke to Howard', *Australian Journal of Public Administration*, 66 (3): 3–16.

Horner, D. (2000). *Defence Supremo: Sir Frederick Shedden and the Making of Australian Defence Policy*, Sydney: Allen & Unwin.

Howard, J. (1998). 'A healthy public service is a vital part of australia's democratic system of government', *Australian Journal of Public Administration*, 57 (1): 3–12.

—— (2002). 'Strategic leadership for Australia: policy directions in a complex world', lecture to the Committee for Economic Development of Australia, 20 November.

—— (2006). 'Transcript of Press Conference' (on Senator Robert Hill's departure), 20 January, Prime Minister and Cabinet website <http://www.dpmc.gov.au/>.

Howe, G. (1994). *Conflict of Loyalty*, London: Macmillan.

Hueglin, T.O. and Fenna, A. (2006). *Comparative Federalism: A Systematic Inquiry*, Ontario: Broadview Press.

Hughes, Billy (1909). 'The case for Labor', *Daily Telegraph*, 24 July.

Hughes, O. (1998). *Australian Politics*, 3rd edition, South Yarra: Macmillan.

Ilbert, C. (1912). *Parliament: Its History, Constitution and Practice*, London: Williams & Norgate.

Jackson, R.J. (1995). 'Foreign models and Aussie rules: executive–legislative relations in Australia', *Political Theory Newsletter*, 7 (1): 1–18.

—— Jackson, D. (2001). *Politics in Canada: Culture, Institutions, Behaviour and Public Policy*, 5th edition, Toronto: Prentice Hall.

—— —— (2006). *Politics in Canada: Culture, Institutions, Behaviour and Public Policy*, 6th edition, Toronto: Prentice Hall.

Jaensch, D. (1997). *The Politics of Australia*, Melbourne: Macmillan.

Jennings, I. (1948). *The British Commonwealth of Nations*, London: Hutchinson.

—— (1957 [1939]). *Parliament*, Cambridge: Cambridge University Press.

—— (1959 [1936]). *Cabinet Government*, Cambridge: Cambridge University Press.

—— (1962 [1941]). *The British Constitution*, Cambridge: Cambridge University Press.

Johnson, N. (2004). *Reshaping the British Constitution: Essay in Political Interpretation*, Houndmills, Basingstoke: Palgrave Macmillan.

Jones, G.W. (1985). 'The prime minister's power', in A. King (ed.), *The British Prime Minister*, 2nd edition, London: Macmillan.

—— (ed.) (1991). *West European Prime Ministers*, London: Frank Cass.

Jones. N. (1999). *Sultans of Spin*, London: Gollancz.

Kaufman, G. (1980). *How to be a Minister*, London: Sidgwick & Jackson.

Kavanagh, D. and Seldon, A. (2000). *The Powers Behind the Prime Minister: The Hidden Influence of Number Ten*, London: HarperCollins.

Keating, M. (2004). *Who Rules? How Government Retains Control in a Privatised Economy*. Annandale, NSW: Federation Press.

Keating, M. and Wanna, J. (2000).'Remaking federalism?', in M. Keating, J. Wanna, and P. Weller (eds.), *Institutions on the Edge? Capacity for Governance*, NSW: Allen & Unwin.

Keegan, W. (2003). *The Prudence of Mr. Gordon Brown*, Chichester, West Sussex: Wiley.

Keith, A.B. (1928). *Responsible Government in the Dominions*, New York: Oxford University Press.

Kelly, P. (1994). *The End of Uncertainty: Power, Politics and Business in Australia*, revised edition, Sydney: Allen & Unwin.

—— (2005). *Rethinking Australian Governance – the Howard Legacy*, Canberra: Academy of the Social Sciences in Australia, Occasional Paper Series Number 4.

Kendle, J. (1967). *The Colonial and Imperial Conferences 1887–1911*, London: Longmans.

Kingston, M. (2004). *Not Happy, John!* Camberwell, Victoria: Penguin Books.

Kipling, R. (1990). *The Complete Verse*, London: Kyle Cathie.

Lake, M. and H. Reynolds (2007). *Drawing the Global Colour Line*, Melbourne: Melbourne University Press.

Lange, D. (1992). *Broadsides*, Wellington: Jonathon Hudson.

—— (1998). 'With the benefit of foresight and a little help from hindsight', *Australian Journal of Public Administration*, 57 (1): 12–18.

—— (2005). *David Lange: My Life*, Auckland: Penguin.

Larby, P.M. and Hannam, H. (1993). *The Commonwealth*, London: Transaction.

Laver, M. and Shepsle, K. (1996). *Making and Breaking Governments: Cabinets and Legislatures in Parliamentary Democracies*, Cambridge: Cambridge University Press.

Lawson, N. (1992). *The View from No. 11*, London: Bantam Press.

Lijphart, A. (1984). *Democracies: Patterns of Majoritarian and Consensus Government in Twenty-one Countries*, New Haven: Yale University Press.

—— (1999). *Patterns of Democracy: Government Forms and Performance in Thirty-six Countries*, New Haven: Yale University Press.

Longford, E. (1983). *Elizabeth R: A Biography*, London: Weidenfeld & Nicolson.

Loughlin, M. (1992). *Public Law and Political Theory*, Oxford: Clarendon Press.

Loveland, I. (1996). *Constitutional Law: A Critical Introduction*, London: Butterworths.

Lovink, J.A.A. (1979). 'Is Canadian politics too competitive?', in R. Schultz, O. M. Kruhlak, and J. C. Terry (eds.), *The Canadian Political Process*, 3rd edition, Toronto: Holt, Rinehart & Winston.

Low, D.A. (1988). 'Introduction: Buckingham Palace and the Westminster model', in D.A. Low (ed.), *Constitutional Heads and Political Crises*, London: Macmillan.

Lowell, A.L. (1927). 'The Imperial Conference', in A.L. Lowell and H.D. Hall, *The British Commonwealth of Nations*, Boston: World Peace Foundation.

Lucy, R. (1985). *The Australian Form of Government*, Melbourne: Macmillan. UK edition 1993.

MAC (Management Advisory Committee) (2004). *Connecting Government: Whole of Government Response to Australia's Priority Challenges*, Canberra: Australian Public Service Commission.

MacCallum, M. (2004). *Run Johnny Run*, Potts Point, NSW: Duffy & Snellgrove.

MacIntyre, A. (1983). 'The indispensability of political theory', in D. Miller and L. Siedentop (eds.), *The Nature of Political Theory*, Oxford: Clarendon Press.

Mackenzie, W. J. M. (1961). *Theories of Local Government*, London: London School of Economics and Political Science, Greater London Group Papers No. 2.

Mackintosh, J. (1968). *The British Cabinet*, 2nd edition, London: Stevens.

MacLeod, R. (1988). 'Introduction', in R. MacLeod (ed.), *Government and Expertise*, Cambridge: Cambridge University Press.

MacMillan, M. (2001). *Peacemakers: The Paris conference of 1919 and Its Attempts to End War*. London: John Murray.

McAllister, I. (2006). 'The personalisation of politics', in R.J. Dalton and H.D. Klingemann (eds.), *The Oxford Handbook of Political Behaviour*, Oxford: Oxford University Press.

McClintock, P. (2003). 'The Australian approach to policy making: response to Mulgan and Zussman', *Canberra Bulletin of Public Administration*, 108 (June): 15–17.

McLeay, E. (1995). *The Cabinet and Political Power in New Zealand*, Auckland: Oxford University Press.

—— (2001). 'Cabinet', in R. Miller (ed.), *New Zealand Government and Politics*, Melbourne: Oxford University Press.

McLeod, R. (1994). *Review of the Public Service Act*, Canberra: AGPS.

McPherson, A. and Raab, C. (1988). *Governing Education*, Edinburgh: Edinburgh University Press.

Maddox, G. (1989). *The Hawke Government and Labor Tradition*, Melbourne: Longman Cheshire.

—— (1991). *Australian Democracy in Theory and Practice*, 2nd edition, Melbourne: Longman Cheshire.

Maddox, M. (2005). *God under Howard: The Rise of the Religious Right in Australian Politics*, St Leonards: Allen & Unwin.

Maley, M. (2003). 'The growing role of australian ministerial advisers', *Canberra Bulletin of Public Administration*, 110, December: 1–4.

Mandelson, P. and Liddle, R. (1996). *The Blair Revolution: Can New Labour Deliver?* London: Faber & Faber.

Manne, R. (ed.) (2004*a*). *The Howard Years*, Melbourne: Black Inc.

—— (2004*b*). 'The Howard years. a political interpretation', in R. Manne (ed.), *The Howard Years*, Melbourne: Black Inc.

Marinetto, M. (2003). 'Governing beyond the centre: a critique of the Anglo-governance school', *Political Studies*, 51 (3): 592–608.

Marr, D. and Wilkinson, M. (2003). *Dark Victory*, Crows Nest, NSW: Allen & Unwin.

Marriott, J.A.R. (1948). *English Political Institutions*, 4th edition, Oxford: Clarendon Press.

Marsh, D. (1980). 'The British political tradition', unpublished manuscript, Department of Government, University of Exeter.

Marsh, D., Richards, D., and Smith, M.J. (2003). 'Unequal plurality: towards an asymmetric power model of British politics', *Government and Opposition*, 38: 306–32.

Marsh, I. (1995). *Beyond the Two Party System*, Cambridge: Cambridge University Press.

Marshall, G. (1986). *Constitutional Conventions: The Rules and Forms of Political Accountability*, Oxford: Clarendon Press (revised paperback edition).

Marshall, G. (2003). 'The constitution its theory and interpretation', in V. Bogdanor (ed.) *The British Constitution in the Twentieth Century*, Oxford: Oxford University Press for the British Academy.

Martin, G. (1995). *Britain and the Origins of the Canadian Federation, 1837–1867,* Houndmills, Basingstoke: Macmillan and UBC Press.

Martin, L. (1995). *Chrétien: The Will to Win,* Toronto: Lester.

Mason, A. (1987). 'Future directions in Australian law', *Monash Law Review,* 13 (3): 149–63.

Matheson, W.A. (1976). *The Prime Minister and Cabinet,* Toronto: Methuen.

May, E. (1844). *A Practical Treatise on the Law, Privileges, Proceedings and Usage of Parliament,* London.

Menzies, R.G. (1960). *The Changing Commonwealth,* Smuts Memorial Lecture, Cambridge: Cambridge University Press.

—— (1967). *Central Power in the Australian Commonwealth,* London: Cassell.

Mill, J.S. (1996 [1843]). *A System of Logic, Ratiocinative and Inductive, Being a Connected View of the Principles of Evidence and the Methods of Scientific Investigation. Volume VIII of the Collected Works of John Stuart Mill,* ed. J.M. Robson, London: Routledge, book 3, chapter 8.

Miller, J.D.B. (1966). *Britain and the Old Dominions,* London: Chatto & Windus.

Mills, S. (1986). *The New Machine Men, Polls and Persuasion in Australian Politics,* Ringwood: Penguin.

Morrison, H. (1964 [1959]). *Government and Parliament: A Survey from the Inside,* 3rd edition, Oxford: Oxford University Press.

Mouzelis, N.P. (1967). *Organization and Bureaucracy,* London: Routledge & Kegan Paul.

Mowlam, M. (2002). *Momentum: The Struggle for Peace, Politics and the People,* London: Hodder & Stoughton.

Mughan, A. (2000). *Media and the Presidentialisation of Parliamentary Elections,* Houndmills, Basingstoke: Macmillan.

—— Patterson, S.C. (eds.). (1992). *Political Leadership in Democratic Societies,* Chicago: Nelson-Hall.

Mulgan, R. (1992). 'The elective dictatorship in New Zealand', in H. Gold (ed.), *New Zealand Politics in Perspective,* 3rd edition, Auckland: Longman Paul.

—— (2002). 'On ministerial resignations (and the lack thereof)', *Australian Journal of Public Administration,* 61 (2): 121–7.

—— (2003). *Holding Power to Account: Accountability in Modern Democracies,* Houndmills, Basingstoke: Palgrave Macmillan.

—— (2004 [1994]). *Politics in New Zealand,* 3rd edition, Auckland: Auckland University Press.

Naughtie, J. (2002). *The Rivals: The Intimate Story of a Political Marriage,* revised edition, London: Fourth Estate.

New Zealand Treasury (1987). *Government Management.* Wellington: Government Printer.

Noble, The Hon G.S. (1995). *Commission of Inquiry into the Collapse of the Viewing Platform at Cave Creek, Punakaiki, West Coast.* Wellington, New Zealand: The Department of Internal Affairs.

Norman, R. (2003). *Obedient Servant? Management Freedoms and Accountabilities in the New Zealand Public Sector,* Wellington: Victoria University Press.

Northcote–Trevelyan (1853). *Report on the Organisation of the Permanent Civil Service*. Reprinted in: Committee on the Civil Service (Fulton 1968), *Report* (Cmnd 3638, London, HMSO), Appendix 3.

Norton, P. (1981). *The Commons in Perspective*. Oxford: Martin Robertson.

—— (1982). *Constitution in Flux*. Oxford: Martin Robertson.

—— (2000). 'Barons in a shrinking kingdom: senior ministers in British government', in R.A.W. Rhodes (ed.), *Transforming British Government, Volume 2: Changing Roles and Relationships*, London: Macmillan.

—— (2003). 'The presidentialisation of British politics', *Government and Opposition*, 38 (2): 274–8.

—— (2005). *Parliament in British Politics*. Houndmills, Basingstoke: Palgrave Macmillan.

O'Halpin, E. (1989). *Head of the Civil Service: A Study of Sir Warren Fisher*, London: Routledge.

Oakeshott, M. (1962). *Rationalism in Politics and Other Essays*. London: Methuen.

—— (1996). *The Politics of Faith and the Politics of Scepticism*, ed. Timothy Fuller, New Haven: Yale University Press.

Oborne, P. and Walters, S. (2004). *Alastair Campbell*. London: Aurum Press.

Official Record (1986). *Official Record of the Debates of the Australasian Federal Convention*: Volume 1, Sydney, 2 March–9 April 1891; Volume 2, Second Session, Sydney, 2–24 September 1891; Volume 3, Adelaide, 22 March–5 May 1897; Volume 4 and Volume 5, Third Session, Melbourne, 20 January–17 March 1898; Volume 6, The Convention Debates 1891–1898: commentaries, indices and guide, ed. Gregory Craven, Sydney: Legal Books.

Onselen, P. van and Errington, W. (2007). *John Howard*, Melbourne: Melbourne University Press.

Orwell, G. (1970*a* [1944]). 'Benefit of Clergy: some notes on Salvador Dali', in *The Collected Essays, Journalism and Letters of George Orwell, Volume III: As I Please 1943–1945*, ed. S. Orwell and I. Angus, Harmondsworth: Penguin Books.

—— (1970*b* [1944]). 'The English People', in *The Collected Essays, Journalism and Letters of George Orwell, Volume III: As I Please 1943–5*, ed. S. Orwell and I. Angus, Harmondsworth: Penguin Books.

Osbaldeston, G. (1989). *Keeping Deputy Ministers Accountable*, Toronto: McGraw-Hill Ryerson.

Palmer, G. (1979). *Unbridled Power: An Interpretation of New Zealand's Constitution & Government*, Auckland: Oxford University Press.

—— Palmer, M. (1988). *Bridled Power: New Zealand's Constitution & Government*, Auckland: Oxford University Press.

Parker, R.S. (1976). 'The meaning of responsible government', *Politics* 11 (2): 178–84 (reprinted in D.W. Lovell, I. McAllister, W. Maley, and C. Kukathas (eds.), *The Australian Political System*, 2nd edition, Melbourne: Longman.

—— (1978). 'The public service and responsible government', in R.F.I. Smith and P. Weller (eds.), *Public Service Inquiries in Australia*, St Lucia: University of Queensland Press.

Parris, H. (1969). *Constitutional Bureaucracy: The Development of British Central Administration since the Eighteenth Century*, London: Allen & Unwin.

Patapan, H. (1997). 'The author of liberty: Dicey, Mill and the shaping of English constitutionalism', *Public Law Review*, 25: 211.

——Wanna, J., and Weller, P. (eds.) (2005). *Westminster Legacies: Democracy and Responsible Government in Asia, Australasia and the Pacific*, Sydney: University of New South Wales Press.

Perez-Diaz, V.M. (1993). *The Return of Civil Society*, Cambridge, Mass: Harvard University Press.

Peston, R. (2005). *Brown's Britain*, London: Short Books.

Peters, B.G., Rhodes, R.A.W., and Wright, V. (eds.) (2000). *Administering the Summit: Administration of the Core Executive in Developed Countries*, Houndmills, Basingstoke: Macmillan.

Peters, G. (1999). *Institutional Theory in Political Science: The 'New Institutionalism'.* London: Pinter.

Pierson, P. (2004). *Politics in Time: History, Institutions, and Social Analysis*, Princeton, NJ: Princeton University Press.

Plato (1974). *The Republic*, 2nd edition (revised).Translated with an introduction by Desmond Lee, Harmondsworth: Penguin Classics.

Plowden, W. (1994). *Ministers and Mandarins*, London: Institute for Public Policy Research.

Podger, A. (2007). 'What really happens: departmental secretary appointments, contracts and performance pay in the Australian public service', *Australian Journal of Public Administration*, 66 (1): 131–47.

Poguntke, T. and Webb, P. (2005*a*). 'The presidentialization of politics in democratic societies: a framework for analysis', in T. Poguntke and P. Webb (eds.), *The Presidentialization of Politics: A Comparative Study of Modern Democracies*, Oxford: Oxford University Press.

——— (2005*b*). 'The presidentialization of contemporary democratic politics: evidence, causes, consequences', in T. Poguntke and P. Webb (eds.), *The Presidentialization of Politics: A Comparative Study of Modern Democracies*, Oxford: Oxford University Press.

——— (eds.) (2005*c*). *The Presidentialization of Politics: A Comparative Study of Modern Democracies*, Oxford: Oxford University Press.

Pollard, S. (2005). *David Blunkett*, London: Hodder & Stoughton.

Pollitt, C. and Bouckaert, G. (2000). *Public Management Reform: A Comparative Analysis*, Oxford: Oxford University Press.

Porter, J. (1963). *The Vertical Mosaic: An Analysis of Social Class and Power in Canada*, Toronto: University of Toronto Press.

Prescott, J. (2008). *Prezza: My Story, Pulling No Punches*, London: Headline Review.

Prime Minister and Cabinet (PM&C) (1998*a*). *Cabinet Handbook*, Canberra: PM&C.

——(1998*b*). *A Guide on Key Elements of Ministerial Responsibility*, Canberra: PM&C.

——(2004). *Cabinet Handbook*, Canberra: PM&C.

Privy Council Office (PCO) (1977). 'Responsibility in the Constitution'. *Submission to the Royal Commission on Financial Management and Accountability.* Ottawa: Canadian Government Publishing.

—— (2003*a*). *Governing Responsibly: A Guide for Ministers and Ministers of State,* Ottawa: PCO.

—— (2003*b*). *Guidance for Deputy Ministers,* Ottawa: PCO.

Pryce, S. (1997). *Presidentializing the Premiership,* New York: St Martin's Press.

Przeworski, A. and Teune, H. (1970). *The Logic of Comparative Social Inquiry,* New York: Wiley.

Public Service and Merit Commission (PSMPC) (2001). *Serving the Nation: 100 years of Public Service,* Canberra: Commonwealth of Australia.

Punnett, R.M. (1977). *The Prime Minister in Canadian Government and Politics,* Toronto: Macmillan.

Pym, F. (1984). *The Politics of Consent,* London: Hamish Hamilton.

Quick, J. and Garran, R. (1901). *The Annotated Constitution of the Australian Commonwealth,* Sydney: Angus & Robertson.

Rawnsley, A. (2001). *Servants of the People: The Inside Story of New Labour,* revised edition, London: Penguin Books.

Rees, J.C. (1977). 'Interpreting the constitution', in P. King (ed.), *The Study of Politics,* London: Cass.

Reid, G.S. (1973). 'The trinitarian struggle: parliamentary–executive relationships', in H. Mayer and H. Nelson (eds.), *Australian Politics: A Third Reader,* Melbourne: Cheshire.

—— (1981). 'Responsible government and ministerial responsibility', in G.R. Curnow and R.L. Wettenhall (eds.), *Understanding Public Administration: Essays in Honour of Robert Stewart Parker and Richard Neville Spann,* Sydney: Allen & Unwin.

—— (1984). 'The Westminster model and ministerial responsibility', *Current Affairs Bulletin,* June: 4–16.

Rentoul, J. (2001). *Tony Blair: Prime Minister,* London: Little, Brown.

Rhodes, R.A.W. (1988). *Beyond Westminster and Whitehall,* London: Unwin-Hyman.

—— (1993). 'State-building without bureaucracy', in I. Budge and D. McKay (eds.), *Developing Democracy: Research in Honour of Jean Blondel,* London: Sage.

—— (1995*a*). 'From prime ministerial power to core executive', in R.A.W. Rhodes, and P. Dunleavy (eds.), *Prime Minister, Cabinet and Core Executive,* London: Macmillan.

—— (1995*b*). 'The institutional approach', in D. Marsh and G. Stoker (eds.), *Theories and Methods in Political Science,* London: Macmillan.

—— (1997). *Understanding Governance: Policy Networks, Governance, Reflexivity and Accountability,* Buckingham: Open University Press.

—— (2001). 'The civil service', in A. Seldon (ed.), *The Blair Effect,* London: Little, Brown, pp. 97–116.

—— (2005). 'The Westminster model as tradition: the case of Australia', in H. Patapan, J. Wanna, and P. Weller (eds.), *Westminster Legacies: Democracy and Responsible Government in Asia, Australasia and the Pacific,* Sydney: University of New South Wales Press.

Rhodes, R.A.W. (2006). 'Old institutionalisms', in R.A.W. Rhodes, S. Binder, and B. Rockman (eds.), *The Oxford Handbook of Political Institutions,* Oxford: Oxford University Press.

—— (2007). 'Understanding governance: ten years on', *Organization Studies,* 28 (8): 1243–64.

—— Binder, S., and Rockman, B. (eds.) (2006). *The Oxford Handbook of Political Institutions,* Oxford: Oxford University Press.

—— Carmichael, P., McMillan, J., and Massey, A. (2003). *Decentralising the UK Civil Service: From Unitary State to Differentiated Polity,* Buckingham: Open University Press.

—— Dunleavy, P. (eds.) (1995). *Prime Minister, Cabinet and Core Executive,* London: Macmillan.

—— Weller, P. (eds.) (2001). *The Changing World of Top Officials: Mandarins or Valets?* Buckingham: Open University Press.

—— —— (2005). 'Westminster transplanted and Westminster implanted: exploring political change', in H. Patapan, J. Wanna, and P. Weller (eds.), *Westminster Legacies: Democracy and Responsible Government in Asia, Australasia and the Pacific,* Sydney: University of New South Wales Press.

—— Wanna, J., and Weller, P. (2008). 'Reinventing Westminster: how public executives reframe their world', *Politics and Policy,* 36 (4): 461–79.

Richards, D. (2007). *New Labour and the Civil Service: Reconstituting the Westminster Model.* Houndmills, Basingstoke: Palgrave Macmillan.

—— Smith, M.J. (2002). *Governance and Public Policy in the UK,* Oxford: Oxford University Press.

Riddell, P. (1989). *The Thatcher Decade,* Oxford: Blackwell.

—— (2001). 'Blair as prime minister', in A. Seldon (ed.), *The Blair Effect,* London: Little, Brown.

—— (2005). *The Unfulfilled Prime Minister: Tony Blair and the End of Optimism,* London: Politico's.

Ridley, F.F. (ed.) (1968). *Specialist and Generalist,* London: Allen & Unwin.

Ridley, N. (1991). *My Style of Government,* London: Hutchinson.

Robertson, G. (2001). *Memoirs of a Very Civil Servant,* Toronto: University of Toronto Press

Rokkan, S. and Urwin, D.W. (1982). *The Politics of Territorial Identity: Studies in European Regionalism,* London: Sage.

Rose, R. (2001). *The Prime Minister in a Shrinking World,* Cambridge: Polity Press.

Rowse, T. (2002). *Nugget Coombs: A Reforming Life,* Melbourne: Cambridge University Press.

Royal Commission on Australian Government Administration (RCAGA) (Coombs) (1976). *Report,* Canberra: Australian Government Printing Service.

Royal Institute of Public Administration (RIPA) (1987). *Top Jobs in Whitehall: Appointments and Promotions in the Senior Civil Service,* London: RIPA.

Rudd, K. (2008). Address to Heads of Department and Members of the Senior Executive Service, Parliament House, Canberra, 30 April <http://www.pm.gov.au/media/speech/2008/speech_0226.cfm>

Savoie, D. (1999). *Governing from the Centre*, Toronto: Toronto University Press.

—— (2003). *Breaking the Bargain: Public Servants, Ministers and Parliament*, Toronto: Toronto University Press.

Sawer, M. (2003). *The Ethical State? Social Liberalism in Australia*, Melbourne: Melbourne University Press.

Scott, D. (2004). *Off Whitehall: A View from Downing Street*, London: Tauris.

Seidman, H. (1975). *Politics, Position and Power*, 2nd edition, Oxford: Oxford University Press.

Seldon, A. (2004). *Blair*, London: Free Press.

—— (ed.) (2007). *Blair's Britain, 1997–2007*. Cambridge: Cambridge University Press.

—— Kavanagh, D. (eds.) (2005). *The Blair Effect 2001–5*, Cambridge: Cambridge University Press.

Senate Select Committee on a Certain Maritime Incident (SSCCMI) (2002). *Report*. Canberra: Senate, October.

Seymour-Ure, C. (2003). *Prime Ministers and the Media. Issues of Power and Control*, Oxford: Blackwell.

Shell, D. (2007). *The House of Lords*. Manchester: Manchester University Press.

Shergold, P. (2003).'Two cheers for bureaucracy: public service, political advice, and network governance', APSC Seminar, 13 June.

—— (2004a). 'Can governments be strategic? The role of the public service', address to ANZSOG, Canberra, July.

—— (2004b). 'Once was Camelot in Canberra? Reflections on public service leadership', Canberra: Sir Roland Wilson Lecture, 23 June.

—— (2005). 'Goodbye to all that?' *The Canberra Times*, 5 April.

Shore, C. (2000). *Building Europe: The Cultural Politics of European Integration*, London: Routledge.

Short, C. (2004). *An Honourable Deception? New Labour, Iraq and the Misuse of Power*, London: Free Press.

Shugart, M. (2006). 'Comparative executive–legislative relations', in R.A.W. Rhodes, S. Binder, and B. Rockman (eds.), *The Oxford Handbook of Political Institutions*, Oxford: Oxford University Press.

Simpson, J. (2001). *The Friendly Dictatorship*, Toronto: McCelland & Stewart.

Singleton, G. (2000). 'Introduction: Howard's Way', in G. Singleton (ed.), *The Howard Government*, Sydney: UNSW Press.

Smiley, D. (1976). *Canada in Question*, 2nd edition, Toronto: McGraw-Hill Ryerson.

—— (1980). *Canada in Question: Federalism in the Eighties*, 3rd edition, Toronto: McGraw-Hill Ryerson.

Smith, B.C. (1985). *Decentralization: The Territorial Dimension of the State*, London: Allen & Unwin.

Smith, M.J. (1999). *The Core Executive in Britain*, London: Macmillan.

Sossin, Lorne. (2006). 'Defining boundaries: the constitutional argument for bureaucratic independence and its implication for the accountability of the public service', in J.H. Gomery, *Restoring Accountability – Research Studies, Volume 2: The Public Service and Transparency* (Gomery Commission), Ottawa: Canadian Government Publishing.

State Services Commission (New Zealand) (2002). *Review of the Centre*, Ministerial Advisory Group, for Ministers Trevor Mallard and Michael Cullen, Wellington, January.

Strøm, K., Müller, W.C., and Bergman, T. (2003). *Delegation and Accountability in Parliamentary Democracies*, Oxford: Oxford University Press.

Sykes, P. (2008). 'Women leaders and executive politics: engendering change in Anglo-American nations', Senate Occasional Lecture Series, Parliament House, Canberra, 7 March.

Taylor, C. (1971). 'Interpretation and the sciences of man', *Review of Metaphysics,* 251: 3–51.

Thomas, P. (2009). 'Parliamentary scrutiny of government performance in Australia', *Australian Journal of Public Administration,* 68 (3): forthcoming.

Thompson, E. (1980). 'The Washminster mutation', in P. Weller and D. Jaensch (eds.), *Responsible Government in Australia*, Melbourne: Drummond.

—— Tillotsen, G. (1999). 'Caught in the act: the smoking gun view of ministerial responsibility', *Australian Journal of Public Administration,* 58 (1): 48–57.

Tiernan, A. (2007). *Power without Responsibility: Ministerial Staffers in Australian Governments from Whitlam to Howard*, Sydney: University of New South Wales Press.

—— Menzies, J. (2007). *Caretaker Conventions in Australasia. Minding the Shop for Government.* Canberra ANU E-Press, ANZSOG monographs.

Timmins, N. (2007). 'Stalinist Brown'. An interview with Sir Andrew Turnbull, Head of the British Home Civil Service, *Financial Times,* 20 March.

Todd, A. (1880). *Parliamentary Government in the British Colonies*, London: Longmans Green.

Tsebelis, G. (2002). *Veto Players: How Political Institutions Work*, Princeton: Princeton University Press and Russell Sage Foundation.

Turnbull, A. (2005). 'Valedictory lecture', 27 July <http://www.civilservice.gov.uk/publications/rtf/sat_valedictory_lecture.rtf\>

Turpin, C. (2002). *British Government and the Constitution: Text, Cases and Materials*, 5th edition, London: Butterworths.

Uhr, J. (1998). *Deliberative Democracy in Australia*, Cambridge: Cambridge University Press.

—— (2006). 'Bicameralism', in R.A.W. Rhodes, S. Binder, and B. Rockman (eds.), *The Oxford Handbook of Political Institutions*, Oxford: Oxford University Press.

—— Wanna, J. (2000). 'The future roles of parliament', in M. Keating, J. Wanna, and P. Weller (eds.), *Institutions on the Edge? Capacity for Governance*, Sydney: Allen & Unwin.

Uhrig Review (2003). *Review of the Corporate Governance of Statutory Authorities and Office Holders.* Canberra: AGPS <http://www.finance.gov.au/financial-framework/governance/docs/Uhrig-Report.pdf>

Ullman, S. (1979). 'Regional political cultures in Canada: a theoretical and conceptual introduction', in R. Schultz et al. (eds), *The Canadian Political Process*, 3rd edition, Toronto: Holt, Rinehart & Winston.

Verney, D. (1991). 'Westminster model', in V. Bogdanor (ed.), *The Blackwell Encyclopaedia of Political Science* (corrected paperback edition), Oxford: Blackwell.

Walker, P. (1991). *Staying Power*, London: Bloomsbury.

Walker, P.G. (1970). *The Cabinet*, London: Cape.

Walsh, P. (1995). *Confessions of a Failed Finance Minister*, Milsons Point, NSW: Random House.

Walter, J. (1986). *The Ministers' Minders*, Melbourne: Oxford University Press.

Wanna, J. (2005). 'New Zealand's Westminster trajectory: archetypal transplant to maverick outlier', in H. Patapan, J. Wanna and P. Weller (eds.), *Westminster Legacies: Democracy and Responsible Government in Asia, Australasia and the Pacific*, Sydney: University of New South Wales Press.

—— (2006). 'Insisting on traditional ministerial responsibility and the constitutional independence of the public service: the Gomery inquiry and the Canadian sponsorship scandal', *Australian Journal of Public Administration*, 65 (3): 15–21.

—— Hanson S. (2005). 'Enabling the Australian cabinet: supporting cabinet capabilities', Political Science Program seminar, Research School of Social Sciences, Australian National University, Canberra, 23 March.

—— Weller, P. (2003). 'Traditions of Australian governance', *Public Administration*, 81 (1): 63–94.

Warhurst, J. (ed.) (2007). *The Howard Decade in Australian Government and Politics*. Special Issue of the *Australian Journal of Political Science*, 42 (2).

—— Chalmers, J. (2003). 'Studying the Hawke government: a bibliographical essay', in S. Ryan and T. Bramston (eds.), *The Hawke Government: A Critical Retrospective*, North Melbourne, Victoria: Pluto Press.

Watson, D. (2002). *Recollections of a Bleeding Heart: A Portrait of Paul Keating PM*, Sydney: Knopf.

Weaver, R.K. and Rockman B.A. (1993). 'When and how do institutions matter?', in R.K. Weaver and B.A. Rockman (eds.), *Do Institutions Matter? Government Capabilities in the United States and Abroad*, Washington, DC: The Brookings Institution.

Weller, P. (1985). *First Among Equals: Prime Ministers in Westminster Systems*, Sydney: Allen & Unwin.

—— (1989*a*). *Malcolm Fraser, the Westminster System and the Separation of Powers*, Research Lecture Series, Griffith University.

—— (1989*b*). *Malcolm Fraser PM.: A Study of Prime Ministerial Power in Australia*, Melbourne: Penguin.

—— (1989*c*). 'Politicisation and the Australian Public Service', *Australian Journal of Public Administration*, 48 (4): 369–81.

—— (1992). *Menzies to Keating: The Development of the Australian Prime Ministership*, London: Hurst.

—— (2001). *Australia's Mandarins: The Frank and the Fearless*, Sydney: Allen & Unwin.

—— (2003). 'Cabinet government: an elusive ideal?' *Public Administration*, 81 (4): 701–22.

Weller, P. (2005). 'Investigating power at the centre of government: surveying research on the Australian executive', *Australian Journal of Public Administration*, 64 (1): 35–40.

—— (2007). *Cabinet Government in Australia, 1901–2006*, Sydney: University of New South Wales Press.

—— Grattan, M. (1981). *Can Ministers Cope? Australian Federal Ministers at Work*, Melbourne: Hutchinson.

—— Bakvis, H., and Rhodes, R.A.W. (eds.) (1997). *The Hollow Crown: Countervailing Trends in Core Executives*, London: Macmillan.

Wheare, K.C. (1953 [1938]). *The Statute of Westminster and the Dominions*, 5th edition, Oxford: Oxford University Press.

—— (1960). *The Constitutional Structure of the Commonwealth*, Oxford: Oxford University Press.

—— (1963). *Legislatures*. Oxford: Oxford University Press.

Wilenski, P. (1983). 'Six states or two nations?', in J. Aldred and J. Wilkes (eds.), *A Fractured Federation? Australia in the 1980s*, Sydney: Allen & Unwin.

Wilson, G. (1994). 'The Westminster Model in Comparative Perspective', in I. Budge and D. McKay (eds.), *Developing Democracy*, London: Sage.

Wilson, H. (1977). *The Governance of Britain*, London: Sphere.

Wilson, R. (1999). 'The civil service in the new millennium', speech delivered at City University, London, 5 May.

—— (2003). 'Portrait of a profession revisited', *Public Administration*, 81 (2): 365–78. Published version of a speech delivered on 26 March 2002 at Admiralty Arch, London.

Winterton, G. (1983). *Parliament, the Executive and the Governor-General*, Melbourne: Melbourne University Press.

Wintringham, M. (2008). 'Striking the balance: public service independence and responsiveness', Address to IPAA National Roundtable, University of Melbourne, 14 March, (and personal communication).

Wishart, I. (2008). *Absolute Power: The Helen Clark Years*, North Shore: Howling at the Moon Publishing.

Wittgenstein, L. (1972). *Philosophical Investigations*, trans. G. Anscombe, Oxford: Blackwell.

Wood, M. (1997). 'John Wayne agonistes', *New York Review of Books*, 24 April.

Woodhouse, D. (1994). *Ministers and Parliament: Accountability in Theory and Practice*, Oxford: Clarendon Press.

—— (2003). 'Ministerial responsibility', in V. Bogdanor (ed.) *The British Constitution in the Twentieth Century*, Oxford: Oxford University Press for the British Academy.

—— (2004). 'UK ministerial responsibility in 2002: the tale of two resignations', *Public Administration*, 82 (1): 1–19.

Wright, V. and Hayward, J. (2000). 'Governing from the centre: policy coordination in six European core executives', in R.A.W. Rhodes (ed.), *Transforming British Government, Volume 2: Changing Roles and Relationships*, London: Macmillan.

Young, L. and Archer, K. (eds.) (2002). *Regionalism and Party Politics in Canada*, Ontario: Oxford University Press.

Author Index

Subject Index